MasterClass in
Geography Education

MasterClass in Geography Education

Transforming Teaching and Learning

Edited by Graham Butt

MasterClass Series

Bloomsbury Academic
An imprint of Bloomsbury Publishing Plc

BLOOMSBURY
LONDON · NEW DELHI · NEW YORK · SYDNEY

Bloomsbury Academic
An imprint of Bloomsbury Publishing Plc

50 Bedford Square	1385 Broadway
London	New York
WC1B 3DP	NY 10018
UK	USA

www.bloomsbury.com

BLOOMSBURY and the Diana logo are trademarks of Bloomsbury Publishing Plc

First published 2015

© Graham Butt and Contributors, 2015

British Library Cataloguing-in-Publication Data
A catalogue record for this book is available from the British Library.

ISBN: HB: 978-1-4725-3572-6
      PB: 978-1-4725-3571-9
   ePub: 978-1-4725-3573-3
   ePDF: 978-1-4725-3574-0

Library of Congress Cataloging-in-Publication Data

Typeset by Newgen Knowledge Works (P) Ltd., Chennai, India
Printed and bound in India

Contents

List of Figures and Tables   vii
Notes on Contributors   viii
Series Editor's Foreword   xi

Part I   CONTEXTUALIZING

1 Introduction   3
Graham Butt

2 Research in Geography Education   15
David Lambert

3 Research and Professional Practice   31
Clare Brooks

Discussion to Part I   45
Margaret Roberts

Part II   CONSTRUCTING

4 Constructing Geographical Knowledge   53
Roger Firth

5 Constructing the Geography Curriculum   67
Charles Rawding

6 What Is the Role of Theory?   81
Graham Butt

Discussion to Part II   95
Gemma Collins

Part III RESEARCHING

7 **Approaches to Research in Geography Education**   103
Paul Weeden

8 **Writing a Research Proposal**   113
Mark Jones

9 **Ethical Considerations**   129
Maggie Wilson

Discussion to Part III   145
John Morgan

Part IV PRODUCING

10 **Getting Underway with Your Research**   151
Simon Catling

11 **Doing Your Research Project**   171
Liz Taylor

12 **Striving for a Conclusion**   185
Gemma Collins

Discussion to Part IV   197
Graham Butt

13 **Conclusions**   205
Graham Butt

Index   213

List of Figures and Tables

Figures

3.1 A model of teaching and learning situations: actors and contexts   37

8.1 Considerations when writing a research proposals   115

10.1 Some aspects of validity   163

10.2 Some aspects of reliability   164

11.1 Relationship between research questions and theory, methods and methodology   172

11.2 Example of research questions and their link to theoretical perspectives, methods and methodology   173

11.3 Example of an article record form   174

11.4 Some possible methods of data collection   177

11.5 Processes of qualitative analysis   180

Tables

5.1 Influence of the geography community on curriculum discourse 1989–99   71

11.1 Examples of methods for accessing students' understandings of geographical topics   178

11.2 Empirical research questions mapped to methods in Claire Kennedy's MEd research   179

Notes on Contributors

Clare Brooks is Senior Lecturer in Geography Education at the Institute of Education, University of London, UK, where her current role is Programme Director of the MA in Education. Her research interest is in how teachers' subject identity influences their professional practice. Her forthcoming publication on the Teachers' Professional Compass reflects this interest. She is Honorary Executive Secretary to the International Geographical Union, Commission for Geography Education, chair of the UK Committee and a founding member of the Geography Education Research Collective (GEReCo).

Graham Butt is Professor in Education and Co-Director of Research at the School of Education, Oxford Brookes University, UK. He is a founding member of the Geography Education Research Collective (GEReCo). Graham's research is predominantly in the field of geography education, although he has also published on assessment, teacher workload and modernisation of the teaching workforce. His books include *Modernising Schools* (2007, with Helen Gunter), *Lesson Planning* (3rd edition) (2008), *Making Assessment Matter* (2010) and, as editor, *Geography, Education and the Future* (2011). Graham is a long-established member of the Geographical Association and an invited member of the UK Committee of the International Geographical Union (IGU).

Simon Catling is Professor Emeritus of Primary Education at Oxford Brookes University, UK. His recent research activity has been in curriculum making in primary geography, children's geographies and geographical understanding, and geography textbook writing. His professional interests are in teaching geography with primary children and he wrote, with Tessa Willy, *Teaching Primary Geography* (2009) and *Teaching Primary Geography for Australian Schools* (2013). He is a Past President of the Geographical Association, UK, and has been involved with primary geography developments for 40 years.

Gemma Collins is Lecturer in Geography Education at the University of Birmingham, UK. A former secondary school teacher and head of department, Gemma is now a teacher educator with responsibility for students on the PGDipEd and MEd Teaching Studies courses. She has also worked with the Ministry of Education in Tanzania, in the areas of curriculum, pedagogy and continuing professional development for teachers.

Roger Firth is Associate Professor and Fellow of St. Anne's College, University of Oxford, UK. Research interests include disciplined knowledge, the school curriculum and subject pedagogy, and closing the attainment gap for disadvantaged pupils. Recent publications include book chapters on Task Design in Geography and Constructing Geographical

Knowledge – the challenges inherent in bringing disciplinary knowledge into the frame of constructivist teaching and learning. He is a member of The Department for Education/ National College for Teaching and Learning two-year research and development project *Closing the Gap: Test and Learn*, which has introduced a range of intervention strategies designed to raise the attainment of disadvantaged pupils.

Mark Jones is Senior Lecturer in Geography Education at the University of the West of England, UK. A former curriculum leader with 18 years' teaching experience in schools in Bristol and South Gloucestershire, he is an active member of the Geographical Association and leads the Secondary Geography PGCE course at UWE. His research and publications focus on student participation, university–school connections and cross-curricular creativity. His most recent publication is the co-edited volume with David Lambert *Debates in Geography Education* (2013).

David Lambert is Professor of Geography Education at the Institute of Education, University of London, UK. He started out as a secondary school teacher of geography, becoming a teacher educator in the late 1980s. He is a former chief executive of the Geographical Association (2002–12). He has published widely on geography in education and amongst his recent work are *Teaching Geography 11–18: A Conceptual Approach* (2010, with John Morgan) and *Knowledge and the Future School: Curriculum and Social Justice* (2014, with Michael Young and colleagues).

John Morgan is Professor of Education at the University of Auckland, New Zealand. Previously he worked as a geography teacher in schools, a teacher educator at the University of Bristol, UK, and a researcher at the Institute of Education, University of London, UK. His most recent book is *Teaching Geography as if the Planet Matters* (2011).

Charles Rawding is Senior Lecturer in Geography Education at Edge Hill University, UK. Prior to becoming involved in teacher training, he was Head of Geography in a large comprehensive school on Humberside. He has written widely on curriculum innovation in geography. His most recent publication is *Effective Innovation in the Secondary Geography Curriculum* (2013). He currently chairs the Teacher Education Special Interest Group of the Geographical Association. After teaching in comprehensive schools in London, Leicestershire and Sheffield.

Margaret Roberts worked at the University of Sheffield, UK, where she co-ordinated the PGCE geography course from 1982 until her retirement in 2006. Her research has focused on the geography national curriculum and on geographical enquiry. In 2011, she led ten courses on 'Inquiry' for teachers in Singapore. Among her publications are two books: *Learning through Enquiry* (2003) and *Geography through Enquiry* (2013). She has been involved in the work of the Geographical Association for many years, on committees, steering groups of projects, as Editor of *Teaching Geography* and in 2008–9 as President.

Liz Taylor is Senior Lecturer at the University of Cambridge, UK, where she coordinates the Geography PGCE course and supervises at Masters and PhD level. Her research interests include young people's understandings of place and space. She writes on various topics in geography education and on the representation of space in children's literature.

Paul Weeden is retired Lecturer in Geography Education at the University of Birmingham, UK. He previously taught in a Bristol Comprehensive School, was an advisory teacher and Lecturer at the University of Bristol. He was a GCSE examiner for many years and until recently Secretary of the Assessment and Examinations Special Interest Group of the Geographical Association. He has written extensively on assessment in geography education.

Maggie Wilson is Senior Lecturer in Education Studies at Oxford Brookes University, UK, where she teaches on the undergraduate Education Studies programme and on the MA programmes in Education and Childhood Studies. She has specialized in research ethics for a number of years and is currently the Research Ethics Officer for the Faculty of Humanities and Social Sciences and a member of the University Research Ethics Committee. She has conducted research on gender and achievement from an international perspective and acted as a consultant in this field. More recently, she has undertaken research into women in educational management and part-time teachers. She is a member of the British Association for Comparative and International Education.

Series Editor's Foreword

This vibrant and engaging book brings together scholarship, critical engagement and 'real life' enquiry within Geography Education in energetic and innovative ways. As both outstanding academic and geographer, Graham Butt has drawn on his extensive expertise to craft and create a volume which informs, challenges and extends thinking in geography education. Using a conceptual framework of *Contextualizing, Constructing, Researching* and *Producing*, Butt demonstrates how research in geography education can be designed and carried out. Each part concludes with a discussion designed to bring about reflective and reflexive responses from the reader, so that this is a volume which invites interaction and rewards that with a deeper and richer understanding of the field, in Butt's words, 'as an insider rather than as an observer'.

Some of the leading names in geography education are featured in this book, all writing within a context of practitioner research in recognition of the ways in which practice is lifted through structured theorizing. The book robustly asserts the place of research in effective teaching and learning. Teachers are not simply 'conduits' for curricula designed by others, but are at the heart of knowledge and professionalism, and practitioner research is the means of achieving this laudable place. Butt has brought together leading scholars in geography education in discussing and demonstrating the powerful position that being both practitioner and theorist offers. In bringing together the creative opportunities that critical engagement can bring, the book reminds us of why we became teachers – because we find learning stimulating and exciting, and want to share that with others. The chapters within this volume all demand careful thought and are often designed to be provocative in claims. Most of all though, the writers in this volume demonstrate the centrality of *involvement* – in ideas, in classroom practices, in shaping the future of geography education. There are urgent questions to be addressed and the audiences for this book are the actors of change. It's a demanding role, and research offers a key route to become that informed and voiced community. Readers are not invited to sit back and relax!

This is a book that urges us to think deeply about geography education and provides the intellectual resource and energy to help us meet that demand. The volume is a model of how to bring clarity and accessibility to key debates whilst maintaining the intellectual integrity of the subject. It is my great pleasure to have this splendid volume, edited by such a renowned geographer and scholar as Graham Butt, as part of the MasterClass series.

Sue Brindley, Senior Lecturer in Education
University of Cambridge, UK

Part I
Contextualizing

Introduction

Graham Butt

Chapter outline

The rationale for *MasterClass in Geography Education*	5
Starting points	6
Working at M level	7
Structure and content	9
Conclusions	11

MasterClass in Geography Education has been written to support education practitioners who are undertaking research in geography education, with a particular focus on those studying on postgraduate courses which offer Masters-level credits. As such, it is primarily aimed at two groups. Firstly, those who have enrolled on a course of initial teacher training, such as a Post Graduate Certificate of Education (PGCE) or Post Graduate Diploma in Education (PGDipEd), where academic work is either partly or wholly assessed at Masters level. Most PGCE and PGDipEd courses contain assignments which are marked against Masters criteria and stipulate that students should engage in data gathering and analysis, often as a formal piece of research, within the assessment process. Secondly, this book will be a valuable resource for anyone completing a full Masters degree – either as a part time, or as full time, student – if the context and content of their work is linked to either geography education or a closely related field of study. *MasterClass in Geography Education* therefore seeks to support the professional development of geography teachers, at whatever stage of their careers, who are working towards achieving postgraduate accreditation – although it will also be relevant for educationists who are interested in furthering their knowledge and understanding of geography education, with or without gaining accreditation. The points raised and issues pursued here are germane to audiences in the United Kingdom, but will also have purchase in countries which share the Euro-American tradition of academic geography and geography education, including much of Europe, Australasia, North America and South Africa (see Butt and Lambert 2014).

This book is built around the concept of the 'teacher as researcher'. Many of the authors are established members of the geography education community, having conducted research as tutors in higher education institutions (HEIs) for a number of years; other contributors are new to the world of research – having only recently trained to enter the teaching profession, or experienced their first year or second as a teacher. Some authors are leaders of Masters courses, whilst others have experience of doctoral level supervision at PhD and/or EdD levels. This is, I believe, what gives depth, breadth and vibrancy to the text – driven as it is by a desire to discuss 'real life' research questions and the quest for their solution. What is clear from the contributors' accounts is that although challenging in terms of time, resources, organization and effort, conducting research in geography education can provide valuable support for the development of one's professional identity. Indeed, most of the contributors note the advantages of engaging in research in terms of encouraging greater critical engagement with teaching and learning, supporting reflexivity, aiding problem solving and enhancing professional learning. Each of the chapters is informed by reference to recent and relevant research in education, both in the field of geography education and beyond, and convey appropriate sensitivity towards teachers' ownership of their professional knowledge.

The broad remit of this book is therefore to explore:

- Masters-level education in geography education;
- the place of subject knowledge in geography;
- the role and function of research in geography education;
- the relationship between research and professional practice;
- practical aspects of researching in geography education and
- the views of 'discussants'/stakeholders in dialogue with geography educationists.

The number of teachers who aspire to gaining a full Masters degree has increased since the early 1990s, although many Masters courses in HEIs have shown rather uneven growth, or may have declined. Numerous teachers still seek Masters status within a few years of initial professional qualification, often as part of their career development. Beck (2009) notes the efforts of previous UK governments to 're-professionalize' the teaching workforce at the start of the twenty-first century; part of this process involved the promotion of evidence-based practice which utilized relevant research evidence. The necessity of creating a modernized teaching workforce, many of whom would be comfortable handling research evidence and engaging with research activity, was also considered important (see Butt and Gunter 2007). However, the political imperative to raise the academic profile of the teaching workforce is arguably not so strong now – for example, teachers recruited to 'free schools' are required neither to have undertaken any professional training, nor to have gained Qualified Teacher Status (QTS), before they start teaching. The official perception of what is required for the appropriate preparation of new teachers has shifted radically. Not all models of teacher training in the United Kingdom fully recognize the importance of beginning teachers undertaking some form of systematic enquiry as part of their training; routes other than the PGCE/PGDipEd may treat preparation for the profession as largely a craft-based activity, comprised of observing classrooms followed by 'trial and error' attempts at teaching. Many involved in the provision of initial teacher education question such models of teacher preparation, favouring the creation of professional teacher-researchers capable of adopting critical, reflective and evaluative ways of problem solving as well as delivering practical excellence in teaching. The value of creating a professional community that has moved beyond basic competency training is surely obvious.

Alongside those students who are in their initial teacher education phase, or who have recently taken up their first teaching post, this book should appeal to practitioners who have some experience of research but who now wish to move to the 'next stage' of research activity. MPhil, EdD and PhD students in geography education – particularly those in the first year(s) of their study – will hopefully also find this book's discussion of research methods, methodologies and issues attractive. Essentially the challenges facing any 'beginning researcher', whether they are working at undergraduate, taught postgraduate or doctoral level, are very similar – particularly if the task is to produce some form of dissertation, or thesis. There is a familiar path of topic selection, identification of aims and objectives, deciding on which research methods to use, designing a methodology, considering ethical issues, negotiating access, collecting, analysing and presenting information, and writing the dissertation (Bell 2010). Brooks (2010a) states this process deceptively simply:

> First, the researcher needs to understand the processes of research. Second, they need to identify something worthy of researching, and finally, they need to identify the resources to enable them to conduct the research. Once these conditions are in place, the research can be undertaken and the results disseminated. (p. 115)

A number of excellent support books and guides already exist for Masters level students (see Hart 2004; Denby et al. 2008; Sewell 2008; Bryan et al. 2010). However, *MasterClass in Geography Education* takes the *geography* specialist beyond these generic approaches to appreciate the particular significance of geography education research.

The rationale for *MasterClass in Geography Education*

As with other contributions to the *MasterClass* series, this book offers a blend of both theory and practice. Its rationale is to help teachers who are studying to gain Masters credits in geography education to engage with the 'big questions' of their subject and its pedagogy: What constitutes subject knowledge in geography and geography education? How might we determine the relevance of educational research in geography? What are considered to be 'appropriate' research methods in geography education? How does one successfully establish and conduct research in education?

The intention has been to provide an appreciation of how teachers engage with their own professional development, grounded in practical case studies and accounts from those who have already undertaken this research journey. In essence, the task is to move teachers 'on' from simply registering the seemingly endless, often apparently tangential, government directives and policy statements to achieving a more critical engagement with what their subject can offer to young learners. In so doing the broad aim is to achieve a contribution to the re-professionalization of the geography teaching workforce. Theoretical and conceptual concerns sit centrally within this text. Chapters which include accounts of novice or 'beginning researchers' illustrate how the formality of undertaking a piece of properly structured, original research can move teachers forward professionally. The intention is to help teachers build upon their regular process of reflection – which all teachers engage with on a day-to-day basis, often when tired, at the end of frenetic working days – to achieve more considered, systematic and structured forms of sustained enquiry. Discussion about the nature of Masters-level education, the place of this qualification within the gamut of professional development initiatives, and the drive towards making teaching a Masters-level profession is still raging – we therefore present observations which contribute to all of these debates.

Starting points

What is the significance of the growing contribution of practitioner research and scholarship in geography education, generated through postgraduate studies? Does such research have any real impact on educational policy and practice? These questions open up a larger debate about the value of much of the educational research conducted in the United Kingdom.

Concerns about the overall quality of research in education have deep roots. Demands for accountability, with regard to quality and excellence of research in HEIs, have resulted in periodic research assessment exercises (RAEs) and research excellence frameworks (REFs) in the United Kingdom. Here assessment criteria for 'originality', 'significance' and 'rigour' are applied to help determine the quality of any individual's research outputs – the consideration of these has some utility for any research activity. On the basis of the RAE/REF findings, which are benchmarked against international standards of excellence, the higher education funding council distributes public money to support research activity in UK institutions. But big questions still persist. Criticism of the quality and relevance of educational research has been marked since the late 1990s (see, e.g., Hargreaves 1996; Hillage et al. 1998; Tooley and Darby 1998; Maclure 2003; Whitty 2005; Thomas 2007), with concerns being targeted at its lack of rigour and culmination, theoretical incoherence and ideological bias, lack of relevance, poor user engagement and low value for money (Whitty 2005). UK governments, even when supporting the creation of evidence-based policies in education, have regularly expressed their unease about the generally poor quality of research findings (Furlong and Oancea 2005). Unfortunately, research in geography education sits rather uneasily in this arena. It has not traditionally attracted much government, funding council or project money – large-scale, generously funded research projects in geography education are unusual, with most research being produced as small-scale, practitioner-based, unfunded work often reflecting the interests of a few individuals. This can be viewed, at best, as offering professional development for individual teachers, rather than opening up strategic, cost-effective and high-impact research activity (Butt 2006). I return to discussions about the quality of research in geography education in Chapter 13.

Brooks (2010b) is realistic about the potential impact of much practitioner research, but celebrates the possibilities of researchers contributing to changing, and potentially improving, teachers' professional practice. Here the links between research, practice and policy making may not be immediately apparent – but the individual benefits are certainly visible. Exploring the differences between practitioner research/scholarship and the types of research often undertaken by academics, she acknowledges differences but poses an important question: does this necessarily *invalidate* the research undertaken by practitioners? In this context we must acknowledge Finney's (2013) assertion that:

> while teacher research is easily positioned as small scale, local, context-bound and complementary to the 'big world of research' legitimated by professional researchers, it could instead claim to be the source of original pathways to pursue, leaping over well-worn approaches to long-standing issues. It needs to be taken seriously. (p. 10)

Working at M level

What are the key characteristics of educational research at Masters level? All HEIs will offer their own guidance about what (for them) constitutes a successful approach to studying for a Masters qualification. Although it is not my intention to cover what is essentially similar ground, a brief outline of the common demands of M level work may prove helpful. When stating the aims of Masters degrees in Education, alongside their learning outcomes and assessment criteria, most institutions also state a number of desirable learner attributes. By far the majority of providers will require students to undertake a sustained piece of research (which may be empirical or literature based) towards the completion of a dissertation (usually between 15,000 and 20,000 words long); other written assignments or examinations will make up the bulk of the degree, each aspect of which will involve elements of research.

When undertaking a dissertation the broad area of research is largely of your choosing; however, you should have the support of a supervisor who will guide you into the choice of appropriate research question(s) and help you to design and prepare a research enquiry.

Different HEIs will approach this in different ways – you may already know your tutor/ supervisor from previous work completed; your supervisor may be completely unknown to you; s/he may be selected because of their particular skills or research interests (which align with your initial research ideas); or they could be randomly selected. A key component of research work involves engaging with appropriate literature – making reference to theories, previous research findings and established education principles – and being able to justify one's views. Therefore, the ability to identify and select appropriate literary sources, analyse these and then evaluate their contribution to your research is crucial. Such sources may be from within your subject discipline (geography, geography education), but may also spread more widely (with an inter-disciplinary or multi-disciplinary focus) according to the nature of your research. For example, a research study into how effectively children with special educational needs engage with fieldwork in geography will require an understanding of literature in both of these areas.

The relationship and interplay between theory and practice is important at Masters level. This is reflected in the assertion that research in geography education should not 'concentrate narrowly on the pragmatic issues of "what works" in geography classrooms' (Butt 2010, p. 80), but seek to consider broader theoretical and methodological questions of 'how', 'why' and 'how ought'. Here the importance of systematic enquiry, validity of methods and procedural rigour come to the fore – within a wider conceptual framework that encompasses an appreciation of the work of those who have attempted to solve similar, or related, questions. To complete assignments and to undertake research for your dissertation will require you to have a firm grasp of research and evaluative methods. This must be fairly comprehensive – it is important to understand the range of quantitative and qualitative approaches available to the researcher, assess their appropriateness to the research question(s) set and to justify the methods used to gather data. This implies some understanding of both ontological and epistemological considerations of the types of research questions posed and the nature of the evidence collected through enquiry.

Just as within the discipline of academic geography, research in (geography) education has shifted from a paradigm which broadly favoured the use of scientific method, positivism, quantification and hypothesis testing to search for the inviolable 'truth', to approaches that have recognized more relative, contested and contestable notions of knowledge (Hickey and Lawson 2005). What constitutes reality and knowledge, and the ways in which we conceive of these notions, must be articulated and defended in our research – actions which often invite qualitative, interpretivist stances to be taken which recognize that truth is rarely simple, given, absolute, verifiable and easily generalizable (Laurence 2013). Importantly, such methods acknowledge that power relationships exist within research (as in all aspects of life), explicitly considering who the research is 'done by', who it is 'done to' and what the consequences of its findings might be. Here the importance of ethical considerations arises. The growth of mixed methods research – where measurement, hypotheses and the use of number blend with interpretivist approaches to explore meaning and to challenge, or create, theories – is arguably a welcome development in the arena of educational research (Onwuegbuzie and Leech 2005).

Successful researchers, at any level, need to develop both knowledge and a range of skills capable of undertaking theoretical analysis and application. They should be adept at devising an appropriate research methodology, applying research methods and then gathering, analysing and discussing the data collected (Robson 2002; O'Leary 2004; Johnson and Christensen 2012). The presentation of this work, either as an assignment or as a dissertation, will follow conventions about how it should be offered to an external audience. An ability to justify standpoints according to established theory is essential. Such work must inevitably 'sit' within the canon produced by others, but it does not have to agree with it! A dissertation must be honest, fair, accurate, comprehensive and clear; it must be a credible account of what you have attempted to research. Research work tends to be 'messy' – things often do not go the way you expect – but it is the role of the researcher to bring 'order into chaos', something that is best achieved if the research work is well planned, and carefully structured. The aim is to move away from anecdote, convention and belief, to more rigorous explanation, analysis and evaluation.

Some Masters degrees in Education (and indeed, some EdD courses) stress the need to develop knowledge with a view to making a practical contribution, based on one's research findings, to a wider professional community. They therefore place some store on planning the potential communication and dissemination of results to a range of colleagues and/or 'community of practice' (Lave and Wenger 1991). Indeed, it is a truism that much research at this level will be in pursuit of a 'local' issue or concern at a personal level, such that the outcomes may have little impact or generalizability beyond this – even though the work undoubtedly adds something to what we know about geography education. Most dissertations remain unpublished, even in part, and do not tend to achieve a readership beyond that of other Masters students or their tutors. The work may be of high quality, theoretically and methodologically, but is rarely appreciated by the wider education community. Some would also seek to draw fairly distinctive lines between 'teacher research' and 'academic research' in terms of their purposes, transferability, reliability and validity (Sachs 2003).

Structure and content

MasterClass in Geography Education is composed of four parts – *Contextualizing, Constructing, Researching* and *Producing* – each of which progressively reveals ways in which research in geography education can be planned, designed and carried out. Each part is concluded with a 'Discussion', which offers a commentary on the points raised in the three preceding chapters; here the reader is invited to reflect upon what has been offered, supported by the thoughts and observations of the discussant. This may help the reader consider their own practice, address new research ideas, concur with the views expressed or adopt a more critical stance. It is hoped that these parts will also encourage the reader to feel a stronger association with the geography education research community, as an insider rather than as an observer. The chapters convey the reader from initial considerations of research ideas, questions and potential areas of investigation, to achieving greater structure and focus for their research – identifying the most pertinent aims and objectives, questions, research design and methods/methodologies. Issues of epistemology, ontology and ethical clearance are considered, as are methods for data gathering, data analysis and writing up. Importantly, advice about the scale of your project (given your available time, costs and the requirements of assessment) is also here. A number of associated themes are covered, in ways which seek to include the views of a wide range of education professionals. Within the parts on *Researching* and *Producing* opportunities are given for recently qualified, ex-Masters students to discuss their experience of Masters-level education. In this way a variety of perspectives are offered to provide a refreshing take on all aspects of provision. There is no necessity to read this book 'cover to cover', but there is logic in the way in which it has been structured – moving the reader/researcher from initial research questions and ideas to the culmination of their project.

In the *Contextualizing* part Graham Butt offers introductory thoughts on being part of a research-based profession, exploring the particular needs of the expected reader and sign-posting the nature of the contributions in the book's parts and chapters. David Lambert provides an overview of the place of research in geography education, its role in the preparation and continuing professional development of geography educators and the importance of this research in maintaining a healthy field of study. Following this, Clare Brooks explores the notion that research contributes a vital component in the link between the practice of geography teachers and their consideration as 'professionals'. By outlining the nature of professional practice she explores what makes geography teachers worthy of being labelled as professionals. Finally Margaret Roberts, as the first discussant, draws this opening part together with comments on the preceding chapters.

The next part, titled *Constructing*, offers contributions from Roger Firth, Charles Rawding and Graham Butt. The discussant is Gemma Collins. Firth explores the place of knowledge in geography education, while Rawding investigates the development of the Geography National Curriculum (GNC) through discourse analysis – in so doing highlighting the extent to which geography curriculum documents incorporate assumptions about geographical knowledge that are either politically or ideologically derived. Butt concludes this part by discussing the place of theory in research in geography education and its role in analysing, structuring and/or interpreting frameworks within which ideas and research methods can be considered. The importance of adopting a theoretical perspective before collecting data is stressed – to help structure the ways in which problems are considered and research questioned defined.

The *Researching* part is comprised of contributions from Paul Weeden, Mark Jones, Maggie Wilson and, as a discussant, John Morgan. Weeden illustrates some commonly used methods for identifying research questions, identifies how research aims can be clarified and how ideas can be framed into research problems that are potentially resolvable. Following this, Jones identifies how a good research proposal provides evidence of sustained conceptual, theoretical and methodological thinking being brought to bear when considering the nature of the research, the research questions and the methodology to be adopted. The particular issues surrounding the positioning of 'insider researchers' are explored with respect to the resolution of ethical questions in the next chapter. Wilson concludes this part by introducing a series of 'moral equations' the researcher must contemplate – starting at the point of designing the research activity, through data collection, data analysis and writing up the study. John Morgan offers closing comments on the dangers of 'methodism' in geography education research.

The final part, on *Producing*, provides the reader with advice on conducting, completing and reporting on their research. Simon Catling's contribution is weighted with practical guidance for the new researcher at Masters level. He considers the steps involved in 'getting going' with research in geography education, which inevitably involves negotiating access (to individuals and institutions) and fore-fronting the potential limitations of the research project. Liz Taylor also addresses the practical aspects of carrying out a research project: ensuring that a consistent approach is adopted through all elements of the research, locating the research project in the appropriate literature, selecting and using the right techniques of data collection and analysis, and establishing and discussing the findings. Finally, Gemma Collins provides a case study of a single Masters student, describing the 'pitfalls and practicalities' he faced when writing up his research project. By utilizing quoted material from the research student this chapter gives a vibrant account of concluding the 'research journey', but with appropriate reference to scholarly and academic work which structures the context for the case study. A brief Discussant comment, followed by a chapter of Conclusions, both by Graham Butt, draws the book to a close.

Conclusions

Following the realignment in 2006 of many PGCE courses to include some accreditation at Masters level (as opposed to *professional* courses), there was a 'spike' in the number of early career teachers studying for higher degrees in England. There was also, at this time, considerable government rhetoric about finally making teaching a Masters-level profession, alongside a steady (but somewhat erratic) flow of established teachers engaging with full Masters courses. Unhappily, this is no longer the case today – the UK government appears to favour a craft-based apprenticeship model for preparing beginning teachers, largely school centred and competency driven. No longer is the achievement of the previous benchmark of QTS seen as a *sine qua non* for teaching in all English state schools. This contrasts strongly with traditional HEI-based teacher education courses, which mix classroom practice with the development of critical and theoretical frameworks, valuing the role of the teacher-researcher and prizing the development of critically reflective practitioners who are expected to both use and generate research in their professional lives. So intransigent has the policy directive been towards placing teacher training in schools rather than letting it remaining in HEIs, over the last 20 years, that some have been drawn to comment that it amounts to a form of 'anti intellectualism' (Lambert and Jones 2013).

It is a truism that all teachers are 'knowledge workers'. They possess valuable reserves of both subject and pedagogical knowledge, and they help to create and exchange knowledge with their students on a daily basis. The research dimension recognizes the need for teachers to consume knowledge, and to adopt a constructively critical stance in their consideration of disciplinary knowledge. This criticality should also extend to research outputs, policy initiatives, government directives and shifts in pedagogic methods. Here is another dimension of knowledge creation – with the 'teacher as researcher' having the agency and capability to mediate policy diktat by the generation of secure evidence that has relevance to professionals in other school settings. Teachers' subject knowledge, which must be stimulated and re-freshed, is crucial – disciplinary and subject knowledge represents more than the simple backdrop to the main acts of teaching and learning; it is central to the whole process of (geography) education in schools (Butt and Collins 2013). These facts have been either misunderstood, sidelined or forgotten by many within education in recent years. Teachers need to work with a clear sense of moral purpose, carrying with them conceptually secure notions of their subject and of education itself (Lambert and Jones 2013).

If, like Hargreaves (1998), we believe that teaching is essentially a research-based profession, there is an imperative to ensure that educational research is prized. Hopefully we have moved on from Naish's observation in the early 1990s, that many teachers saw educational research as irrelevant to addressing their professional concerns: 'teachers sometimes claim that research tells them what they already know' (Naish 1993, p. 64). Your research will be expected to be original, rigorous in design and execution, and of high quality. It may struggle to meet the expectations of large-scale funded research projects – particularly with respect to user engagement, knowledge generation and/or synthesis, impact, sustainability and wider professional development. However, one can always aspire to methodological and theoretical excellence – quality is partly determined by purpose, intended audience and overall aims – factors which can and must be addressed in any small-scale research. Achievement of excellence is possible.

Let me conclude by restating an important point made by David Lambert (2010) about the field (if such a thing exists) of geography education research. He asserts that it must be 'more substantial than education research with a geographical hue' (p. 85), being concerned as it is with two big ideas (geography and education) and how these relate to each other. This phrase serves as both a description and an endorsement of the content commissioned for this book.

References

Beck, J (2009) Appropriating professionalism: restructuring the official knowledge base of England's modernized teaching profession. *British Journal of Sociology of Education* 30(1): 314.

Bell, J (2010) *Doing Your Research Project*, 5th edition. Maidenhead: McGraw-Hill.

Brooks, C (ed.) (2010a) *Studying PGCE Geography at M Level*. London: Routledge.

— (2010b) How does one become a researcher in geography education? *International Research in Environmental and Geographical Education* 19(2): 115–18.

Bryan, H, Carpenter, C and Hoult, S (2010) *Learning and Teaching at Masters Level: A Guide for Student Teachers*. London: Sage.

Butt, G (2006) How should we determine research quality in geography education? In Purnell, K, Lidstone, J and Hodgson, S (eds.) *Changes in Geographical Education: Past, Present and Future*, pp. 91–5. Proceedings of the International Geographical Union Commission on Geographical Education Symposium. Brisbane, Australia: IGU-CGE.

— (2010) Perspectives on research in geography education. *International Research in Environmental and Geographical Education* 19(2): 79–82.

— (ed) (2011) *Geography, Education and the Future*. London: Continuum.

Butt, G and Collins, G (2013) Can geography cross 'the divide'? In Lambert, D and Jones, M (eds.) *Debates in Geography Education*, pp. 291–301. Abingdon: Routledge.

Butt, G and Gunter, H (eds.) (2007) *Modernizing Schools: People, Learning and Organizations*. London: Continuum.

Butt, G and Lambert, D (2014) International perspectives on the future of geography education: an analysis of national curricula and standards. *International Research in Geographical and Environmental Education* 23(1): 1–12.

Cohen, L, Manion, L and Morrison, K (2000) *Research Methods in Education*. London: Routledge Falmer.

Denby, N, Butroyd, R, Swift, H, Price, J and Glazzard, J (2008) *Masters Level Study in Education*. Maidenhead: McGraw-Hill.

Finney, J (2013) Music teachers as researchers. In Finney, J and Laurence, F (eds.) *MasterClass in Music Education*, pp. 3–12. London: Bloomsbury.

Firth, R and Morgan, J (2010) What is the place of radical/critical research in geography education? *International Research in Environmental and Geographical Education* 19(2): 109–13.

Furlong, J and Oancea, A (2005) *Assessing Quality in Applied and Practice-Based Educational research*. Oxford: OUDES.

Guba, E (1990) Subjectivity and objectivity. In Eisner, E and Peshkin, A (eds.) *Qualitative Enquiry in Education: The Continuing Debate*. New York: Teachers College Press.

Hargreaves, D (1998) A new partnership of stakeholders and a national strategy of research in education. In Rudduck, J and McIntyre, D (eds.) *Challenges for Educational Research*, pp. 114–36. London: Paul Chapman.

Hart, C (2004) *Doing Your Masters Dissertation*. London: Sage.

Hickey, M and Lawson, V (2005) Beyond science? Human geography. Interpretation and critique. In Castree, N, Rogers, A and Sherman, D (eds.) *Questioning Geography: Fundamental Debates*. Oxford: Blackwell.

Hillage, J, Pearson, R, Anderson, A and Tamkin, P (1998) *Excellence in Research on Schools*. London: DFEE.

Johnson, B and Christensen, L (2012) *Educational Research: Quantitative, Qualitative and Mixed Approaches*. London: Sage.

Lambert, D (2010) Geography education research and why it matters. *International Research in Environmental and Geographical Education* 19(2): 83–6.

Lambert, D and Jones, M (2013) Introduction: geography education, questions and choices. In Lambert, D and Jones, M (eds.) *Debates in Geography Education*, pp. 1–14. Abingdon: Routledge.

Laurence, F (2013) Doing research in music education. In Finney, J and Laurence, F (eds.) *MasterClass in Music Education*, pp.13–23. London: Bloomsbury.

Lave, J and Wenger, E (1991). *Situated Learning: Legitimate Peripheral Participation*. Cambridge: Cambridge University Press.

Lincoln, Y and Guba, E (1985) *Naturalist Enquiry*. California: Sage.

Maclure, M (2003) *Discourse in Educational and Social Research*. London: McGraw-Hill.

Morgan, J and Firth, R (2010) 'By our theories shall you know us': the role of theory in geographical education. *International Research in Environmental and Geographical Education* 19(2): 87–90.

Naish, M (1993) 'Never mind the quality – feel the width' – How shall we judge the quality of research in geographical and environmental education? *International Research in Environmental and Geographical Education* 2(1): 64–5.

O'Leary, Z (2004) *The Essential Guide to Doing Your Research Project*. London: Sage.

Onwuegbuzie, A and Leech,N (2005) On becoming a pragmatic researcher: the importance of combining quantitative and qualitative research methodologies. *International Journal of Social Research Methodology* 8(5): 375–87.

Robson, C (2002) *Real World Research*. Oxford: Blackwell.

Sachs, J (2003) *The Activist Teaching Profession*. Maidenhead: Open University Press.

Sewell, K (2008) *Doing Your PGCE at M Level*. London: Sage.

Thomas, D (2007) *Education after Theory*. London: McGraw-Hill.

Tooley, J and Darby, D (1998) *Educational Research: A Critique*. London: OfSTED

Whitty, G (2005) *Education(al) Research and Education Policy Making: Is Conflict Inevitable?* Presidential address to BERA conference, 17 September 2005, University of Glamorgan.

Research in Geography Education

David Lambert

2

Chapter outline

Some initial distinctions and setting the scene   16

An overview of geography education: what counts as 'research' and
   where do we start?   18

Demarcating a 'field' of GER   21

Some 'ways in' to GER priorities   24

Conclusions   25

This chapter aims to provide an overview of research in geography education. It discusses the *place* of research within the context of a large and diverse field of professional practice focused on the teaching of geography in primary and secondary schools and sixth form colleges. The field of 'geography education' extends to further and higher education sectors as well, but we are largely concerned here with the years of compulsory education which in England is officially to 17 years of age, rising to 18 years in 2015.

The view developed in the chapter is that those intending to teach, especially (but not only) those who acquire Masters credits through their training, should be guided by research (see Brooks 2010). In some ways this is an unremarkable case to make: surely any professional body is anchored by a specialist knowledge base, and this is created and refined through research and scholarship. But teaching is unusual in this case: some policy makers and even educationists have conflicting views on this to the extent that they argue that teachers need no training or professional development at all, just an enthusiasm to impart their subject knowledge. It is without doubt true that some brilliant teachers are simply 'born'. But that is a flimsy reason to be against the notion of requiring all teachers to acquire a professional qualification. The fact that occasionally unqualified individuals have circumvented the rules to become practising doctors, and even airline pilots, does not mean it is right or just, nor the basis for robust, trusted service provision to 'allow' this to happen as an 'alternative pathway' into the profession. Thus, wrong doers are rooted out and professional defences, in the form of regulations and qualifications, strengthened. But in teaching it appears possible for some to contemplate an entirely practice-based profession based on instinct, experience and enthusiasm. This certainly undermines the notion that research and scholarship should inform teaching.

So on what basis can we claim research in geography education is important? The case I would make is that it is the critical engagement with research that both deepens and extends our appreciation and understanding of day-to-day practices – which can so easily become habitual and unresponsive to changing circumstances. 'Engagement' can mean doing research if circumstances allow. It can also mean reading research; that is, engaging with the scholarly contribution of others including maybe those undertaking higher degrees. The increasing number of practising teachers who go on to complete their Masters degree, which normally involves writing a Report or Dissertation, conduct research of their own and in so doing contribute to the body of research intelligence and our collective understanding of the field. This is especially so if additional steps are taken to get the research published through a professional or academic journal and therefore communicated after 'peer review' to the wider community of practice. However even if this is not the case, the process of reading and writing research in geography education is the principal means by which the field develops: and develop it must, as both the discipline of geography and the idea of education continue to evolve in response to economic, environmental, political, social and technological change.

Some initial distinctions and setting the scene

It is important to make some clear distinctions from the outset. In the introduction I chose to say that teachers, or teaching, should be 'evidence-led': I preferred the phrase 'guided by research'. The distinction is important not least because much of the policy narrative in education (from government, from Ofsted and from the National College for Teaching and Leadership) places emphasis on the notion of evidence-led practice (notwithstanding contradictory counter-currents in the 'glorious amateur' sentiments mentioned in the previous paragraphs). Of course, 'evidence-led' is in some ways a difficult notion to quibble with, especially if we want to promote the significance of research in geography education. After all, research usually gathers data, or evidence, about a particular question or issue; it sifts and analyses this and often then relates this to an aspect of professional practice, often overtly seeking some kind of improvement. However, in education we are usually faced with enormously difficult challenges about the generalizability of such evidence. As we shall see, very little research in geography education is large scale; indeed, not much extends beyond single school settings or even individual classrooms. Thus, much educational practice is highly context specific, based on unique encounters and relationships. This is not to say that we only study singularities in geography education research (GER) or that the application of research findings across contexts is impossible: far from it. But it does mean we have to be wary of the tendency sometimes perceived that education can or should follow a kind of 'medical' model, leading to the diagnosis and treatment of teaching and learning issues. Evidence-led rhetoric is often uncritically based on research findings of 'what works'. However, what works for me (in *this* classroom, with *these* children, with *those* resources) may not quite work in the same way for you (in that classroom, with those children, with these resources). In other words, evidence of 'what works' needs to be treated with a pinch of salt.

In a similar way, I would not advise teachers to search for 'evidence' before introducing some form of curriculum or pedagogic change. Education as a field of scholarship is not like medicine, engineering or dentistry as it is more ideographic (focusing on individual cases or events) than nomothetic (searching for general statements that account for larger patterns) in its approach. Judgements can be made about particular events and settings and of course teachers are in a good position to pursue the critical scholarship on which to base such judgements. In passing, it is very well worth noting that *geographers* are especially familiar with the significance of the ideographic: that is, the need to respect and understand the uniqueness of place. This does not mean that geographers only study places as singularities. They acknowledge universal processes operating at a variety of scales including the global, while at the same time acknowledge that these play out differently in different places depending on the unique combination of physical and human geography. Interestingly, Andrew Kirby (2014) has recently argued for a return to a greater emphasis on the particularity of place context in the study of cities:

> Practitioners have studied the city and done so in an ideographic, contextual manner, which is what will be demanded in the future. Geography has the ability to integrate its understanding of both human and social systems in a way that other disciplines do not. (p. 18)

Insert 'classrooms' for 'the city' and we have a reasonable approximation of an approach to GER which guards against merely the application of so-called evidence-led good practices such as the 'three part lesson' or 'always declare your objectives at the beginning of the lesson'.

However, this does not mean we cannot learn from research, nor that research conducted by others in different contexts and settings cannot slowly build and refine our professional knowledge and judgement. Indeed, there is clearly a case for nomothetic approaches to

GER, not least because the larger-scale studies that these imply refine our understanding of the broader contexts in which particular events and settings exist. Again, it is perhaps worthwhile explicitly to draw attention to the parallel that exists here between the fields of geography and education. As we have noted, in geography we are acutely aware of the way universal or general processes play out differently in different places: this is one reason why 'case studies' are so important in geography. As we shall see, case study research makes a significant contribution to GER too, for similar reasons.

This chapter attempts to say something about what we have learnt from GER and points to some current and future research priorities. There are times when it is appropriate and helpful systematically and carefully to gather some evidence, perhaps to evaluate a particular curriculum or pedagogic innovation. This may be entirely for local reasons – to improve your own teaching or simply to satisfy your curiosity. But it is much more communicable when this at least aspires to build on what we know (or think we know) already and to contribute to the greater good. This is one of the challenges that the Geography Education Research Committee (GERC) of the *Roadmap for 21st Century Geography Education Project* sought to address in the United States (Bednarz et al. 2013), as we shall see later in this chapter. It is one of the purposes of the purely voluntary creation of the UK-based Geography Education Research Collective (GEReCo: http://gereco.org).

An overview of geography education: what counts as 'research' and where do we start?

As I have pointed out elsewhere (Lambert 2013), overviews of geography education tend to be in the form of teacher 'handbooks' assuming the role of textbooks. These typically have a section on the justification of geography in the school *curriculum* and its philosophy, followed by the main bulk of the book on *pedagogy* and *assessment*. Though often well referenced and research based, these books are aimed mainly at a professional audience and often stress practical techniques. Based more on principle and heavily dependent on conceptual research and development rather than on empirical 'evidence', these books are mainstays and are influential in teacher education and training. In the United States, Gersmehl (2006) provides a detailed account of some principles and practices of geography teaching. This book also contains explanations of geographical content and concepts and in this sense is quite different from its counterpart in the UK context, where for example Lambert and Balderstone (2010) address geography graduates, perhaps taking for granted a high level of 'subject knowledge'. In addition to professional handbooks, however, there is a growing literature aimed at the teacher educators, mentors and researchers in education, including Masters and postgraduate research students. Butt (2011) is a good example from the United Kingdom, as is another edited collection, Lambert and Jones (2013), which attempts to provide an overview of contemporary debates and disputes in geography education. These books and other similar sources over the years (Balderstone 2006; Smith 2002) are a good 'way in' to the field of geography education generally, and to research in this field. This is, of course, partly because chapters are by and large well referenced and take us into the wider literature, including journal articles: see for example the specific chapters on research by Lofthouse and Leat (2006) and Roberts (2002).

Journals can be classified in at least two ways. First, we can distinguish between subject specialist journals such as those within the 'field' of geography education (see the next part) and those that are more generic and concerned with general educational processes. It is possible to find articles in general education research journals concerning geography: often these are of special significance, because the author has chosen to communicate their research beyond the more familiar (and perhaps 'safer') subject specialism. It takes some courage to write to an 'external' audience: but it is important that geography educationists do so, for the risk with highly specialist fields such as geography education is that the discourse may become 'internalist', and full of insider orthodoxies and unchallenged assumptions.

Secondly, we can distinguish between 'professional' journals, of which *Teaching Geography* would be a good example, and 'academic' journals, of which *Geography* and *International Research in Geographical and Environmental Education* (IRGEE) are leading examples (see the more complete listing at the end of this chapter). While the former aims very consciously at teaching practices, usually through well-illustrated, short (c. 1,000–1,500 words) articles, the latter is oriented around reporting research through articles often exceeding 5,000 words in length and which include careful elucidation of the methodological approaches adopted and origin of the theoretical frameworks used to conceptualize the research and its findings.

We may conclude from this short section that much of the published writings on geography education, though research based or at least referenced to wider debates, are 'professional' rather than 'academic' in purpose and in form. This is not to privilege one against the other, for both are important. But this raises the question of what 'counts' as research. For if we are to *read* research, let alone *write* it, it may be helpful to say something indicative of what we mean by research. We cannot be completely cut and dried about this; indeed, it would not be helpful to offer a hard and fast rigid definition, for there are many grey areas. The following illustrate this with an inevitably personal response:

- Does research *have to* contain 'data'?
- 'No' is my answer, for research can be entirely conceptual, using philosophical or methodological frameworks in order to tease out and clarify important distinctions or meanings. One reason why such research is important is that it helps keep our attention on the level of goals and purposes rather than the nitty-gritty of day-to-day practice. The latter also is important, but focuses only on that and we can finish up with accumulations of evidence about 'what works' but in a relative vacuum.

- Are professionally oriented enquiries and writings by definition 'not academic' and therefore *not* research?
- My answer again is 'No'. Carefully conducted Action Research, for example, can be entirely class-room based, perhaps on a single teacher and single small group of students. Both the process and the products of such enquiries can be illuminating, and can be adopted or adapted by others in other settings.

Bearing in mind the challenges of grasping and assimilating such debates (or 'grey areas') what can we say about GER which is a little more definitive? There are a number of things:

- Research is usually based on an explicit *methodology* that is justified in terms of its fitness for pur-pose. One overarching purpose of the methodology is usually to show that care has been taken (a) to 'distance' the researcher from what is being researched and (b) to avoid overstating what can be concluded from the research. To put this another way, in what way can the study claim to be more than a collection of personal reflections and/or opinions? Can it be 'trusted' in some way? Positivistic science usually requires validity and reliability, perhaps delivered through the application of tried and tested techniques on randomized and suitably sized sample populations. More qualita-tive studies would probably emphasize steps taken to ensure the data as portrayed are accurate and the conclusions drawn dependable. To do this the researcher takes steps to show a disinterest in the findings: disinterest offers no guarantees, but at least it helps show that the research findings were not predetermined.
- Research also usually shows a high level of what we may call 'systematicity' – that is, it is connected, usually through an extensive literature review, to a wider set of ideas, concepts or theories. In other words, the research is 'located' and is not just a 'one off'. Another way of looking at this is that good research tries to 'stand on the shoulders of others': only very rarely do we begin with a blank sheet.
- Research is usually driven by a clear 'research question' or aim (sometimes with a small number of sub-questions) that is carefully situated and justified. In other words, we do not simply set out hoping to find something, hoping for the best. Research is focused by a clear sense of what needs to be found. This requires a lot of 'front loading' in the research journey – that is, a considerable mental effort (usually involving reading and writing) in order to achieve conceptual clarity before the data-gathering stage.
- A good place to begin a literature search is with the Geographical Association. Marsden and Foskett (1997) produced a comprehensive bibliography of research in geography education which has been complemented by the Geographical Association's (GA's) Geography Geography Trainer Induction Programme (GTIP) pages which now features an online 'library' of journal articles. http://www.geography.org.uk/gtip/library/

Having made some introductory remarks about the field of geography education, and how to enter this field through the literature, we have now made some observations about what constitutes research. We are now in a position therefore to say something about the particu-lar field of geography education research (GER).

Demarcating a 'field' of GER

Geography is not a singular concept. It exists in many forms across educational settings. Thus although it is in some ways a common-sense and straightforward matter to demarcate the field of GER, it can become rather more tricky in practice. This is especially so internationally, as we shall see. But first, let's start with a common-sense frame of mind: GER is educational research conducted within the context of geography as a school subject. We can, for example, visit the unofficial website of the on-line MA Geography Education at the Institute of Education where it advises the following in relation to choosing dissertation research topics:

> In the MA GeogEd we insist that the research enquiry addresses questions or issues within, broadly, the field of geography education. The grand overarching questions that shape this field are 'what is the relationship between geography and education?' and 'in what ways does the study of geography contribute to education?' This encompasses issues to do with teaching and learning, technology and assessment, media and resources, environment and citizenship and many more besides . . . but always within the field of geography education. (http://mageoged.webs.com/dissertations.htm)

This is, arguably, a bit circular. But it does allude to one of the enduring clusters of questions in GER – at least among Masters students – which is to do with the nature of geography: what is being taught and learnt in geography, and how do teachers, parents and students perceive this? It is remarkable that a settled answer to these questions appears so elusive. However, what is important to acknowledge is that there is a story to tell: we are never starting such enquiries on a blank piece of paper. Thus, Alastair Bonnett (2008) tackles the question 'what is geography?' in a way that is inclusive, even of popular geographies, characterizing geography as an 'ancient idea'. This is quite different from Matthews and Herbert (2008) who prefer to describe geography perhaps more straightforwardly as a coherent academic discipline (in mainly the UK context) or Tim Cresswell (2013) who takes a historical approach to his very informative account of the evolution of geographical thought. Thus in any investigation of geography in education, questions concerning the nature of geographical knowledge are germane. The principles guiding the selection of what to teach in schools vary significantly between national jurisdictions, depending partly on how geographical knowledge is conceptualized and valued. Occasionally, journal articles have attempted to overview these differences, such as Gerber (2001) and the 2014 special issue of *International Research in Geographical and Environmental Education* (Butt and Lambert 2014). From the US perspective, Golledge (2002) seeks to identify the unique qualities of geographical knowledge, whilst Hanson (2004) opts to emphasize the value of geographical perspectives, coining the term the 'geographic advantage' (utilized to good effect by the *Roadmap* project: Bednarz et al. 2013). In the United Kingdom, Roger Firth (2011) has explored in a very timely manner the epistemic features of geography as a discipline from a social realist perspective (in the context of a 'knowledge-led' national curriculum following the 2010 Coalition government). He argues persuasively that teachers need closer engagement with the discipline, and partly to this end Peter Jackson (2006) has written from his position as a leading cultural geographer about the nature and value of 'thinking geographically' as an educational goal (which has parallels to Susan Hanson's 'geographic advantage').

Now it could be argued that the research agenda outlined above and which I have attempted to place in a wider disciplinary context is *so far* removed from a 'what works' agenda that it is destined to be of parochial ('internalist') interest only. By this I mean it is essentially inward looking: some may even say self-absorbed. This is a possibility that the GERC of the *Roadmap for 21st Century Geography Education Project* confronted and sought to address in the US context (Bednarz et al. 2013). The GERC reviewed current research being conducted in geography education and found:

> . . . that it is unfocused, parochial and disconnected from other education research. (NGS 2013, p. 14)

It may be possible to make a similar claim for GER in the United Kingdom although there are several notable contemporary exceptions (that nevertheless may serve to 'prove the rule'). Thus, geography educators have published research that draws perspectives from philosophy (Firth 2011; Winter 2006, 2010, 2013a, 2013b), cultural studies (Morgan 2007, 2008b), childhood studies (Biddulph 2011; Martin and Catling 2011), and cognitive and conceptual development (Bennetts 2005; Taylor 2011) . . . there is undoubtedly more GER that can be cited, for example, intersecting with: curriculum studies (Rawling 2001; Roberts 1996; Morgan 2008a), learning styles and pedagogy (Leat and Higgins 2002; Roberts 2013), technologies including GIS (Fargher 2013), personalization (Jones 2013), fieldwork (Rickinson et al. 2004; Dunphy and Spellman 2009), development education (Lambert and Morgan 2011), assessment and evaluation (Butt et al. 2011). This is an illustrative rather than exhaustive list.

This emergent list can also be used to reinforce the other point made by the GERC, about *focus*. Whilst all the above are certainly opportunities that arise for researchers in geography education, what this list does not do is help the lone researcher, perhaps a Masters student, prioritize in a way that would really help build our 'collective research intelligence' as I described it earlier in the chapter. What I am saying here is that the field of GER, though obvious to define in one sense (i.e. it is to do with *geography* in education), is in the end impossible to delimit in any meaningful way because geography education overlaps with pretty much every educational question and across the whole range of issues under curriculum, pedagogy and assessment. The risk here is worth spelling out. It is sometimes observed in Masters dissertations that the research has taken on a generic aspect of education (say, inter-culturalism, formative assessment, teacher talk in the classroom, challenging gifted learners . . . the list is potentially endless and may in the end be determined to some extent by the priorities identified by the senior leadership team of a school – in turn, sometimes in response to the perceived demands of Ofsted). The research is conducted in the context of geography, but can finish up as simply that: a generic study with a geographical hue. Arguably, this does not contribute significantly to research and scholarship in geography education, which ought to be driven by its own questions and priorities.

The US Roadmap GERC confronted this issue by identifying, following an extensive literature search and discussion, its research priorities for geography education. In summary, these are organized under five headings:

- learning progressions,
- effective teaching,
- exemplary curricula,
- impact of fieldwork and
- teacher preparation.

Furthermore, the GERC proposed that these priorities be shaped by four key research questions. In other words, individuals conducting their own research in locations across the country (hopefully under one of the five headings above) would be encouraged to think how their research would contribute in some way to these overarching research questions:

- How do geographic knowledge, skills and practices develop across individuals, settings and time?
- How do geographic knowledge, skills and practices develop across different elements of geography?
- What supports or promotes the development of geographic knowledge, skills and practices?
- What is necessary to support the effective and broad implementation of the development of geographic knowledge, skills and practices?

It is important to recognize that these questions and priorities relate to the United States. In the US school geography is organized (some would say 'lost') under the social studies curriculum, often playing second fiddle to US and world history and only very rarely being taught by specialist geographers even in secondary schools. This has obvious implications, for example, on how 'subject knowledge development' of teachers is understood. In England, where the majority of geography lessons in secondary schools are taught by teachers with a degree in geography, we have a different set of assumptions which includes the preparedness of teachers to take responsibility for curriculum making: in the United States we cannot assume teachers of geography have an adequate grasp of geography *as a discipline* beyond everyday conceptions of the subject in the popular imagination. However, important though it is to acknowledge differences, we should do this with due caution. Secondary school teachers of geography in England may have a degree in the subject: but does that mean they do not have to continue to think hard about the nature of geographical knowledge and its potential role in education? Or about the relationship between geography as expressed in the national curriculum (and/or examination specifications) and the discipline? Or about the relationship between the national curriculum documents and the localized curriculum, as enacted in a particular school context? These are vital concerns and questions partly because geography in education is not (and in my view must never become) a settled, 'given' body of knowledge.

Thus, we may take the US *Roadmap* GERC priorities and key research questions as a working template applicable to other settings, including England. These are not educational research questions 'with a geographical hue'. Rather, they set a clear set of priorities for GER – and a potential for some meaningful international comparisons.

Some 'ways in' to GER priorities

In this final section we explore in broad brush terms the main GER priorities as identified by the US Roadmap and listed in the previous section (with the exception of 'teacher preparation', which arguably is beyond the scope of this book). It almost goes without saying that what follows is not definitive. Its purpose is twofold: (a) to illustrate to some extent the scope of these 'priorities' as subfields in their own right and (b) to provide some form of baseline of literature as possible entry points to at least some aspects of these subfields.

Learning progressions (I include assessment under this category)

- There is a large professional literature on assessment in geography, and Butt and Weeden (2009) is a good example. There is relatively little empirical research on assessment methods and approaches in the specific field of geography, although Davies (1995) presents important articles on national testing in geography (in England's national curriculum context); Butt et al. (2011) contain research on assessment practice.
- Equally important is conceptual work on what we actually mean by 'progression'. Bennetts (2005) made an important contribution clarifying what we mean by 'making progress' in learning geography. If *assessment* is concerned mainly with the measurement of attainment, usually of the acquisition and application of geographical knowledge, understanding and skills, *evaluation* is concerned with the making of judgements about effectiveness or even efficacy of geographical courses of study. Edelson et al. (2013) develop these distinctions clearly. Evaluation often draws on evidence in the form of student assessment scores, but it can also combine this with broader indicators including direct classroom observations and interviews.

Effective teaching ('pedagogy')

- The development of pedagogy and pedagogic technique has been of great interest to geography educationists, and it would be a mistake to assume that this is only a recent phenomenon. Fairgrieve, a key figure in geography, wrote arguably the most influential book of its time (Fairgrieve 1926) merging a vision of geography as a subject with assertions about how it should be taught in school. The development of active learning pedagogies expanded in the second half of the twentieth century. A groundbreaking book in this regard, theoretically robust and deeply influential to this day, is Slater (1982). In more recent times, further developments in our understanding of learning through developments in psychology have been harnessed in Leat (1998) a well-known, but in some ways controversial handbook. Roberts (2013) is an altogether more rounded account of how effective pedagogies can be deployed to enhance geographical knowledge development.

- In the United States, and in other jurisdictions, there has been an enormous interest in spatial cognition, illustrated by the interesting paper and ensuing discussion in Gersmehl and Gersmehl (2006). But there has been a longstanding interest in this aspect of geography education in the United Kingdom too, for example, through scholarly works like Boardman (1983) and more recently Wiegend (2006), partly related to children's spatial abilities providing a ready empirical base for applying Piagetian theories of learning in geography, as in Blaut (1997).

Exemplary curricula

- For research purposes we can conceptually distinguish curriculum (what to teach) from pedagogy (how to teach), although it is clearly recognized that in practice the two ideas are blended and often inseparable. We also distinguish curriculum design and development (which need not happen inside school and may not involve teachers directly) from curriculum making (which definitely does take place locally and involves teachers in different classroom settings). Thus, as a field of scholarship, curriculum is extensive and complex.
- An early attempt to implement the idea of rational curriculum planning and development in geography is Graves (1979), a book that still repays reading today. It became part of the conceptual platform for what Rawling (2001) called the 'golden age' of curriculum thinking in the United Kingdom, partly a result of several significant government-funded (Schools Council) curriculum projects in geography. Roberts' (1996) research is highly significant to the present day as it signalled very clearly the limited impact of (simply) issuing national standards in order to reform the curriculum without investing in teacher development at the same time (as, arguably, the curriculum projects did).

Impact of fieldwork

- The role of fieldwork has been a prominent concern in the United Kingdom since the nineteenth century – perhaps reflecting the heritage of the idea of geography itself, requiring the active exploration, discovery, description and classification of the world and its features. Fieldwork is currently a target for empirical research as evidenced by, for example, Nundy (1999) and Oost et al. (2011) and many more.

Conclusions

This chapter has attempted a *tour d'horizon* of GER. It is a field of highly specialized scholarly enquiry and as such can never be expected to grow and mature into anything other than an important niche interest. Even specialist fields such as science education and mathematics education research, both fields of education that attract strong political interest and therefore funding, are comparatively young (they didn't really exist 40 or 50 years ago) and relatively small. They are important however, because teaching a subject is a specialized activity requiring deep critical deliberation and thoughtful practice: research and scholarship needs to be undertaken and to develop steadily in order to nourish this. Specialist subject research such as GER is not simply educational research with a geographical slant: it is fundamentally about the significance of geographical knowledge and thought in education and ways in which we can implement this to our satisfaction – and with maximum benefit for our students.

I wish to end with a thought in relation to this final comment. I have written before (Lambert 2010) about the uselessness of research for research's sake, preferring the notion of 'consequential validity' to steer decisions about what research to do, and how, when and so on. I firmly believe that researchers need to occupy a space of ideas and that this carries with it some risk: ideas that seemed to hold promise can sometimes run into the sand. That's fine, because we almost certainly learn a great deal along the way. The 'useless' research I have in mind is more to do with research that does not take any risks: where we accumulate data on this or that because it is possible, accessible and can be done. The research question is, as we have discussed, of vital importance – more important than identifying gatherable data. It is apposite to keep in mind the question: what is the consequence of this enquiry? This entails addressing further questions such as: What can we learn from it? Why does it matter?

Key sources

Here is a summary of the principal 'ways in' to the field of GER.

1. Websites

There are many websites dedicated to geography education, including many associated with particular individuals or schools. Many of these are interesting, especially as a source of teaching ideas. In terms of more deliberative websites that can help students, teachers and researchers wade through the mass of often freely available resources on the internet, we can turn to the learnt societies and subject associations. In the United Kingdom, the Geographical Association (GA) was established in 1893 and is arguably now the leading advocate of geography education in the United Kingdom. In the United States, the National Council for Geographic Education was established in 1915 to celebrate and promote geography in education. Since the 1980s the National Geographic Society has supported an extensive network of Geographic Alliances in every US state committed to 'bringing geography back to K-12 education'. For geography education internationally, two reference points are the relatively recently established (1979): Eurogeo, which has extensive links and networks, and the International Geographical Union (IGU), which has a very active Commission for Geographical Education.

- Eurogeo: http://www.eurogeography.eu
- Geographical Association: http://www.geography.org.uk/

- The International Geographical Union: http://www.igu-online.org
- National Council for Geographic Education: http://www.ncge.org
- Association for American Geographers: http://www.aag.org
- National Geographic Society: http://education.nationalgeographic.co.uk/education/program/geography-alliances/?ar_a=1&force_AR=True
- The Royal Geographical Society: http://www.rgs.org/OurWork/Schools/Schools+and+education.htm

2. Journals

There are many research journals dedicated to geography and its many cognate disciplines and specializations. Geography education is a comparatively small – and recent – subfield of geography with a very small number of specialist research journals. The leading journal in this subfield is *International Research in Geographical and Environmental Education* (IRGEE), established in 1991. Even more recent than IRGEE is *Research in Geographical Education* (RGE), which is dominated by American research activity. The *Journal of Geography in Higher Education* (JGHE) has a wider remit than education and is not often concerned with education in primary and secondary schools, but recognizes the importance of curriculum, pedagogy and assessment in higher education. The Geographical Association's academic journal *Geography* has, for many years, had an interest in educational issues and developments but combines this with scholarly articles on geography: it rarely reports educational research studies per se. It can be compared with its counterpart from the NCGE in the United States, the *Journal of Geography*. More professionally oriented journals serving geography education are rather more in number than those addressing research, usually serving a national or regional audience meeting the particular needs of teachers and educationists in specific jurisdictions. Thus, *Teaching Geography* is a well-established, refereed journal aimed at supporting the development of classroom practice mainly in secondary geography. An interesting recent development is the advent of online, open access journals such as *Review of Geographical Education Online* (RIGEO) and *European Journal of Geography* (EJG).

- *European Journal of Geography*: http://www.eurogeographyjournal.eu/
- *Geography*: http://www.geography.org.uk/Journals/Journals.asp?journalID=1
- *International Research in Geographical and Environmental Education*: http://www.tandfonline.com/toc/rgee20/current#.UcIeEBbYiwE
- *The Journal of Geography*: http://www.ncge.org/journal-of-geography
- *The Journal of Geography in Higher Education*: http://www.tandfonline.com/toc/cjgh20/current#.UcIfvBbYiwE
- *Research in Geographic Education*: http://www.geo.txstate.edu/grosvenor/
- *Review of Geographical Education Online*: http://www.rigeo.org/
- *Teaching Geography*: http://www.geography.org.uk/journals/journals.asp?journalID=3

References

Balderstone, D (ed.) (2006) *Secondary Geography Handbook*. Sheffield: Geographical Association.

Bednarz, S W, Heffron, S and Huynh N T (eds.) (2013) *A Roadmap for 21st Century Geography Education Research*, A Report from the Geography Education Research Committee. Washington, DC: Association of American Geographers http://natgeoed.org/roadmap

Bennetts, T (2005) The links between understanding, progression and assessment in the secondary geography curriculum. *Geography* 90(2): 152–70.

Biddulph, M (2011) Young people's geographies; implications for school geography. In Butt G (ed.) *Geography, Education and the Future*, pp. 44–59. London: Continuum.

Blaut, J (1997) Children can. *Annals of the Association of American Geographers* 87(1): 152–8.

Boardman, D (1983) Spatial concept development and primary school work. In Boardman, D (ed.) *New Directions in Geographical Education*, pp. 119–34. London: Falmer Press.

Bonnett, A (2008) *What Is Geography?* London: Sage.

Brooks, C (ed.) (2010) *Studying PGCE Geography at M Level*. London: Routledge.

Butt, G (2000) *Continuum Guide to Geography Education*. London: Continuum.

— (ed.) (2011) *Geography, Education and the Future*. London: Continuum.

Butt, G and Lambert, D (2014) International perspectives on the future of geography education: an analysis of national curricula and standards. *International Research in Geographical and Environmental Education* 23(1): 1–12.

Butt, G and Weeden, P (2009) *Assessing Progress in Your School Curriculum*. Sheffield: Geographical Association.

Butt, G, Weeden, P, Chubb, S and Srokosz, A (2011) The state of geography in English secondary schools: an insight into practice and performance in assessment. *International Research in Geographical and Environmental Research* 15(2): 134–48.

Catling, S and Martin, F (2011) Contesting powerful knowledge: the primary geography curriculum as an articulation between academic and children's (ethno-) geographies. *Curriculum Journal* 22(3): 317–35.

Cresswell, T (2013) *Geographic Thought: A Critical Introduction*. Chichester: Blackwell-Wiley.

Davies, P (1995) An inductive approach to levels of attainment. *International Research in Geographical and Environmental Education* 4(1): 47–65.

Dunphy, A and Spellman, G (2009) Geography fieldwork, fieldwork value and learning styles. *International Research in Geographical and Environmental Education* 18(1): 19–28.

Edelson, D C, Shavelson, R J and Wertheim, J A (eds.) (2013) *A Road Map for 21st Century Geography Education: Assessment*. A Report from the Assessment Committee of the Road Map for 21st Century Geography Education Project. Washington, DC: National Geographic Society.

Fairgrieve, J (1926) *Geography in Schools*. London: UTP.

Fargher, M (2013) Geographic Information (GI); how could it be used? In Lambert, D and Jones, M (eds.) *Debates in Geography Education*, 206–18. London: Routledge.

Firth, R (2011) Making geography visible as an object of study in the secondary school curriculum. *The Curriculum Journal* 22(3): 289–316.

Gerber, R (2001) The state of geographical education around the world. *International Research in Geographical and Environmental Education* 10(4): 349–62

Gersmehl, P (2006) *Teaching Geography*. New York: Guilford Press.

Gersmehl, P and Gersmehl, C (2006) Wanted: a concise list of neurologically defensible and assessable spatial-thinking skills. *Research in Geographic Education* 8: 5–38.

Golledge, R (2002) The nature of geographical knowledge. *Annals of the Association of American Geographers* 92(1): 1–14.

Graves, N (1979) *Curriculum Planning in Geography*. London: Heinemann.

Hanson, S (2004) Who are 'we'? An important question for geography's future. *Annals of the Association of American Geographers* 94(4): 715–22.

Hopwood, N (2004) Pupils' conceptions of geography: towards an improved understanding. *International Research in Geographical and Environmental Education* 13(4): 348–61.

Jackson, P (2006) Thinking geographically. *Geography* 91(3): 199–204.

Jones, M (2013) What is personalized learning in Geography? In Lambert, D and Jones, M (eds.) (2013) *Debates in Geography Education*. pp. 116–28. London: Routledge.

Kirby, A (2014) Geographical leadership, sustainability and urban education. *Geography* 99(1): 13–19.

Lambert, D (2010) Geography education research and why it matters. *International Research in Geographical and Environmental Education* 19(2) (special issue on research in geography education).

— (2013) 'Education (K-12) geography', *Oxford Bibliographies*. In Geography Warf, B (ed.) New York: Oxford University Press, http://www.oxfordbibliographies.com/

Lambert, D and Balderstone, D (2010) *Learning to Teach Geography*, 2nd edition. London: Routledge.

Lambert, D and Jones, M (eds.) (2013) *Debates in Geography Education*. London: Routledge.

Lambert, D and Morgan, J (2011) *Geography and Development: Development Education in Schools and the Part Played by Geography Teachers*, DERC Research Paper 3. London: Institute of Education.

Leat, D (1998) *Thinking through Geography*. Cambridge: Chris Kington Publishing.

Leat, D and Higgins, S (2002) The role of powerful pedagogical strategies in curriculum development. *The Curriculum Journal* 13(1): 77–85.

Lofthouse, R and Leat, D (2006) Research in geographical education, In Balderstone, D (ed.) *Secondary Geography Handbook*. Sheffield: Geographical Association.

Marsden, B and Foskett, N (1998) *ABibliography of Geographical Education 1970-1997*. Sheffield: Geographical Association.

Matthews, J and Herbert, D (2008) *Geography: A Short Introduction*. Oxford: Oxford University Press.

Morgan, J (2007) School geography and the politics of culture. *Geography Compass* 1(3): 373–88.

— (2008a) Contesting Europe: representations of space in English school geography. *Globalisation, Societies, Education* 6(3): 281–90.

— (2008b) Curriculum development in 'New times'. *Geography* 93(1): 17–24.

NGS (2013) *Charting the Course: A Roadmap for 21st Century Geography Education, Executive Overview*. National Geographic Society, www.natgeoed.org/roadmap

Nundy, S (1999) The fieldwork effect: the role and impact of fieldwork in the upper primary school. *International Research in Geographical and Environmental Education* 8(2): 190–8.

Oost, K, De Vries, B and Van der Schee, J (2011) Enquiry-driven fieldwork as a rich and powerful teaching strategy: school practices in secondary school geography education in the Netherlands. *International Research in Geographical and Environmental Education* 20(4): 309–25.

Rawling, E (2001) *Changing the Subject: The Impact of National Policy on School Geography 1980–2000*. Sheffield: Geographical Association.

Rickinson, M, Dillon, J, Teamey, K, Morris, M, Choi, M, Sanders, D and Benefield, P (2004) *A Review of Research on Outdoor Learning*. London: National Foundation for Educational Research and Kings College London.

Roberts, M (1996) Interpretations of the Geography National Curriculum: a common curriculum for all? *Journal of Curriculum Studies* 27(2): 187–205.

— (2002) The role of research in supporting teaching and learning. In Smith, M (ed.) (2002) *Teaching Geography in Secondary Schools*. London: Routledge Falmer.

— (2013) *Geography Through Enquiry*. Sheffield: Geographical Association.

Slater, F (1982) *Learning through Geography*. London: Heinemann.

Smith, M (ed.) (2002) *Teaching Geography in Secondary Schools*. London: Routledge Falmer.

Taylor, L (2011) Investigating change in young people's understandings of Japan: a study in learning about distant place. *British Educational Research Journal* 37(6): 1033–54.

Weigend, P (2006) *Learning and Teaching with Maps*. London: Routledge.

Winter, C (2006) Doing justice to geography in the secondary school: deconstruction, invention and the national curriculum. *British Journal of Educational Studies* 54(2): 212–29.

— (2010) Places, spaces, holes for knowing and writing the earth: the geography curriculum and Derrida's Khora. *Ethics and Education* 4(1): 57–68.

— (2013a) Enframing geography: subject, curriculum, knowledge, responsibility. *Ethics and Education* 7(3): 277–90.

— (2013b) 'Derrida Applied': Derrida meets Dracula in the geography classroom. In Murphy, M. (ed.) *Social Theory and Education Research: Understanding Foucault, Habermas, Bourdieu and Derrida*. London: Taylor and Francis.

Research and Professional Practice

Clare Brooks

Chapter outline

What is meant by professional practice?   31
Geography teachers' professional knowledge   32
Problems with research as part of professional practice   34
Geography education research   35
What's wrong with 'what works'?   35
Reading research   38
Do our definitions exist?   38
The value of teachers acting as researchers   39
What are the implications of this argument?   41

In this chapter, I explore the relationship between research and professional practice specifically for geography teachers, with the argument that research is a vital component for a geography teacher's practice to be considered 'professional'. I acknowledge that research is not the primary focus of a geography teacher's work (after all that should be teaching geography!), but in order to teach geography well (or 'professionally'), teachers require an ongoing relationship with research: one that is dynamic, challenging and nourishing of their practice.

What is meant by professional practice?

To outline my argument, I want to begin by being clear on what I mean by professional practice and how that might be different from practice that is not considered professional.

The debate as to whether teaching is a profession or quasi-profession has been somewhat superseded by the abundance of the use of professional in everyday language. 'Profession' was a term traditionally reserved for specific prestigious occupations such as law and medicine. Now high streets are full of professional drycleaners, printers and plumbers' merchants. Marketing materials will often boast of 'professional services' attached to a variety of occupations. The proliferation of the term in everyday language reflects a trend for it to mean a high standard of service in a variety of occupations.

This notion of quality is dominant in both traditional and modern uses of the word 'professional'. Whilst you may take umbrage at someone behaving 'unprofessionally' towards you, this use implies that their behaviour fell short of the expected standards of politeness and service. Within the traditional use of the term however, professionalism had a particular meaning. A professional was expected to have a specialist body of knowledge, and to have proved him/herself worthy of becoming part of the profession through a rigorous and self-governed selection process. Professionals served society through their expert knowledge and practice (both of which were beyond that of the layperson). Professions were self-governed and self-regulated.

This traditional view of both the professional and professions has evolved. Whitty (2008) notes how government policies have introduced a notion of accountability into the professions, a move which some have seen as being ultimately deprofessionalizing. Others however have called for teachers to reprofessionalize or to become 'activist professionals' (Sachs 2003).

As Abbott (1988) outlines, society has expectations of the groups that it defines as 'professionals'. Professionals are expected to help diagnose and resolve problems in society, through the skilled use of their expert knowledge. If we relate this to the work of geography teachers, we can see that society expects geography teachers to teach geography well, to define and resolve issues and problems pertinent to geography teaching when they arise, and to do so by drawing on their expert knowledge. The questions I wish to pose are:

- What is the specialist expert knowledge of the geography teacher?
- How do geography teachers develop and use this specialist knowledge?

It is only after answering these questions that we can start to see the important role that research can play in teachers' professional practice.

Geography teachers' professional knowledge

There has been much debate about what constitutes a teacher's professional knowledge, with some work specific to geography education. Shulman identified seven knowledge bases for teachers which included content knowledge, general pedagogical knowledge, curriculum knowledge, pedagogical content knowledge, knowledge of learners and their characteristics, knowledge of educational contexts, and knowledge of educational ends, purposes and values (Shulman 1987). Subsequently, there has been debate about these knowledge bases, and their construction and validity (e.g. see Beck 2009; McEwan and Bull 1991; Sockett 1987). Within geography education, research on geography teachers' knowledge has tended to focus on their subject knowledge and how it relates to practice (Corney 2000; Barrett Hacking 1996; Rynne and Lambert 1997; Martin 2008; Brooks 2010). Whilst this work has helped to explore the relationship between subject expertise and teachers' practice, it has only focused on one aspect of geography teachers' knowledge.

The Geographical Association (GA) has promoted the idea of curriculum making as a way of understanding the three 'ingredients' in the curriculum-making process. They explain:

Teachers make it happen in the classroom by drawing from their knowledge of:

- *teaching approaches and specific teaching techniques*
- *students and how they learn*
- *the subject – geography – and what it is for (GA Website accessed 19/9/2013 http://www.geography.org.uk/cpdevents/curriculummaking/)*

If we take these 'ingredients' as indicators of both a geography teacher's knowledge and skilled use of that knowledge, it would be safe to say that, as a minimum, a professional geography teacher requires knowledge in these three main areas:

- their subject area, geography as both an academic discipline and a school subject;
- their knowledge of students, and in particular their own students, and their needs and
- their knowledge of pedagogy, or teaching approaches and techniques.

I do not want to suggest that these three areas are distinctively different or that there is just one 'right' knowledge of any of these areas. The act of teaching requires teachers to bring these three areas together through their practice. The choices that teachers make – such as what to include, what to leave out, what examples to offer, what metaphors or analogies will help illustrate, what activities to give students – are all examples of these three areas of professional knowledge working together. Teachers' decisions may be due to their knowledge of any of the three areas outlined above and indeed one likely to be made at the intersection between all three. In other words, the relationship of knowledge to action is not easily attributable to bounded pieces of 'knowledge' but in how they interplay together, influenced by teachers' values and beliefs: this is what undergirds a geography teacher's professional practice. Without knowledge in these areas, geography teachers are operating with a deficit specialist knowledge which may affect the professional standard of their practice: put simply, without specialist knowledge in these areas they might not teach geography very well. Professional knowledge is key to professional practice. So what role can research play in helping geography teachers to develop and use their professional knowledge?

Problems with research as part of professional practice

The notion that research and professional practice are linked may cause some readers some consternation. Questions may arise such as:

- Where does a teacher find the time to undertake research?
- Do teachers have the appropriate knowledge about research in order to undertake research well?
- How can teachers get access to research reports or publications?
- What instances have there been that research in geography education has had any impact on practice?

To answer these questions, I want to make a clear distinction between the research work of academics and teachers, and to make an honest assessment of the value of geography education research to date.

Educational research is a specialist and complex field, and teachers can be concerned that being involved in research may take them away from their primary focus on teaching, or require them to become professional researchers. It is not feasible or desirable to suggest that teachers should seek to be professional education researchers, alongside their teaching duties and responsibilities. Sachs (2003) argues that it is important not to confuse the research work of practitioners and academics, as they conduct research for different purposes and for different audiences. The research work they undertake is focused in different areas: teachers tend to concern themselves with problems of practice, whereas academics can concern themselves with problems of theory, or of the field: the research lens is differently focused. Therefore, whilst I shall outline below the need for teachers to be involved in research, I am not suggesting that research work becomes their *primary* task or focus.

The 'usefulness' of education research is an issue that requires clarification. The value of education research came under much criticism in the late 1990s for not representing good value for money, or for having an impact on practice. Pring (2004) suggests that there are four factors that led to these criticisms:

- that education research does not provide the answers to questions about the best ways to organize education;
- that education research does not help solve professional problems (like the best way to teach children to read);
- that education research is fragmented, starting in different places, with different methodologies and does not offer a coherent perspective or message and
- that education research is often politically motivated and ideologically driven.

Pring argues that as a result of these factors, there is a gap between the work of educational researchers and the experience of practitioners. Within the field of geography education, this gap is arguably even wider.

Geography education research

Despite attempts to disseminate findings, the field of geography education research has had little impact on the practice of geography teachers. There have been various publications to promote research in Geography Education and to make it accessible for practitioners. For example, under the guidance of the International Geographical Union-Commission for Geography Education, the GA published three bibliographies which included research and professional publications in the field (1972, 1998, 2001). The aims of these publications were to support geography teachers and researchers in finding reports on appropriate research. Publications like Geography and Teaching Geography also seek to emphasize research in geography education.

In the United States, the *Road Map Report* on Geography Education (Bednarz et al. 2013) draws upon previous reviews of geography education research, and highlights persistent criticisms of the field – that it is:

- parochial,
- inward-looking,
- disconnected from educational research in other disciplines,
- small scale (i.e. small number of study participants),
- asynchronous (i.e. few longitudinal studies) and
- descriptive and anecdotal, limited in quantity (but not in quality) (ibid., p. 32).

The limited nature of geography education research conducted can mean that the body of knowledge it reports is not immediately supportive to practitioners seeking answers to their questions of 'what works' in geography education. But this perspective misrepresents how geography education research contributes to the professional knowledge base of geography teachers. The role of geography education research is not to tell teachers 'what works' but to offer a range of different perspectives and challenges that enables individual geography teachers to make more informed decisions about their professional practice.

What's wrong with 'what works'?

The debate in the late 1990s on the efficacy of educational research focused on the extent to which educational research was informing practice: telling teachers 'what works' and making gains in the quality of education raised some important questions about our expectations of educational research.

In his lecture to the Teacher Training Agency in 1996, David Hargreaves argued that education research should be more like medical research: it should involve practitioners and be directed at specific problems to identify 'what works'. The lecture sparked a flurry of 'evidence-based' or 'evidence informed' initiatives, but was also criticized for misunderstanding the relationship between research findings and practice. For example, Hammersley (1997) highlights the differences between medicine and education as fields of enquiry; social science and the practice of medicine draw from different ways of viewing and understanding the world. In Hargreaves' original account he represents the field as having the potential to be cumulative: that education research, piece by piece, can reveal the effective ways for teachers to behave, and for learners to learn. Underpinning his argument is an assumption that there is a 'right way' to teach and that this can be 'revealed' through appropriate research. Indeed, Hammersley critiques the view of teaching that underpins this assumption, describing teaching as 'engineering', a technical activity that can be improved through the use of particular tactics and techniques.

As a professional activity, teaching is not easily reducible to a set of tactics and techniques, as it requires immediate decision making (described by Eraut (1994) as 'hot action'), as well as intellectual endeavour and consideration. These 'thinking' activities are hidden from much education research, as they are grounded in the complexity of a teacher's professional knowledge. Hammersley argues that teachers do not practise in particular ways because of the results of evidence, but through understandings, influenced by their knowledge, values and attitudes.

This debate reveals that the relationship between research and practice is not just centred on the quality of education research or in its dissemination, but on how the findings of research are used by practitioners: how it adds to or challenges their established professional knowledge. The body of research in education is often constructed and enacted by academic researchers, and published for other researchers or policy makers. The teacher is often characterized as the object of research study. Cochran-Smith and Lytle (1999) argue that the teacher's voice and experience is hidden from such research outcomes. Such research then may be able to report successes with particular strategies but are unable to explain why it has been successful.

Margaret Roberts (2000) shows the different ways that research in geography education can be useful for practitioners (see Figure 3.1). Her perspective is one that starts with the actors and contexts of research, and in how research can be 'useful' for teaching and learning geography. The diagram and her analysis reveals that there has been relatively little research on actual classroom and field practice, and hence little on how teachers and students interact in geography.

In presenting geography education research in this way, Roberts shows the potential for research to speak directly to the practitioner. But Roberts is not suggesting that such research is adopted uncritically. Teachers have to engage with research not as technicians, but to be sceptical in their adoption of research findings. Roberts argues:

> Ultimately, deciding what is worth teaching is a matter of judgment, for both the researcher and the teacher; it is determined and justified by one's values and not by evidence. The fact that an activity "works" does not necessarily mean that it is worth doing. (ibid., p. 93)

This perspective places professional geography teachers in the role of 'informed consumers' of research who use their expert knowledge and skilled judgement to evaluate the findings

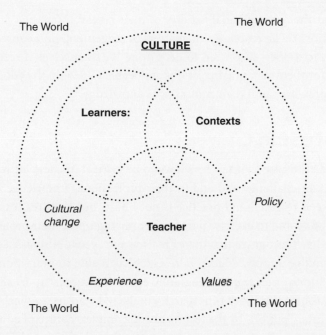

The World   The World

The World   The World

Figure 3.1 A model of teaching and learning situations: actors and contexts (after Roberts 2000)

of research and its applicability to their practice. A key dimension of this is the geographical nature of the research conducted: how it contributes to our understanding of geography in education and not just what happens in a geography classroom. Engaging with research enables teachers to critique and challenge their practice, and assumptions about their practice, but in doing so it can also add to their knowledge base.

Roberts' perspective has implications for researchers. If practitioners are encouraged to use their judgement, then it is also up to researchers to consider the impact their research may have on practice and to lay bare the factors that may affect this. Lambert (2010) refers to this as consequential validity. He contrasts the field of geography education research with the better-funded (and more established) mathematics education research (MER). More research has taken place within MER, and there are more outlets for the publication of such research. However, the debates as to its efficacy are similar to those in geography education research. The gap between research work and practice may be exacerbated by the small-scale nature of geography education research, but this does not mean it is necessarily any worse off than other research fields.

Lambert (2010) argues that researchers need to be clear about the field itself: that geography education research must be more than research that happens to take place in the geography classroom. Research that is so closely aligned with practice needs to consider the consequences of the research findings, and not just the outcomes of such research (i.e. the consequential validity). For Lambert, this means developing research questions about the distinctive contribution of geography in the curriculum. To some extent researchers are at pains to point out the consequential validity of their research (as they discuss its significance and limitations). The emphasis on 'matters of judgement' and consequential validity highlights that practitioners also need to determine for themselves if research has consequential validity for their own practice, if it is applicable to geography education, and to do this they will be drawing upon their professional knowledge.

Reading research

So far I have made the case that teachers have to be critical 'readers' of research, and that in doing so they can challenge and add to their professional knowledge. In addition, the relationship between research and practice is not linear, but requires teachers to consider consequential validity and to exercise judgement drawing upon their professional and geographical knowledge. I recognize that there are time and accessibility issues in making education research (and geography education research) available to practitioners (although as noted GA publications often feature geography education research). In addition, however, there are issues around the types of research conducted and its applicability to teachers. Practitioners are often 'put off' by the technical and complex nature of education research.

The problems that guide research would benefit from being informed by practitioner perspectives. Teachers, as part of the geography education community, could contribute to research in the field by using their critical insights into practice to guide and inform research agendas.

Do our definitions exist?

In her review of geography education research, Francis Slater (1994) posed the question as to whether our definitions (of education research) exist. This challenge was in response to what Slater described as rigid distinctions between different research genres: positivistic, interpretativist and postmodern. Writing the introduction to a research monograph that featured three pieces of research, each broadly representative of the categories of each genre, Slater considered whether the distinction between these positions was helpful. The three pieces of research featured were not pure versions of the research categories they stemmed from, but showed that in our attempts to find out more about geography education there are a wide variety of research paradigms and options open to us. Research design should reflect the research questions posed and the type of enlightenment sought, rather than bearing rigid witness to the 'rules' of research.

Slater's argument was that whilst categories of education research are useful starting points, much valuable research crosses definitional boundaries. It is true to say that most research self-identifies as being part of a research tradition. The terminology for this varies: Robson (2011) uses the terms positivist, post-postivist and critical realist. Williams (1998) refers to the Habermasian distinction between positivist, hermeneutic or critical.

And it is not uncommon for researchers to discuss data as being qualitative, quantitative or from mixed methods. In addition, research textbooks will explore hybrid and new forms of educational research (see Cohen et al. 2011). With this plethora of technical terms and approaches, it is useful to see these categories as referring to different approaches to systematic research enquiry. For example, research that utilizes quantitative data can reveal powerful trends and large-scale developments in geography education (e.g. see Weeden and Lambert's (2010) research into the distribution of GCSE geography candidates). Research with qualitative data can help to illuminate why such patterns exist and/or provide the backbone to understanding them in greater detail. For example, Hopwood's (2004) account of students' conceptions of geography reveals the inherently personal nature of meaning-making. Alternatively, action-orientated practitioner research helps to illuminate the processes and outcomes of trying to elicit change and evaluate its impact (see, e.g., Richard Bustin's (2011a, 2011b) accounts of teaching with the geographical concept of third space).

Slater argued that it is not always useful to stick to rigid distinctions of research paradigms, but that the view of research as 'any systematic critical and self-critical enquiry which aims to contribute to the advancement of knowledge' (see Stenhouse 1975, p. 156) may require more eclectic approaches of investigation.

This is not to suggest that the rules and conventions around education research should be ignored, but that research should be seen as a coherent story: where the data collected, methods of analysis and conclusions drawn are in line with the kinds of questions asked and the problems posed. The best way to develop an understanding of this approach is to engage in small-scale research enquiry (as is often required on postgraduate Masters programmes), as the process of undertaking research is a valuable way of understanding research processes as well as engaging in systematic reflective practice, a popular model of teacher development and learning (Moore 2004).

The value of teachers acting as researchers

So why should a busy geography teacher participate in research?

Engaging in research is a recognized form of sustainable teacher development that can be traced back to Stenhouse's Humanities Curriculum Project and his use of the term 'teacher-as-researcher' (see Elliott 2009). Stenhouse (1975) emphasized the importance of teachers acting as co-researchers alongside academics. He argued that only by engaging teachers in the research could there be a long-term lasting change in teacher practice, and hence success in curriculum development initiatives. Stenhouse's work has been significant as it privileged the status of teacher knowledge, making it more visible and important to locally generated reform (Ruthven, 2005).

It was in the 1980s that teacher research also started to be seen as a form of teacher professional development. Teacher research was seen as a valuable way of encouraging teachers' growth and change. In addition, influenced by the work of Donald Schön, teacher research was seen as a way of developing critical reflection on action and thereby promoting professional development. Moore (2004) notes how the terms 'reflection on action' and 'reflection in action' became important buzzwords for teacher education as a process of developing professional growth and knowledge, and how reflective practice has become an influential way of understanding how teachers learn and grow within their professional contexts. Engaging in research requires teachers to reflect critically on their practice and established forms of knowing.

This is not to suggest that teacher research has been without critics. Hulme et al. (2009) argue that it can be used as a reprofessionalizing strategy to enhance self-regulation and intensify teachers' work. They note how teacher research is enmeshed in debates about what constitutes legitimate knowledge and knowers. Critiques of teacher research tend to fall into three main areas (as summarized by Cochran-Smith and Lytle (1999)):

- the knowledge critique: which questions the value of the knowledge generated from teacher research;
- the methods critique: which questions the methodology used by teachers engaging in research and in particular the interpretative nature of this research; and
- the ends critique: which questions the value of the research and whether it is purely instrumental in nature and whether it connects with larger social and political agendas.

In addition, the widespread inclusion of teacher research as a form of professional development has provoked some criticism. For example, Elliott (2009) has been particularly critical, describing current trends in practitioner research in teacher education as a 'marriage of convenience'. Despite being a supporter of practitioner research, he argues that 'What is now called "practitioner research" tends to be understood as an inquiry into how to drive up standards in the classroom' (ibid., p. 179). Elliott argues that this form of practitioner research tends to focus on practice issues, and as such is often shaped by an objectivist and instrumentalist rationality: one that views (practitioner) research as 'how to' endeavours rather than systematic enquiries. For research to contribute to professional knowledge in the way outlined in this chapter, it needs to take these criticisms seriously. The implications for teachers involved in research are that they must drive (or at least contribute to defining) the research agenda; use research as an opportunity to enhance and critique their understanding of practice and engage in research in a critically reflective manner. It is important for practitioners to recognize that professional knowledge can be flawed (and may sometimes be based on assumptions that are incorrect), as such practitioners need to be as circumspect about their professional knowledge as they are about research findings.

Cochran-Smith and Lytle (1999) have argued that teacher research is an important way of privileging teachers' knowledge and is a key driver in initiating educational change. However, they emphasize that this requires teachers to have high levels of research literacy and to be conscious of their ownership of their research knowledge and how professional practice is defined. They see research as an embedded part of professional practice referring to 'inquiry as stance': researching as an empowering part of teachers defining their knowledge base:

> Rather we mean that teacher research can help to question and reinvent the whole idea of a knowledge base, disrupting the existing relationships of power among knowers and known – who decides what 'knowledge' and 'practice' mean? . . . The point here is not to develop a new set of standards to determine whether teacher research is 'good' or 'good enough' but to figure out more contextually what it means to be 'good' and what teacher research might be 'good for'. The point is not to determine whether teacher research 'counts' but what it counts for, not whether it is 'interesting', but whose interests it serves. (ibid., p. 33)

This vision of the relationship between professional knowledge, practice and research builds upon Sach's (2003) distinction between research conducted by academics and that conducted by teachers, and argues for their parity. Research conducted by practitioners is often differently conceived, developed, designed and has different impacts on funded research. For example, in his review of the impact of the small-scale practitioner research conducted as part of the Best Practice Research Scholarships, Furlong (2003, 2005) highlighted that whilst there was little evidence that these research projects had any impact beyond the local, they were of good quality and clearly had been personally transformative.

For geography teachers, engaging in practitioner research that is 'personally transformative' and being a critical reader of published research are both important and valuable activities that contribute to their professional knowledge (and subsequently professional practice). Teachers require a systematic way of enquiring about their own practice, but they also need to engage with developments and new understandings within the field of geography education. The combination of the two is powerful as it connects the individual practice of the geography teachers with the field of geography education.

Sachs (2003) has used the term 'activist professionals' to describe the active role that teachers must play as decision makers and practitioners. Engagement with research is a key dimension of this as it encourages teachers to exercise their professional judgement and local knowledge. Teachers who engage in a research approach to their work, or 'inquiry as stance', are on the way to developing the reflective practice that, Schön (1987) suggested, is so important for expert professionals.

What are the implications of this argument?

So, what would it look like for a geography teacher to be engaged in this kind of professional practice? Is it reasonable to expect teachers to be reading academic journals and to be conducting research into their practice? It is often argued that teachers do not have the time to engage in this kind of practice, or that they are subjected to many other initiatives and requirements that are more pertinent to their work in schools. In addition, there is some scepticism about the value of reading and engaging in research, as it is seen as far removed from practice, and that having your 'head stuck in a book' would not help you to become a better teacher (see Brooks et al. 2012). I have sympathy that the day-to-day demands of the classroom are not trivial and require serious attention. However, it is important to consider the alternative.

As outlined above, Abbott (1988) in his work on the professions describes the relationship that society has with the professions. He argues that society expects the professions to perform three functions, to be able to:

1. diagnose 'problems',
2. reason and infer using professional knowledge about those problems and
3. effectively treat the problems.

Abbott argues that should a profession be seen to be failing in any of these roles, then another profession will rise up to assume the responsibility. With reference to education, Grossman (2008) argues that if education is not seen to handle and resolve its own problems, then other 'professional bodies' will be brought in to deal with them. In the worst-case scenario, we run the risk that 'fashionable', trendy or ill-thought through initiatives get incorporated into schools under the umbrella of 'what works' without being subjected to sufficient critical scrutiny. For geography education we need to ask ourselves how the field of geography education research helps us to better understand the professional challenges of teaching geography.

References

Abbott, A (1988) *A System of Professions*. Chicago: University of Chicago Press.

Barratt Hacking, E (1996) Novice teachers and their geographical persuasions. *International Research in Geographical and Environmental Education* 5(1): 77–86.

Beck, J (2009) Appropriating professionalism: restructuring the official knowledge base of England's 'modernised' teaching profession, *British Journal of Sociology of Education*, 30(1): 3–14.

Bednarz, S W, Heffron, S and Huynh, N T (eds.) (2013) *A Road Map for 21st Century Geography Education: Geography Education Research*, A Report from the Geography Education Research Committee of the Road Map for 21st Century Geography Education Project. Washington, DC: Association of American Geographers.

Brooks, C (2010) Why geography teachers' subject expertise matters. *Geography*. 95(3): 143–8.

Brooks, C, Brant, J, Abrahams, I and Yandell, J (2012) Valuing initial teacher education at Master's level. *Teacher Development: An International Journal of Teachers' Professional Development* 16(3): 285–302.

Bustin, R (2011a) Thirdspace: exploring the 'lived space' of cultural 'others'. *Teaching Geography* 36(2): 55–7.

— (2011b) The living city: thirdspace and the contemporary geography curriculum. *Geography* 96(2): 60–8.

Cochran-Smith, M and Lytle, S L (1999) The Teacher Research Movement: a decade later. *Educational Researcher* 28(7): 15–25.

Cohen, L, Manion, L and Morrison, K (2011) *Research Methods in Education*. London: Routledge.

Corney, G (2000) Student Teachers' Pre-conceptions about teaching environmental education and their implications for pre-service teacher training. *Environmental Education Research* 6(4): 313–29.

Elliott, J (2009) Research based teaching. In Gewirtz, S, Mahoney, P, Hextall, I and Cribb, A (eds.) *Changing Teacher Professionalism*. London and New York: Routledge.

Eraut, M (1994) *Developing Professional Knowledge and Competence*. London: Falmer Press.

Foskett, N and Marsden, B (eds.) (1998) *A Bibliography of Geographical Education: 1970–1997*. Sheffield: Geographical Association.

Furlong, J (2005) New labour and teacher education: the end of an era education and the Labour Government: an evaluation of two terms. *Oxford Review of Education* 31(1): 119–34.

Furlong, J, Salisbury, J and Coombs, L (2003) *The Best Practice Research Scholarship Scheme*, An Evaluation and Final Report to the DfES. University of Cardiff School of Social Sciences.

Grossman, P (2008) Responding to our critics: from crisis to opportunity in research on teacher education. *Journal of Teacher Education* 59(1): 10–23.

Hammersley, M (1997) Educational research and teaching: a response to David Hargreaves's TTA Lecture. *British Educational Research Journal* 23: 141–61.

Hargreaves, D (1996) Teaching as a research-based profession: possibilities and prospects, Teacher Training Agency Annual Lecture (London, Teacher Training Agency).

Hopwood, N (2004) Pupils' conceptions of geography: Towards an improved understanding. *International Research in Geographical and Environmental Education* 13(4): 348–61.

Hulme, M, Baumfield, V and Payne, F (2009) Building capacity through teacher enquiry: the Scottish Schools of Ambition. *Journal of Education for Teaching: International Research and Pedagogy* 35(4): 409–24.

Lambert, D (2010) Geography education research and why it matters. *International Research in Geographical and Environmental Education* 19(2): 83–6.

Lukehurst, C T and Graves, N J (1972) *Geography in Education. A Bibliography of British Sources, 1870–1970*. Sheffield: Geographical Association.

McEwan, H and Bull, B (1991) The pedagogic nature of subject matter knowledge. *American Educational Research Journal* 28(2): 316–34.

Martin, F (2008) Knowledge bases for effective teaching: beginning teachers' development as teachers of primary geography. *International Research in Geographical and Environmental Education* 17(1): 13–39.

Moore, A (2004) *The Good Teacher: Dominant Discourses in Teaching and Teacher Education*. London: Routledge Falmer.

Pring, R (2004) *Setting the Scene: Criticisms of Educational Research in Philosophy of Educational Research*. London: Continuum.

Roberts, M (2000) The role of research in supporting teaching and learning. In Kent, W A (ed.) *Reflective Practice in Geography Teaching*. London: Sage.

Robson, C (2011) *Real World Research*, 3rd edition. Chichester: John Wiley.

Ruthven, K (2005) Improving the development and warranting of good practice in teaching. *Cambridge Journal of Education* 35(3): 407–26.

Rynne, E and Lambert, D (1997) The continuing mismatch between student's undergraduate experiences and the teaching demands of the geography classroom: experience of pre-service secondary geography teachers. *Journal of Geography in Higher Education* 21(1): 187–98.

Sachs, J (2003) *The Activist Teaching Profession*. Milton Keynes: Open University Press.

Schön, D A (1987) *Educating the Reflective Practitioner*. San Francisco: Jossey-Bass.

Shulman, L E E S (1987) Knowledge and teaching: foundations of the new reform. *Harvard Educational Review* 57(1): 1–23.

Slater, F (1994) *Do Our Definitions Exist?* Reporting Research in Geography Education Monograph No 1, 5–8. Department of Economics, Geography and Business Education Institute of Education, University of London.

Sockett, H (1987). Has Shulman got the strategy right? *Harvard Educational Review* 57(2): 208–19.

Stenhouse, L (1975) *An Introduction to Curriculum Research and Development*. London: Heinemann.

Weeden, P and Lambert, D (2010) Unequal access: why some young people don't do geography. *Teaching Geography* 35(2): 74–5.

Whitty, G (2008) Changing modes of teacher professionalism: traditional, managerial, collaborative and democratic. In Cunningham, B (ed.) *Exploring Professionalism*, pp. 28–49. London: Institute of Education, University of London.

Williams, M (1998) Review of research in geographical education. In *Issues for Research in Geographical Education, Research Forum I Textbooks*. London IGU Commission on Geographical Education and University of London, Institute of Education.

Discussion to Part I
Margaret Roberts

Chapter outline

The political and cultural context   46
Teacher as researcher   47
Geography education research   48
Conclusions   50

The UK Labour Government of 1997–2010, in setting up a new Masters qualification in 'Teaching and Learning', had the ambition that eventually teaching would become an all Masters profession (DCSF 2007). Its plans were not implemented as envisaged, yet the number of student teachers and teachers studying at M level has increased. This is because, in response to the requirements of the Framework for Higher Educational Qualifications that came into effect in 2004, many higher education institutions (HEIs) offer Masters Credits within postgraduate certificate in education (PGCE) courses. Teachers with M level credits have been able to continue their studies and gain a full Masters qualification. The proposals for a Masters in Teaching and Learning, together with the award of M level credits in PGCE courses, have provoked an ongoing debate about the value for teachers of studying at M level. The authors in the first part of this book contribute to this debate, raising issues related to the training of teachers, professionalism, research quality and the nature of geography education research. In this chapter, I want to focus my discussion around three themes related to these issues: the current educational context in England; practitioner research and M level research into geography education.

The political and cultural context

All three authors in this part emphasize teachers as professionals. Butt refers to 'professional identity', 'professional practice', 'professional learning', 'professional knowledge' and 'professional community'. Brooks usefully explores what it means to be 'professional' and writes about professions being 'self-governed and self-regulated'. Lambert refers to 'professional knowledge and judgement'.

The concept of teacher professionalism has been challenged by UK government policies and by prevailing discourses about teachers and teaching. Policies introduced in England since 2010 by the coalition government have reinforced the managerial approaches introduced by the 'New Labour' Government (1997–2010). In spite of rhetoric about increasing freedom for schools and professional autonomy for teachers, highly prescriptive systems of accountability have been maintained. They are managed through Teachers' Standards, OfSTED inspections, frequent public tests and examinations, performance indicators and league tables. Policies introduced by the coalition government emphasize leadership, management, enterprise and choice at the same time as encouraging a return to more traditional curriculum and pedagogy. But as Ball et al. (2012) write, 'Policies rarely tell you exactly what to do, they rarely dictate or determine practice, but some more than others narrow the range of creative responses' (p. 3). The managerial context in which teachers are working means that the spaces within which they can exercise their professional judgements are narrower and teachers, as practitioners, might well feel constrained by this. Teachers as researchers, however, should be encouraged to feel free to challenge and to adopt a constructively critical stance.

UK government policies over the last 30 years have contributed to prevailing discourses about teaching. Moore (2004) has identified two current discourses: teacher as competent craftsperson and teacher as reflective practitioner. The present managerial culture tends to emphasize the former. Those arguing for teachers as reflective practitioners are not disputing the need for teachers to be competent. They emphasize, however, as Lambert does, that teaching is 'a specialist activity requiring deep critical deliberation and a critical, questioning stance'. Teachers need a range of skills but they also need to reflect on what they are doing if they are to develop as professionals capable of making their own judgements and contributing to educational thinking.

Butt points out that most teacher education courses in HEIs 'prize the development of critically reflective practitioners who are expected to both use and generate research in their professional lives'. Courses that offer M level credits require students to think more critically and deeply. However, the increase in M level study among teachers is threatened by two policies of the coalition government. First, a shift in England towards more school-based training will mean that fewer of those training to become teachers will be required to study at M level. Second, academies and free schools, which are increasing in number, have been permitted to employ people without a teaching qualification, undermining as Lambert points out the notion that 'teaching should be informed by research and scholarship'. The idea that teachers might not need training is related to a third popular discourse identified by Moore: that of the charismatic teacher, linked to a belief that teachers are born rather than made. The fact that this belief is frequently voiced does not give it substance. The idea that teachers might not need training belittles what is involved in teaching. The coalition government's policy of enabling unqualified teachers to work in academies and free schools contrasts starkly with the previous government's ambition to make teachers an all Masters profession. It also contrasts with policies of other countries, including notably Finland and Singapore – often referred to in international comparisons – that put great emphasis on the professional training of teachers.

Teacher as researcher

All three authors in this part identify ways in which engaging with research, that is, both reading accounts of research and carrying out research, is of value to teachers. It promotes their professional development by enabling them to be more critically reflective about teaching and learning and by deepening their understanding of day-to-day practices. It enables them to focus on real-life research questions.

As mentioned by Brooks, our thinking about 'teacher as researcher' can be traced back to the work of Lawrence Stenhouse. His ideas are relevant to this book. Stenhouse's primary concerns were how educational research could contribute to the betterment of schools and how research might guide educational action and curriculum development. He believed that curriculum research and development 'ought to belong to the teacher' (Stenhouse, in Ruddock and Hopkins 1985, p. 92) because real classrooms 'are in the command of teachers not of researchers' (ibid., p. 126). He envisaged classrooms as 'laboratories' in which teachers, in collaboration with professional researchers, could develop a research stance towards their work and put curriculum development ideas to the 'test of practice'. Such a stance involved teachers in constant 'systematic questioning' and 'thoughtful study' of their own practice. Insights gained from such research were always provisional, to be further tested and modified by practice.

For Stenhouse 'curriculum development' was not only about improving teaching; it was also about teacher self-development. Writing about the Schools Council's curriculum development projects, he claimed that 'no group of teachers who experiment seriously, cooperatively and doggedly, with any of the curricula described in this book, could fail to strengthen themselves as practitioners in the art of teaching' (Stenhouse 1980, p. 251). He argued that such involvement encouraged teachers to reflect on and monitor their own practice so that they could rely on their own judgements rather than those of others. Although Stenhouse's ideas were informed by his thinking about curriculum research and development, the value he placed on teacher involvement in small-scale research is relevant to all practitioner research.

Brooks makes a useful distinction between the purposes of practitioner and academic research, the former being focused on problems of practice and the latter on problems of theory. Not only is practitioner research 'differently focused', but the different purposes for which the research is carried out have implications for methodologies used and criteria used to judge quality. Practitioner research, unless it uses large secondary data sets, is inevitably small scale. Lambert explores a range of possibilities of what might count as research in this context. Only some of the criteria used for assessing the quality of academic research, referred to in Butt's opening chapter, are applicable to practitioner research. Oancea and Furlong (2007) in considering issues related to quality in practice-based research identified three 'domains of quality': theoretical; technical and practical. It is worth considering the extent to which criteria within each of these domains might apply to M level research. In the theoretical domain, concerned with the process of research, practitioner research can be expected to be rigorous and trustworthy but the knowledge it produces is usually neither generalizable nor widely significant. The technical domain includes criteria related to accountability and impact. Those related to accountability, including cost-effectiveness, marketability and competitiveness, would not apply to practitioner research. Criteria related to impact, however, could apply; practitioner research could suggest possible solutions to practical problems and lead to changes in practice. Findings could be shared with colleagues or published to widen their potential impact. Criteria in the practical domain are related to capacity building and value for the person carrying out the research. These can be judged according to whether the research promotes self-reflection and self-development; encourages a questioning, critical attitude towards practice and its underpinning rationale; exposes tacit understandings underpinning practice; develops practical wisdom and is attuned to the concrete and current problems of practice. All these criteria could be used to judge quality of M level research. Oancea and Furlong argue that it is not enough for practice-based research to satisfy theoretical and technical criteria of quality; it also needs to satisfy criteria within the practical domain. It is in this domain that practitioners, because they are 'attuned to the concrete and current problems of practice' (Oancea and Furlong 2007, p. 132) are at an advantage.

Geography education research

People studying for an M level qualification need to take into account the generic issues related to contexts and quality discussed above. But if the focus is to be on geographical education, they need to consider how to build on what is already known and to decide what to investigate and how.

The authors in this part all acknowledge the limitations of the knowledge base on which the researcher in geography education can build. It tends to be limited in amount, fragmented, descriptive and on a small scale. The US Roadmap (Bednarz et al. 2013, p. 32) laments these characteristics. In spite of these limitations, it is evident from Lambert's extremely useful list of sources of information on geographical education research that there is quite a lot to draw on. Indeed, the novice researcher might well be daunted by how much background reading they need to carry out to become acquainted with a particular field of research rather than being concerned about the limitations of the field.

The fact that much geography education research is on a small scale is an advantage to M level practitioner researchers, as this is the scale at which they will inevitably be working.

Research reports of small-scale studies can indicate the scope of such studies and suggest appropriate methodologies. David Lambert argues persuasively for the use of case study research in geographical education, making an interesting comparison with their use in academic geography. All aspects of geographical education, including schemes of work, departments, classrooms, textbooks and assessment, although subject to similar processes to those operating in other contexts, can be fully understood only within the specific cultural contexts in which they are situated. Stenhouse argued that 'case studies are important as evidence' (Stenhouse in Ruddock and Hopkins 1985, pp. 53–4) arguing that 'descriptive case studies of any kind provide documentary evidence for the discussion of practice'.

Although it is important for those researching geographical education to build on existing research in this field, this is not the only possible starting point. Precisely because the field is relatively limited, it is worth drawing on three other fields: generic research, academic geography research and research related to other school subjects. There is a large body of high-quality generic research of relevance to geography education which could easily be overlooked if practitioner researchers limited their reading to journals and books focused on geographical education. For example, there has been a substantial amount of research over the last 40 years into language and learning, which would be very valuable to those researching any aspects of language and learning in geographical education. Other examples of relevant generic research include research into the curriculum, child development and assessment. A second possibility for extending background reading is to make use of research published by academic geographers. Anyone investigating a specific theme or place studied in school geography would do well to draw on ways in which they are studied and understood by academic geographers. A third fruitful field on which to draw is research focused on other school subjects. This is likely to suggest aspects worth studying and ways of investigating them. Among examples relevant to geographical education I would suggest reports of research published in *Teaching History* and extensive research in science education focused on children's thinking and on argumentation.

Deciding what to investigate can be a problem. The best starting point for research is genuine curiosity. This might arise from a practitioner's own experience or might be stimulated by background reading. There are many possibilities in geographical education for the focus of an investigation. M level students might want to work on an aspect already well researched, for example, the use of maps, the value of fieldwork or the gap between school and academic geography, in order to bring findings up to date or to apply previous research in their own particular context. On the other hand, there are some significant gaps in geographical education research. These tend to be in aspects for which it is more difficult for academic outsider researchers to gain sustained access, for example, related to particular schools, classrooms, teachers and students. Less well-researched areas include: the influence of school culture and location on geographical education within a school; how geography teachers think about and practice 'curriculum making'; how students use and make sense of geographical source materials found in textbooks and on computers; how students make sense of statistical information; students' understandings and misconceptions of key geographical concepts; how classroom discussion and dialogic teaching can contribute to geographical education and how students learn to 'think geographically'. It is in these areas that practitioner researchers, who have access to their own schools, departments, classrooms and students, can make a really valuable contribution to geography education research.

Conclusions

The value of 'evidence' from research into geographical education, whether it be from reports of qualitative studies, from detailed case studies or from large-scale quantitative studies, should not be conceptualized only in technical, utilitarian terms. I share the view of all three authors in this part that geography education research should go beyond 'what works'. This is not only because, as Lambert rightly points out, what works in a particular context, with a particular class and particular students, might not 'work' in a different context. It is also because 'what works' is underpinned by assumptions about what is thought to be important 'to work' either by teachers or by policy makers. As Carr (2007) writes: 'Education is a practice and that to engage in this practice always presupposes an interpretation of what education is and what it is for' (p. 276). Research in geographical education might guide policy and practice, but it is necessarily underpinned by views about what geographical education is for and what it ought to be. Research in geographical education has a role in encouraging practitioners to question policy and practice and in enabling them to expose the tacit, taken-for-granted beliefs and understandings inherent in what they do.

References

Ball, S J, Maguire, M and Braun, A (2012) *How Schools Do Policy: Policy Enactments in Secondary Schools.* Abingdon: Routledge.

Bednarz, S, Heffron, S and Huynh, N T (eds.) (2013) *Roadmap for 21st Century Geography Education: Geography Education Research.* Washington, DC: Association of American Geographers. Available from http://education.nationalgeographic.com/media/file/NGS_RoadMapConcept_GERC_07.pdf

Carr, W (2007) Educational research as a practical science. *International Journal of Research and Method in Education* 30(3): 271–86.

DCSF (Department for Children, Schools and Families) (2007) *The Children's Plan: Building Brighter Futures.* London: HMSO.

Moore, A (2004) *The Good Teacher: Dominant Discourses in Teaching and Teacher Education.* Abingdon: Routledge.

Oancea, A and Furlong, J (2007) Expressions of excellence and the assessment of applied and practice-based research. *Research Papers in Education* 22(2): 119–37.

Ruddock, J and Hopkins, D (eds.) (1985) *Research as a Basis for Teaching: Readings from the Work of Lawrence Stenhouse.* London: Heinemann Educational Books.

Stenhouse, L (1980) *Curriculum Research and Development in Action.* London: Heinemann Educational Books.

Part II
Constructing

Constructing Geographical Knowledge

Roger Firth

Chapter outline

Debates about knowledge   57
The influence of constructivism   59
A realist perspective on knowledge   60
The importance of the epistemic   61
Disciplinary constraint   62
Conclusions   63

In his aim to encourage teachers to reflect on the nature of 'thinking geographically', John Morgan (2013) begins with a discussion of the nature of geographical knowledge. He makes a distinction between two epistemological theories, what we might call 'objectivism' and 'social constructivism'. He states:

> Much teaching in schools proceeds from the position that there is an objective 'real world' which is studied by geographers to produce knowledge which is then transmitted in schools. However, since at least the early 1970s, and influenced by research in the 'sociology of knowledge', it has become possible to argue that geographical knowledge does not innocently reflect the 'real world' but instead reflects the subjective interests of geographers. This is to point out that geographical knowledge is 'socially constructed'. (p. 274)

I'm not sure how teachers think about the 'real world' or reality; whether it is understood as largely independent of us, as 'socially constructed' or in terms of some gradation of constructionist commitment in between. Morgan is highlighting the question of the relationship between the world and our knowledge of it, but more particularly, making a distinction between two conceptualizations of knowledge.

Much of the current conceptual landscape around knowledge is rooted in terms of a choice between a 'traditional' view of knowledge and knowledge as socially constructed. With the traditional view, knowledge is largely understood to be objective, certain, neutral and independent of the socio-historical context in which it is developed. It is also largely associated with the academic disciplines. Social approaches to knowledge assume that whatever knowledge is, it is intrinsically social. These approaches all share an opposition to the 'traditional' view of knowledge as a set of disembodied, reified facts about the world. The Geographical Association (GA) consultation process during the recent review of the National Curriculum highlighted how for many teachers the coalition government's curriculum policy and emphasis on core knowledge was seen as a return to this 'traditional' approach to knowledge. As a consequence, such knowledge can be viewed as inherently authoritarian, abstract, conservative, even elitist – and not fit as a basis for a twenty-first-century curriculum.

Alternatively, knowledge can be seen as socially constructed within particular cultural and historical conditions; it conveys an active and experience-driven conception of itself. It brings notions of meaning, interpretation and social context into consideration. Such a view is more sceptical about the possibility of objective knowledge and places an emphasis on the situated and contextual nature of knowledge production, whereby knowledge has only relative, subjective value according to differences in perception and consideration. This is seen as offering a more progressive view of geographical knowledge and the curriculum.

In his chapter Morgan (2013) sets out not to convince teachers that there is a single way of thinking geographically but rather to illustrate through examples from the academic discipline, some of what 'thinking geographically' might entail. His hope is that the value of some disciplined (a reference to the academic discipline) reflection on the wider purposes of geographical teaching and learning will also be recognized. In connecting the nature of geographical knowledge and its different conceptions to 'thinking geographically', he draws attention to the fact that both change 'over time in relation to, and in response to, shifting societal configurations and needs' (p. 174).

The identification of different approaches to the theorization of knowledge sets the scene for this chapter, which considers how different conceptions of knowledge imply and encourage different approaches to teaching and learning in geography. In particular, the chapter takes up the idea that knowledge is 'socially constructed': in relation to the 'realities of the tension that teachers must navigate between disciplinary modes of thought and the less formally disciplined beliefs of students' (Stemhagen et al. 2013, p. 58). In similar fashion to Morgan, it is also hoped that the value of disciplined reflection will be recognized here, and specifically the idea of disciplined knowledge. It is likely, however, that an alternative more powerful influence will be at play regarding teachers' thinking about geographical knowledge in relation to students' learning, namely constructivism. In recent decades constructivism has emerged as a very powerful discourse for explaining the development of human knowledge and how students learn (knowledge construction). Its influence developed through reaction against 'traditional' views about the nature and status of knowledge, which saw the student as a *tabula rasa* upon which the educational process should inscribe the essential features of the world, and gave foundation to a developmental stage model of cognitive/intellectual growth which was seen as implying deterministic limitations to children's capabilities. From here the influence of constructivism as a reform-oriented theory grew rapidly, as did its associated body of literature. Initial teacher education and the former government's education policy and national strategies have also played their part, whereby constructivist perspectives were presented to teachers as the foundation for reforming teaching and learning. The discourses of constructivism that reached schools through government policy, however, often bore little relation to the theoretical implications of their parent theories.

As a theory of learning, constructivism has epistemological, psychological and pedagogical dimensions: though as Stemhagen et al. (2013) suggest 'it is likely that some trouble with the term stems from misunderstandings as to which form of constructivism is at play' (p. 57). In the development of its tenets in geography education, the focus has been on the learner and the learning process and the idea that students are active constructors of knowledge. But in consequence other considerations seem to fade from view, if not out of the picture altogether. That is to say, the psychological and pedagogical dimensions of constructivism have been most influential, while discussions about knowledge (epistemological considerations) have been sidelined.

This chapter also addresses what might be called 'the problem of knowledge' in teaching and learning. What is meant by this is the significant weakening of the concept of knowledge in the last decade or so and its impact on what and how geography is taught in schools.[1] It puts the spotlight on 'constructivism' and the ways in which it has been influential regarding teachers' thinking about knowledge and pedagogical strategies. It gives emphasis to how, through initial teacher education and government strategies, constructivist approaches to teaching and learning are often understood to be applicable uniformly across all subject disciplines of the school curriculum. The argument presented here is that constructivist pedagogy is constrained by the nature of the subject disciplines themselves.

Constructivism has brought important and helpful attention to the ideas that students bring with them to the classroom and 'has placed student understanding as a central goal of education. As such, the theory has helped [teachers] to reorient the hierarchical structure of teaching and learning into a more horizontal one in which students constructions of knowledge play a more central role' (Stemhagen et al. 2013, p. 57). However, one might be critical of over-simplified applications of constructivism, which can prevent what Morrow (2007) has described as 'epistemological access to knowledge in the modern world' (Lotz-Sisitka 2009, p. 57). Epistemological access refers to the sophisticated approaches to mediating between disciplinary knowledge represented in abstract form ('styles of reasoning' and 'epistemes') and everyday knowledge, or, between the situated activity of knowledge construction and subject matter. There are two forms of consideration here (as the brackets above suggest): the 'styles of reasoning' within the discipline, which emphasizes the relational connections between disciplinary concepts, and the way disciplinary knowledge is produced (its epistemes). Students need access to both of these if they are to move beyond a focus on isolated examples of content.

Morrow (2007), amongst others, has argued the need for a realist approach to the theorization of knowledge but does not elaborate on what such a realist approach might mean (Lotz-Sisitka 2009, p. 57). Realism is presented as an alternative to forms of constructivism. Constructivism has introduced notions of meaning making, interpretation and social practices into the debate about knowledge. Knowledge, it is emphasized, must be understood in relation to knowers, whether construed in individual ('the knowing subject') or collective terms ('epistemic' or 'disciplinary communities') and may be seen as analytically prone to reducing knowledge claims to power relations amongst socially positioned actors. It stands in opposition to the principle that disciplines can build on previous knowledge or, what Young (2008) has called, 'knowledge growth'. Realism is also concerned with the social nature of knowledge but rather than the focus on knowers it re-centres knowledge itself and is concerned with its systematization and epistemic relations. Using analytical ideas from a realist perspective, the main purpose of this chapter is to draw attention to a small but potentially important improvement to the way we think about the constructivist learning process, one that builds on the manner in which academic disciplines produce new knowledge.

Consideration is given to how we might move beyond a one-sided emphasis on an active constructive approach to knowledge, which by implication avoids consideration of disciplinary knowledge itself. The focus is on how teachers who engage with constructivist theory and its practical applications to pedagogy balance the pressing need to motivate their students, enable them to be active participants in the learning process rather than receivers of knowledge, while maintaining their responsibility to introduce students into discipline-based thinking. In order to help teachers become more aware of the discipline and its approach to knowledge, emphasis is given to the idea of *disciplinary constraint* (Stemhagen et al. 2013) and on the ways in which pedagogy and discipline interact in praxis (Morrow 2007). In choosing to emphasize the disciplinary facets of student learning, a stronger conception of knowledge is necessary.

Whatever one's view about the role of knowledge in the education of young people, recent government policy to re-establish its place in English schools and the establishment of a 'core-knowledge' National Curriculum from September 2014 has consequences for teaching and learning (whether the new programmes of study offer the best opportunity for the development of an authentic knowledge-based curriculum is another question – not considered here). What is clear is that the review of the National Curriculum and the consultation process facilitated by the GA made obvious the importance of knowledge and how we might conceptualize it. In parallel the GA attempted to engage teachers with the idea of disciplined knowledge. When the review was announced, David Lambert (then chief executive of the GA) described it as 'a knowledge turn in schools' and raised an important question about the theoretical resources available to teachers to interpret 'a return to knowledge' (Lambert 2011).

Two interrelated arguments encourage teachers to think about their own pedagogic assumptions and the discourses that affect them: (1) an epistemological argument about the conceptualization of knowledge and (2) an educational argument about the importance of disciplinary knowledge and epistemological access. The epistemological argument is about the need for a stronger conception of knowledge – one which enables the disciplined nature of knowledge to be emphasized as well as seeing students as active constructors of knowledge. It argues that increased theoretical specificity regarding the nature of disciplinary knowledge within the constructivist learning process (Ford 2010, p. 266) is vital if teachers are to enable epistemological access to knowledge and to support teachers in the development of a subject/disciplinary specific pedagogy.

The educational argument is the justification for the epistemological argument; this underpins the discussion in the chapter rather than being given specific consideration. The educational argument is whether, by denying students access to disciplined or theoretical knowledge, we are effectively denying them access to society's conversations about itself and its possible futures (Wheelahan 2010). It is through knowledge that young people move beyond their understanding of things and the relations between them and 'develop the capacity to engage in the distinctive modes of investigation and analysis through which human experience is differentiated and extensions of human understanding [of the world] are achieved' (Kirk and Broadhead 2007, para 39). Access to such knowledge (epistemological access) is thus a question of distributional justice (Wheelahan 2010). In saying this, I am not arguing that knowledge is all there is to young people's education.

Debates about knowledge

The issue of knowledge has featured strongly in the sociology of education for a decade or more – where relativist conceptions of knowledge have been challenged along with the development of a distinctive realist approach to the social nature of knowledge. The label 'social realist' describes the loosely shared set of assumptions of this community (as John Morgan mentioned). The term itself is not important; its attention to the under-theorized nature of knowledge is, alongside the argument that to understand education we need to understand knowledge. Like constructivism, knowledge is seen as socially produced, but it is concerned with exploring the social grounds for the objectivity of knowledge – the very possibility of which is often denied by social constructivism. It is realist in emphasizing the normativity (intrinsic evaluability) of knowledge that is based at least partially on how the world is. Knowledge is thus fallible and revisable in the light of new evidence (Wheelahan

2010, p. 11). Social realism's commitment to the existence of an objective reality, and thus to objective knowledge, is the basis for its arguments about the curriculum and pedagogy.

Theoretical considerations about the epistemological nature of knowledge (how it is produced, how we know) have also been recurrent in some disciplinary subjects of the school curriculum, especially science and mathematics. It is widely recognized in science education and mathematics education that an understanding of the epistemic nature of the discipline is a vital aspect of student learning. Such considerations, however, have remained under-examined in geography education, and the development of students understanding of the epistemic nature of the discipline has never really been an explicit aim of geography education. During the consultation phase of the National Curriculum review, however, the GA sought to engage teachers with the idea of disciplinary or disciplined subject knowledge. This was done through a series of articles in the GA journals and as the focus of the 2011 GA Annual Conference. In arguing against a 'core knowledge curriculum', the GA (2011a, p. 2) suggested that it would be helpful to distinguish three types of knowledge:

- Core knowledge: the extensive world knowledge of geography.
- Content knowledge: the main content of the geography curriculum – its key concepts, ideas and generalizations (what Schwab (1978) calls substantive knowledge).
- Procedural knowledge: what is described as 'thinking geographically', which is a distinctive procedure – it is not the same as thinking historically, or scientifically, or mathematically (etc.). The teacher can model this by example, but it is also learnt through exposure to, and direct experience of, high-quality geographical enquiry which might include decision making or problem solving.

In selecting what to teach, the GA emphasized that all three types are important: 'Moreover, they intersect and are mutually dependent: they cannot be taught in isolation of each other, but all should be taught' (p. 2).

Of significance for the arguments in this chapter is the identification of procedural knowledge, though here the GA seems to be giving more attention to the distinctive ways of reasoning within the discipline than procedural knowledge itself. The nature of procedural knowledge is described somewhat differently by the GA (2011a, 2011b, 2012a, 2012b) on a number of occasions. It is closest to describing procedural knowledge in Schwabian terms in the GA Curriculum Proposals and Rationale:

> Developing procedural knowledge is key to making geographical meaning because it entails a growing realisation of the disciplinary practices that create, interpret and use geographical knowledge. In schools we have, over the years, come to refer to this as 'enquiry learning'. Though this approach has acquired varied forms, at its heart lies the deceptively simple idea that pupils identify, gather and process data in order to draw conclusions which may be open to challenge and debate. (2011a, p. 3)

There are three points. First, the reference to disciplinary practices and their possible types is unusual in itself. Second, besides the emphasis on styles of reasoning there is now reference to disciplinary practices of knowledge production ('create geographical knowledge'), though what this might mean remains obscure. And third, the GA claims that in schools the development of students' procedural knowledge has come to be known as enquiry learning. This can be questioned, in that the concern with how disciplinary communities construct knowledge has little, if any, emphasis within the literature about geographical enquiry. The argument here is that procedural knowledge entails epistemological awareness of the discipline, that is to say the norms of knowledge production. This is distinct from the process knowledge (of learning) emphasized in the notion of geographical enquiry. Curiously perhaps, the GA (2012a) document 'Thinking Geographically' – which demonstrated how essential content can be used to develop students' conceptual understanding of geography and represents 'a strong and succinct rationale for the subject in schools, as well as the basis for curriculum planning' (GA, 2012b) – made no mention of procedural knowledge. In some ways the problem of knowledge was highlighted during the consultation phase of the review of the National Curriculum.

The influence of constructivism

Constructivism emphasizes the cultural basis of skills, tasks and practices and of the knowledge that is the consequence of these practices. It draws attention to the experiential, which means that the contextual and situated take priority. At the core of constructivist epistemological assumptions is a conception of knowledge as socially dependent, in which:

1. the truth of a belief is not a matter of how things stand with an 'independently existing reality';
2. its validity is not a matter of its evaluation by systematic procedures of rational assessment and
3. knowledge necessarily depends at least in part on the contingent social and material setting in which the belief is produced or maintained. (after Boghossian 2006, p. 6)

'The most influential versions of social dependence views of knowledge', as Boghossian emphasizes, 'have been formulated in terms of the ubiquitous notion of social construction. All knowledge, it is said, is socially dependent because all knowledge is socially constructed' (ibid.). The different forms of constructivism share three basic premises about knowledge:

1. knowledge is a product of social practices
2. different kinds of knowledge can be reduced to different kinds of practices
3. the social practices of knowledge producers and other kinds of social actors are commensurable so that the knowledge produced by the former has no special 'authority' compared to that of the later (Wheelahan 2010, p. 115).

The consequence is that knowledge does not have transcendent features beyond the social context in which it was produced. Constructivist theories vary in the extent to which they are based on postmodernism and hence share its concern with unequal power relations to the same degree (ibid., p. 113). In this way knowledge is sidelined in favour of knowing and knowers (Maton 2006).

While there are various forms of constructivism within education, the literature commonly emphasizes how teaching is conceived less in terms of direct instruction and more in terms of indirect (radical constructivist) facilitation, or social constructivist mediation of students' construction of knowledge. Radical constructivism focuses on the individual construction of knowledge, on how learners, as individuals, impose intellectual structure on their world, whereas social constructivism views knowledge as primarily a cultural product and is concerned with how knowledge is constructed through interaction with others. By bringing together these different versions learning is understood as an active construction of knowledge by both individual interpretation and meaning making with other individuals.

The instructional trajectory stemming from constructivism has seen the development of 'active learning' as a pedagogical construct and discourse. The learner is conceived as an active participant in the learning process rather than a receiver of knowledge, and much progress has been made in developing pedagogical techniques for encouraging students to be active learners (Ford 2010, p. 265). Like Golding (2011) 'I take the essential feature of this theory to be its opposition to a mimetic view of teaching [and learning], or what Freire calls the banking concept of education, where [extant] knowledge is transmitted ready-made to students' (p. 468). This is not to say that teaching practices are wholly constructivist or transmissive. The pressure on teachers to prepare older students for examinations, for example, may set limits on the take-up of constructivist approaches to teaching and learning. The point here is that when constructivism is in play, knowledge is understood in relation to knowers (learners), in which individually and as co-learners they actively construct knowledge and understanding. But the epistemic nature of disciplinary knowledge is not in view.

A realist perspective on knowledge

There are two issues about which the realist perspective on knowledge and constructivism agree:

1. like constructivism, it rejects the 'traditional' view that knowledge is timeless, universal and independent of the social context in which it is produced
2. it accepts the constructivist premise that knowledge is socially produced by communities of knowledge producers and these communities are characterised by struggles around power and competing interests (Wheelahan 2010, p. 8).

However, as Wheelahan goes on to argue, this is not the end of the matter. Constructivist arguments that knowledge is a product of social practices have led to two problematic conclusions:

1. More specifically, knowledge is reduced to the experiences and interests of the groups whose perspective knowledge it is held to represent. In this way, knowledge is conflated experientially with knowing

and with knowers. Furthermore, the distinction between disciplinary/theoretical and everyday knowledge can be collapsed because both are a product of social practices.

2. More generally, there is no 'independent existing reality' and all knowledge has equal validity. This denies the possibility of objectivity in knowledge. In this way, there is no privileging of knowledge in terms of its ability to more reliably describe and explain the real world.

In this way, knowledge is reduced to the meaning making of individuals (independently or collaboratively in groups), or communities, at specific points in history (Derry 2013, p. 54). This is not to suggest that teachers necessarily collapse the difference between everyday knowledge and disciplinary knowledge, but when the emphasis is on individual meaning making disciplined knowledge tends to get lost from view. The consequence of the attentiveness on the learner, the learning process and individual meaning making has led to three issues in teaching geography:

1. The epistemic nature of geographical knowledge, and specifically the manner in which new knowledge is constructed (how disciplinary communities generate new knowledge claims) has been ignored.
2. The personal and the social is given priority over 'how the world is', whereby concepts and ideas can be more self-referential than structured by any reference to reality.
3. Notions of 'truth' are able to be replaced by the concept of 'viability' (Osborne 1996, p. 54); as Ford (2010) explains, this is 'a tension between allowing students to construct their own sense of disciplinary ideas and ensuring that the sense they make is "correct"' (p. 265).

In arguing that all knowledge is fallible, but in failing to recognize that judgements about the worth of such knowledge are possible, constructivism offers no guidance or mechanism on adjudication between theories – on how one theory may be considered to be more reliable than another (Osborne 1996, p. 53). What is missing from the constructivist account is any understanding of the norms and practices that guide the construction of knowledge in disciplinary communities.

In geography education we have not acknowledged the limits of constructivism, or rather identified its weaknesses along with its strengths. It has had considerable success in its critique of traditional ways of teaching and learning; moreover, the alternative strategies it offers have made an important contribution to our understanding of the learner and the learning process. With respect to knowledge it has served to destabilize deeply entrenched premises about the independence of knowledge from the social context in which it was produced. However, as a theoretical referent for theoretical/disciplined knowledge, it will always be inappropriate.

The importance of the epistemic

Perkins (2006) draws our attention to the fact that disciplines are more than just concepts, theories and facts: 'They have their own characteristic *epistemes*' (p. 42). As Perkins argues, students will probably have never heard the word episteme, but they deal with epistemes tacitly all the time – 'An episteme can be defined as a system of ideas or way of understanding that allows us to establish knowledge' (ibid.). He draws attention to the work of Schwab (1978), among others, who has emphasized the importance of students understanding the syntactic structure of the disciplines they are studying (what the GA has called 'procedural knowledge').

The point is that what Perkins calls the 'epistemic game' of knowledge production needs to be surfaced and activated; students need to know about the game and how to play it knowingly. In this way, learning is a process of enculturation, with a focus on learning *to be* rather than learning *about* (Bielaczyc and Kapur 2010, p. 20). Epistemes are activity systems that animate disciplinary content. In this way, content becomes more than the *finished product* of disciplinary knowledge/school geography. In what follows, the idea of disciplinary constraint is used to illustrate ways in which teachers might think about the relationship between student knowledge constructions and the construction of disciplinary knowledge and the way they can introduce students to the 'epistemic game'.

The idea of disciplinary constraint, as outlined by Stemhagen et al. (2013) and Ford (2010), is intended to draw attention to the relation between constructivist pedagogy and epistemology; how the epistemic nature of a discipline 'constrains the pedagogical choices open to teachers' (Stemhagen et al. 2013, p. 58). It is also an inducement to help teachers become more aware of their discipline: its unique approach to knowledge production and how to help students learn to employ the epistemic tools provided by the discipline.

Disciplinary constraint

Disciplined judgement is the framework or tool that Stemhagen et al. (2013) have formulated to put disciplinary constraint into practice. It serves two purposes: the first is to orient secondary school teachers towards the discipline and its approach to knowledge; the second, when activated within learning tasks, is to help students to employ the conceptual tools provided by the discipline, arguing 'that constructivist classrooms must balance the individual judgements that students apply during the course of their work with the normalising tools of judgement as employed within the particular discipline in question' (p. 58). What these normalizing tools of judgement are becomes clear when they state 'disciplined judgement . . . describes the application of criteria that emerge from the institutional context of each discipline to judge the worth of knowledge construction' (ibid.). In this way, students become skilled, not only at constructing knowledge, but also at evaluating it – judging its worth – in disciplined ways. The implementation of this approach requires that teachers understand disciplinary knowledge in a more dynamic way, not as a static entity that students either acquire or fail to acquire. It is a crucial scaffold for students disciplined learning. The contention of Stemhagen et al. is 'that the inclusion of judgement is the fulfillment of the promise of empowerment and meaningfulness that is implicit in learner-centred constructivist pedagogy' (ibid.). In similar fashion to Stemhagen et al. Ford (2010) also notes a tension in constructivist pedagogy and asks 'if certain ideas are considered correct [more reliable] by experts, should students internalise those ideas instead of constructing their own' (p. 265). The process of disciplinary critique is described by Ford as an implication of the way disciplinary communities generate new knowledge claims. Therefore, a crucial aspect of the active learning of school subjects is challenging or questioning knowledge claims in ways that the discipline does.

> In this way, the model of disciplinary practice on the interpersonal level (between persons in a disciplinary community) can be used to highlight what the process of learning and justification on the persona level (an individual learner) must include. The reasons why one believes a knowledge claim in science (i.e. its relations to evidence) are precisely the features of the claim that provide its meaning. (ibid.)

This approach to pedagogy 'does not assume that those students possess, in their everyday knowledge stores, sufficient resources for constructing their own understanding of content' (p. 276). By providing explicitly the critique resources that students lack (disciplinary norms), pedagogy can then support students to use critique to actively make appropriate sense of the content. And in this way, students learn to actively challenge their emerging understanding of content, whereby epistemic authority is gradually offloaded from the teacher, while retaining the source of logistical authority in the classroom (p. 278). Indeed, 'pedagogy should involve students in critique processes, which make clear the epistemic demands of the discipline and how they are met by the methods and give rationale to the content', for 'without critique the student would not learn to hold his or her sense-making accountable' (p. 277).

Key to Ford's arguments is that constructivism has emphasized *continuity* between what he terms 'lay' (everyday) knowledge and disciplinary knowledge. He highlights ways in which disciplinary knowledge is *distinct* from everyday knowledge and draws implications from this for the learning process. Everyday knowledge has a more direct relation between meanings and a specific material base; it is likely to be more individual and develops through *implicit critique*. Disciplinary knowledge, on the other hand, is public and develops through *explicit critique*. Because of this, Ford emphasizes, 'disciplinary knowledge is a different kind of thing than everyday knowledge – and the nature of this difference implies that disciplinary critique is an important proactive aspect of learning disciplinary knowledge' (p. 266). Furthermore, this is important for understanding not only 'how we know' (the epistemological aspect of disciplinary knowledge), but also 'what we know' (the content itself) (ibid.).

Conclusions

With reference to teaching geography, the GA's (2011b) 'Geography Curriculum Consultation Full Report' states that 'The best geography teaching is based on stimulating the curiosity of children and young people in order to ask questions and to generate a 'need to know' about the wider world' (p. 6). This chapter has argued that young people also need to be curious about the ways in which geographical knowledge is produced if they are to understand how geography helps them to make sense of the world.

The purpose of the chapter is to begin to consider the challenges inherent in bringing disciplinary knowledge into the frame of constructivist teaching and learning. Attention has been called to the fact that knowledge has receded from view in geography classrooms, apart from the focus on 'content'. The concern has been to highlight the limits of constructivist approaches to geographical learning by highlighting the epistemic nature of disciplinary knowledge. Emphasis has been given to some specific theoretical possibilities about the way the discipline produces new knowledge and how the idea of disciplinary constraint might have a potentially important bearing on teachers' thinking about teaching and learning in geography. By concentrating on the manner in which the academic discipline produces new knowledge, teachers gain an understanding of how knowledge is produced and justified as well as the constraining and norming processes that can be applied in the classroom. Discussion has emphasized how the tools of disciplined judgement and disciplinary critique are possible starting points to complement existing approaches to lesson planning, task design and assessment. While research is needed on the subject of how student judgement and critique might be used in the classroom, it is also important to illustrate how teachers can become more epistemologically aware of their discipline and its approaches to knowledge.

The epistemological status of the student in geography education is a concern. It should be emphasized that rather than attempting to resolve the inherent tension between disciplinary and everyday knowledge, the employment of disciplined judgement and critique in a constructivist pedagogy encourages teachers to accept this tension as both inevitable and useful. It is useful because it helps to bring the knowledge that has been constructed – both student and disciplinary – into sharper relief for both teachers and learners (Stemhagen et al. 2013, p. 59). The active production of knowledge by students is always a 'double move' (Daniels 2001, p. 97), which progressively enables the epistemic dimensions of knowledge construction to be more clearly formulated and infused within geographical learning. It is also a 'double move' in that students are invited into a community of inquirers and knowledge producers, where they are encouraged to take on the role not only of creators but also of evaluators of ideas. Students therefore come to recognize and account for differences through normative practices. Taking this tension seriously necessitates that we give credence to meta-criteria (norms) of knowledge production, recognizing that we are all playing the same knowledge game. Moreover, this points to 'knowing how to go on' – a capability not likely to be developed through constructivist pedagogy and the concern with individual meaning making.

The discussion within this chapter is based on the view that we need to better understand knowledge, the subject disciplines and how they can be used as resources for learning in educational settings. There is a need for a more theoretically informed articulation of knowledge and of the relation between knowledge, the curriculum and pedagogy.

Note

1. Theoretical or disciplinary knowledge has come in for a hard time of late, both as an educational aim and as a matter of public value. While knowledge remains important in contemporary society, its nature, status and validity are under threat. This is reflected in the way it is implicated in the social, cultural and economic wellbeing of societies on the one hand, but at the same time there are doubts about its truthfulness and objectivity on the other (Wheelahan 2010, pp. 87–8). The previous government's curriculum policy and national teaching strategies threw some doubt on the educational importance of disciplinary or schooled knowledge. The loss of priority given to discipline-based theoretical knowledge in society and the school curriculum is the result of complex and iterative social changes over recent decades which have impacted on the way knowledge is conceptualized, produced and used.

References

Ball, L D, Thames, M H and Phelps, G (2008) Content knowledge for teaching: what makes it special? *Journal of Teacher Education* 59(5): 389–407.

Bielaczyc, K and Kapur, M (2010) Playing epistemic games in science and mathematics Classrooms. *Educational Technology* 50(5): 19–25.

Boghassian, P (2006) *Fear of Knowledge: Against Relativism and Constructivism*. Oxford: Clarendon Press.

Daniels, H (2001) *Vygotsky and Pedagogy*. London: Routledge/Falmer.

Derry, J (2013) *Vygotsky: Philosophy and Education*. Chichester: Wiley-Blackwell.

Ford, M J (2010) Critique in academic disciplines and active learning of academic content. *Cambridge Journal of Education* 40(3): 265–80.

Geographical Association (2011a) *The Geography National Curriculum: GA Curriculum Proposals and Rationale*. Sheffield: Geographical Association.

— (2011b) *Geography Curriculum Consultation Full Report*. Sheffield: Geographical Association.

— (2012a) *Thinking Geographically*. Sheffield: Geographical Association.

— (2012b) *Geographical Association Curriculum Consultation Feedback Report*. Sheffield: Geographical Association.

Golding, C (2011) The many faces of constructivist discussion. *Educational Philosophy and Theory* 43(5): 467–83.

Hopkin, J (2013) Framing the geography national curriculum. *Geography* 98(2): 60–7.

Kirk, G and Broadhead, P (2007) Every child matters and teacher education: A UCET position paper. Occasional Paper no. 17. London: UCET.

Lambert, D (2011) Reviewing the case for geography and the 'knowledge turn' in the English National Curriculum. *Curriculum Journal* 22(2): 243–64.

Lotz-Sisitka, H (2009) Epistemological access as an open question in education. *Journal of Education* 16: 57–79.

Maton, K (2006) On knowledge structures and knower structures. In R. Moore, M. Arnot, J. Beck and H. Daniels (eds.) *Knowledge, Power and Educational Reform: Applying the Sociology of Basil Bernstein*. London: Routledge.

Morgan, J (2013) What do we mean by 'thinking geographically'? In Lambert, D and Jones, M (eds.) *Debates in Geography Education*. Abingdon: Routledge.

Morrow, W (2007) *Learning to Teach in South Africa*. Cape Town: HSRC Press.

Osborne, J (1996) Beyond constructivism. *Science Education* 80(1): 53–82.

Perkins, D (2006) Constructivism and troublesome knowledge. In Meyer, J H F and Land, R (eds.) *Overcoming Barriers to Student Understanding*. Abingdon: Routledge.

Schwab, J J (1978) Education and the structure of the disciplines. In Westbury, I and Wilko, N J (eds.) *Science, Curriculum and Liberal Education*. Chicago: University of Chicago Press.

Stemhagen, K, Reich, G and Muth, W (2013) Disciplined judgment: toward a reasonably constrained constructivism. *Journal of Curriculum and Pedagogy* 10: 55–72.

Wheelahan, L (2010) *Why Knowledge Matters in Curriculum*. Abingdon: Routledge.

Young, M (2008) *Bringing Knowledge Back In: From Social Constructivism to Social Realism in the Sociology of Education*. Abingdon: Routledge.

Constructing the Geography Curriculum

Charles Rawding

5

Chapter outline

The Geography National Curriculum	69
The 1995 GNC	70
The 1999 GNC	71
The 2008 GNC	72
The 2014 GNC	74
Conclusions	77

This chapter intends to look at the development of the subject content of the English Geography National Curriculum (GNC) through the lens of discourse analysis (Fairclough 2003) to highlight the extent to which curriculum documents incorporate a range of politically or ideologically derived (whether conscious or unconscious) assumptions about geographical knowledge.[1] A discursive approach to knowledge 'entails careful attention to . . . the ways in which humans construct *meanings* (or . . . 'discourses') to make sense of our world', while recognizing that 'scientific practice, interpretation and dissemination are socially constructed and deeply political actually *strengthens* knowledge claims' (Hickey and Lawson 2005, p. 97). Hickey and Lawson consider that 'social categories are not natural or essential but are constructed through power relations, cultural practices and representational processes' (Hickey and Lawson 2005, p. 102). Such an analysis relates to both everyday life and specialist subject knowledge. For instance, they ask the thought-provoking question: 'how would mainstream development be practised differently if "overconsumption" were the central problem defined by the development establishment rather than "overpopulation"?' (Hickey and Lawson 2005, p. 111). Harvey (1996, p. 206) considers discourses to be 'diverse representations of social life which are inherently positioned – differently positioned social actors 'see' and represent social life in different ways, different discourses'.

Putting such considerations into a wider context, it has become increasingly clear that direct government involvement in education policy over the last 40 years has had a significant influence on curriculum in ways that were much less evident previously.[2] Most recently, for many politicians, education has come to be seen as part of a neoliberal drive for global competitiveness, in itself an ideological discourse. Sayer (2000, pp. 4–5) highlights the ideological bias of phrases such as a 'globalising knowledge-driven economy', and the notion that countries must become highly competitive to survive, while Fairclough (2003, pp. 203–4) points out that a new vocabulary including terms such as 'the knowledge economy', 'globalization', 'flexibility' and 'employability' are 'endowed with the performative power to bring into being the very realities [they claim] to describe'. Such developments are the consequence of pressures on politicians to be seen as having 'successful' education policies – increasingly in a global context and perhaps in relation to Programme for International Student Assessment (PISA) outcomes.[3]

Adopting discourse analysis highlights the absence of neutrality in curricular positions, by asserting that 'all knowledge is produced in specific circumstances and that those circumstances shape it in some way' (Rose 1997, p. 305). As Harvey (1996) rightly states: 'One of the mysteries of the dialectics of discourse is the process in which what begins as self-conscious rhetorical deployment becomes "ownership" – how people become unconsciously positioned within a discourse' (Harvey 1996, p. 208). The purpose of such an exposition is to assist the teacher to evaluate both what they may be required to teach and also to raise their awareness of the ideological implications of the position they adopt. It can therefore be seen as important to situate knowledge 'as a means of avoiding the false neutrality and universality of so much academic knowledge' (Rose 1997, p. 306).

Discourse analysis is crucial to understanding the nature of developments within the school curriculum. For instance, Rawling (2001) provides an interesting array of press releases, newspaper articles and snippets from television shows highlighting the wide variety of media influences on discourses relating to geography teaching in schools. All these influences will have varying impacts on actual policies and practices at any given time. Butt (1997) offers us an appreciation of the inner workings of the original Geography Working Group of the GNC based on a number of interviews of Group members. However, these are not the only influencing factors, and it would be a mistake to see the academic discipline as something of a fixed entity being manipulated by political discourses. As Lambert (2004) states in discussing the much-debated nature of geography, the subject seems to have a 'persistent identity crisis'.

The Geography National Curriculum

Having briefly outlined the nature of discourse analysis, this chapter will now turn to the various iterations of the GNC as it has evolved since the introduction of the original National Curriculum in 1991. Initially, it might be useful to consider what is meant by the term 'curriculum' in this context, bearing in mind that the concept itself is far from unproblematic (Biddulph 2013). In the English school system, the term 'curriculum' has generally been used to describe the overall framework for what should be taught in state schools. Levels of prescription have varied over time from the highly prescriptive original 1991 version with its 183 statements across five attainment targets, through to the 2008 curriculum which was contained in only four pages. It was only with the 1999 version that the curriculum was first given a specific set of aims and purposes. It should be stressed that this chapter does not intend to critique these curricula per se, but to focus solely on the changing structure of geographical knowledges within them. Indeed, it could be argued that the latest (2014) version is not a curriculum in the true sense of the word, but merely an itemization of content that needs to be incorporated within any geography curriculum that is developed by a school.

The introduction of a new curriculum is inevitably surrounded by contestation, whether at the level of amicable discussion within a friendly and functional geography department or a more confrontational resistance to the imposition of nationally determined curriculum content. At the same time, in the case of a nationally imposed curriculum, the expectations of politicians may or may not be achieved as their intentions are mediated through a range of actors, sometimes resulting in unexpected outcomes.

Rawling (2001) has provided a detailed analysis of curriculum change from the 1970s, including an extensive discussion of the political machinations associated with the introduction of the original national curriculum following the 1988 Education Reform Act. She highlights the conflicting viewpoints of the groups involved in the creation of the curriculum at the level of national policy, asserting that the 1988 Education Reform Act was a key element in changing the nature of curriculum discourse in England. Butt (1997) agrees, noting that this Act gave far more power to the state than had ever previously been the case. As a result, Rawling (2001) considers that 'the story of the making of the GNC 1989–91 undoubtedly illustrates the confident assertion of central control over curriculum content' (Rawling 2001, p. 64).[4]

Interestingly, Roberts (1995) identified differing responses to the imposition, for the first time in an English context, of the original GNC in a range of different geography departments. She identified three categories of departments with varying approaches to curriculum: *Content rich* departments that thought of the curriculum as knowledge to be learnt, *Framework* departments that thought of the curriculum as a more complex framework of ideas, skills and values, and *Process* departments that thought of the curriculum as a developmental process for students (Roberts 1995, p. 190). In the conclusion to her study she refers to all three departments studying settlement in Y7; the students 'were learning very different things in the three schools. Only the outline theme was the same. The aspects of settlement which were studied, and the particular settlements studied, were all different' (Roberts 1995, p. 203). A key finding of her work is what she terms 'the gap between intention and practice' (1995, p. 188). While it is not the purpose of this chapter to discuss the ways in which the curriculum has been implemented, it is important to bear in mind that the classroom teacher remains central to the interpretation of any curriculum document, a situation that has been termed 'regulated autonomy' (Biddulph 2013, p. 132).

This chapter builds on Rawling's (2001) analysis of the original GNC by investigating more recent iterations under Conservative (1991–7), Labour (1997–2010) and Coalition (2010–) governments to identify the key drivers that have resulted in certain elements of curriculum content being introduced/removed, highlighted/marginalized and how the version of geography proposed by government could not be seen as neutral. As Rawling (2001, p. 8) notes: 'The 1990s were characterised by continuing and often heated debates over the details of subject content for both history and geography. Ministers and their political advisors have sometimes seemed to stand in direct opposition to the views of professional educators in both disciplines'. The prevailing curriculum vision for the original GNC was a cultural restorationist, or absolutist, one (Firth 2013), aiming to reassert the prominence of 'traditional'[5] academic subjects and resulting in a document where 'key ideas were lost in the weight of specific facts' (Rawling 2001, p. 81). Such an approach equates to a transmission model of knowledge where there is 'an objective "real world" which is studied by geographers to produce "knowledge" which is then transmitted to students in schools' (Morgan 2013, p. 274).

Commentators on the Left criticized the original GNC in strident terms: 'With its undertones of assimilation, nationalism and consensus around the regressive re-establishment of past glories, restorationist national curriculum geography isolates students in time and space, cutting them off from the realities of the single European market, global economic dependencies and inequalities and the ecological crisis' (Ball 1994, p. 37). Such a critique of the discourse of the 1991 curriculum identifies a number of worldviews which were incorporated into the curriculum, either explicitly or implicitly, at the expense of others.

The 1995 GNC[6]

The development of the 1995 GNC was underpinned by a rather different discourse. Political pressures on the national curriculum for simplification, a reduction in content and the introduction of greater flexibility were combined with teacher concerns about increasing workload to produce a much slimmer and less prescriptive document. However, in relation to geographical content, changes were much less evident. Indeed, an explicit requirement was to retain the geographical rationale behind the original Order (Battersby 1995). The only significant shifts in focus relate to the inclusion of enquiry-based approaches identifying geographical questions and issues along with a more explicit emphasis on environmental issues, with the term 'sustainable development' being introduced for the first time.

The 1999 GNC

The shift in political direction heralded by the election of a New Labour Government in 1997 led to education policies which explicitly linked educational improvement directly with economic growth, emphasizing skills for employment in order to create a highly skilled workforce. Unlike the 1991 and 1995 versions of the GNC, the 1999 version explicitly referenced learning across the curriculum with detailed listings in relation to the promotion of pupils' spiritual, moral, social and cultural development through geography, alongside the promotion of citizenship and key skills through geography. At the same time, there was a noticeable shift in approaches to knowledge as absolutist views began to be replaced by social constructivist approaches (Roberts 2013) which focused on building upon the known world of the pupils. This shift was completed by the time of the 2008 GNC.

Rawling (2001, p. 126) suggests that government thinking was linked to the promotion of a dynamic economy with a skilled workforce, alongside the development of a cohesive and inclusive civil society where ideas of citizenship were important and where the challenges and implications of globalization were taken seriously. This was the educational equivalent of neoliberal economics blended with social responsibility which epitomized New Labour thinking at the time. Alongside the changing political emphasis, there was also a change in the role of the geography subject community. Such a change had occurred progressively throughout the 1990s (see Table 5.1). The Geographical Association responded very actively when the draft curriculum was put out to consultation, issuing a detailed 'position statement' (Geographical Association 1999).

The 1999 GNC included a number of changes in relation to geographical knowledge. In part 3 under the heading of 'knowledge and understanding of places', pupils were required to be taught 'to explore the idea of global citizenship'. This is a form of place-based knowledge very different from that considered under the previous two GNCs (the sets of maps prescribing specific knowledge were removed). The revised curriculum also included the requirement to develop 'knowledge and understanding of environmental change', while

Table 5.1 Influence of the geography community on curriculum discourse 1989–99

1989–90 Working group	Geography subject community was allowed very little involvement in the process.
1992–3 Advisory group	Geography subject community had constrained influence within tight remit and schedule.
1998–9 Task group	Geography subject community was able to have considerable influence on details and to build on the groundwork laid 1995–8.

Source: Rawling (2001, p.76).

strengthening the wording in relation to the study of sustainable development. Such modifications indicated a more overt form of environmentalism.

At the same time, the heightened emphasis on geographical enquiry and skills included pupils being taught to 'appreciate how people's values and attitudes, including their own, affect contemporary social, environmental, economic and political issues, and to clarify and develop their own values and attitudes about such issues'. For many this was an important updating of the curriculum to take account of the latest developments in geoscience (in relation to climate change) and to address key geographical issues facing the planet (sustainable development); for others this was an attempt at 'green-washing' by moving away from true geographical knowledge towards a geography based on moral and ethical education (Standish 2003).

A more critical view of these changes was developed on the Right,[7] as epitomized by Standish (2007, p. 29): 'In the notion of global citizenship many geographers have found a new niche for their subject. They have jumped on the internationalisation bandwagon and re-invented geography as a subject that teaches students about these "new" global processes and issues . . . Students are not only being taught about how the world is, but also how it ought to be'. He continues: 'If an important aim of education has become the formation of the values and attitudes of students, how does this change the nature and goals of geographic education'? In many ways, this is the key question and underpins discourse analysis, since without determining the 'goals of geographic education', any construction of a geography curriculum becomes extremely problematic.

The 2008 GNC

Rawling (2001, p. 19) observed that 'the national curriculum in England is a subject-based curriculum and, despite two reviews and the amendments made, it still bears the strong imprint of the original (1988) ten-subject structure'. By the time of the 2008 curriculum, it was no longer possible to assert this. The National Curriculum (2008–13) had a much stronger cross-curricular element to it, with the ten subjects famously diminished to a single line in the 'Big Picture' diagram (Big Picture 2008) which was intended to summarize the whole curriculum. Indeed, had the New Labour government retained power in 2010, it is highly likely that this chapter would have a very different interpretation of current subject discourses. Significantly, one of the first things the new Government of 2010 did was to abolish the 'Big Picture' as part of a reassertion of the primacy of a structure based on academic disciplines.

In relation to the 2008 GNC, the changes identified between the 1995 and 1999 versions can be seen to have been further developed. As part of an introductory, two-paragraph statement on 'The Importance of Geography', the curriculum states: 'Geography inspires pupils to become global citizens by exploring their own place in the world, their values and their responsibilities to other people, to the environment and to the sustainability of the planet'. At the same time, notions of place within the 2008 GNC were heavily influenced by developments in cultural geography (Cresswell 2004). The explanatory notes regarding 'place' state: 'Every place has unique physical and human characteristics which can be interpreted and represented in different ways'. This way of thinking about *place* (as opposed to *places*) reflects postmodern approaches to the topic and is a very long way removed from the notions of place contained within the 1991 and 1995 versions of the GNC.

In addition to the distinctly postmodern approach to *place*, the inclusion of 'cultural understanding and diversity' also reflected more recent paradigm shifts within academic geography (Cresswell 2013), with an increased emphasis on values and attitudes when compared to the 1999 GNC. The explanatory notes included questions for pupils to consider such as 'Who am I?'; 'Where do I come from?' and 'Who is my family?' adopting an essentially phenomenological approach to personal geographies from a social constructivist perspective – a very different approach to the impersonal subject content of the first three versions of the GNC. On the other hand, the subject-specific innovations of the 2008 curriculum were focused almost entirely in human geography, while many aspects of physical geography appeared to be marginalized. This was perhaps a reflection of the socially constructed knowledges of those geographers influential in the creation of this particular iteration of the curriculum.

Running alongside these curriculum developments was a re-engagement of government with subject associations. This was epitomized by *The Action Plan for Geography* (2006–11) which was government funded with the purpose of 'enhancing the teaching and learning of geography at school'. The plan was jointly implemented by the Geographical Association and the Royal Geographical Society (2011). It was also during this period that the Geographical Association (2014) introduced notions of 'curriculum making' in an attempt to provide teachers with appropriate guidance for a new period of teacher independence and autonomy (Lambert and Morgan 2010).

While all these changes were broadly welcomed by the groups that had been so critical of the earlier versions of the GNC, to commentators with more absolutist views of knowledge, the changes were seen as an ethically engaged agenda linked to 'specific non-academic values that tend towards the replacement of knowledge with morality as the central focus of the curriculum' (Standish 2007, p. 39). Interestingly, Standish (2007, pp. 44–5) chooses to highlight the study of environmental impacts such as the use of carbon footprints, and the study of *Fair Trade*, as exemplars of everything he considers to be inadequate about the changing nature of the geography curriculum. The timing of the publication by *Civitas* (other chapters covered Science, Mathematics, Modern Foreign Languages, History and English) had presumably been intended, by the editors, to influence the discourse in the run-up to the 2008 GNC.

At one level the Right is arguing against more recent post-structuralist interpretations of society – interpretations that have been very evident in the 'cultural turn' in geography (and the spatial turn in the social sciences) since the 1990s (Duncan et al. 2008). It is within the contrasting approaches to structures of knowledge highlighted by the polarized positions of post-structuralist and absolutist approaches that many of the shifts in curriculum content can be situated. On the one hand, Standish argues that: 'if knowledge can no longer be abstracted from the particular social context in which it arose, it cannot be separated from the prejudices or values of the individual who constructed it. In this sense post-structuralism holds a limited social interpretation of knowledge' (2007, p. 42). But as Firth (2013, p. 68) rightly states: 'absolutism emphasises the objectivity of knowledge but ignores the socio-historical basis of knowledge'. Interestingly, the restorationists' position is directly opposed to that stated by the Geographical Association in its *Different View* manifesto, where it argued that the curriculum 'is a moral concern and should reflect what we think we should be teaching' (2009, p. 27). On the other hand, social realists would argue that this is a false dichotomy and that rather than considering 'either/or', we should be incorporating 'both/and' (Maton and Moore 2010, p. 2).

The 2014 GNC

If we now turn our attention to the 2014 GNC, there are a large number of fundamental changes in direction when compared with the trends previously identified over the period 1991–2008. A changing political complexion is vividly demonstrated at the personal level, where a group that was very much on the margins in 2007 (Civitas) was actively engaged with the construction of the 2014 curriculum. In the case of Geography, Alex Standish now describes himself as 'Curriculum advisor to the Department for Education and CIVITAS'.[8]

We shall now turn our attention to the underpinning discourses that have been influential in the construction of this document. A number of key characteristics can be seen clearly in the 2014 National Curriculum. Firstly, there has been an explicit (re)articulation of a physical–human binary to the subject – with the introductory *Purpose of study* requiring pupils to acquire 'a deep understanding of the Earth's key physical and human processes. As pupils progress, their growing knowledge about the world should help them to deepen their understanding of the interaction between physical and human processes'. At the same time, one of the two subject-specific aims states that pupils should: 'understand the processes that give rise to key physical and human geographical features of the world, how these are interdependent and how they bring about spatial variation and change over time'. While it is indisputable that physical and human processes are fundamental to geography, recent perceptions of the school subject have tended towards a threefold approach, incorporating environmental geographies as an addition to the two traditional strands of the subject.[9] The study of environments within the curriculum is clearly circumscribed. The *Purpose of study* states: 'Teaching should equip pupils with knowledge about diverse places, people, resources and natural and human environments', while the *Aims* do not mention the word environment. Such an approach accords with calls for a more 'anthropocentric approach' where environments are seen as arenas for human activity rather than more independent entities.

In the subject content sections, discussion of environments is restricted to knowledge of environmental regions which is clearly framed within the second dominant element of the new curriculum, namely regional geography.

At Key Stage 1 (the under 7s), children are required to study 'the human and physical geography of a small area of the United Kingdom', and 'a small area in a contrasting non-European country'. This is followed at Key Stage 2 (7–11) by the study of the 'human and physical geography of a region of the United Kingdom, a region in a European country, and a region within North or South America'. Finally, in the early years of secondary school (Key Stage 3, pp. 11–14), 'the study of human and physical geography of a region within Africa, and of a region within Asia' is specified.

The history of geographical thought is well documented (Livingstone 1992; Unwin 1992) and it is interesting to note that Cresswell (2013), in adopting a chronological approach to the changing geographical paradigms within the academic discipline, writes about regional geography in chapter four (of 13). He identifies the period of maximum influence for regional geographies as the period between the two world wars, with increasing criticisms of the approach during the 1950s and 1960s leading to its rejection as an effective paradigm for geographical understanding by the 1970s. The re-emergence of regional approaches in school geography can be attributed once again to the influence of absolutists within the Conservative party.[10]

The explicit statement relating to the requirement to study industry using a primary/secondary/tertiary/quaternary classification (with only limited additional direction on what might be taught) came as something of a surprise to many geographers given the dated nature of such a categorization. Does such a categorization have any place in twenty-first-century capitalism where it is often impossible to separate research, design, manufacture and marketing (e.g. within the corporate structures of Apple, Google and Facebook)? Yet the proposal to study industrial development in such a context can be understood in an almost nostalgic desire to return to a world of industrial certainties (although, in fact, such certainties merely reflect a relatively short period of industrial capitalism following the emergence of a significant service sector in the period after the Second World War). Such certainties were certainly being challenged by the growing importance of computer-based technologies by the 1980s. As Fairclough (1989, p. 170) states: 'The position of the producer may be problematized as to *contents* where some discrepancy arises between the producers common-sense (ideological) representations of the world, and the world itself. This may happen because of changes in the world, for instance, or when the producer's representations come into contact with other incompatible representations'.

An alternative discourse can be identified by the (re)introduction of the regional paradigm within the GNC. Here it becomes clear that we are dealing with a nostalgic/reactionary view of geography. Any incorporation of regional geography raises fundamental issues about defining regions, as well as considering which regions of the world should be taught. The argument of advocates of this approach usually runs along the lines of stressing the importance of studying the 'major' regions of the world, without ever attempting to define any corresponding 'minor' regions. Such a paradigm is often argued to be common sense by its supporters – yet as Hall (2001) points out, commonsense in itself is ideological. To illustrate this issue, when the regional paradigm was predominant Britain was moving from being a colonial power to a period of post-colonialism. This was clearly reflected in the selection of 'major' regions to study and perhaps more significantly those regions *not* studied. Throughout the period 1945–89, study of the Soviet Union and the Communist bloc remained fundamentally problematic,[11] yet it would be ridiculous to suggest that this area was only a 'minor' region. The 2014 GNC skirts such issues by citing the need to study the 'world's major countries' and 'globally significant places', without ever defining what these locations might be. Again, it will be interesting to see how schools interpret such vague terms and whether there is clear evidence for a similar 'gap between intention and practice' that Roberts noted in 1995.

Alongside subject-specific discourses, it is also possible to identify more general educational discourses which may have an impact on curriculum provision. For instance, the 2014 curriculum has far more emphasis on acquiring detailed factual content in the primary years (which has been described in terms of 'driving up standards'). But this approach is highly contested, as demonstrated by a letter to the *Daily Telegraph* expressing serious concerns about the teaching and testing of very young children and the vehement government response to the criticisms.[12] For the geographer, a consideration of 'seasonal and daily weather patterns in the United Kingdom' might be deemed beyond the ability of a 6-year-old, while the study of 'biomes and vegetation belts' would appear very challenging for 10-year-olds.

The production of a curriculum document does not in itself result in the development of a coherent curriculum. For instance, the 2008 National Curriculum was constructed around what its designers regarded as the central concepts of geography, focusing on notions such as place, space and environment. In reality it is difficult to conceive of an effective geography lesson without reference to place (but see Roberts 2010). This does not mean that a coherent curriculum will result simply from ensuring that place is covered in every lesson. Equally, the rather different approach taken in the 2014 National Curriculum provides a list of content to be covered. To take just one example, at Key Stage 3 pupils are required to: 'understand geographical similarities and differences through the study of human and physical geography of a region or area within Africa and a region or area within Asia'. Quite reasonably, a geography department might choose to look at urban issues in Cairo and nomadic herders in the Sahara Desert to conform to these requirements, yet such an approach does not produce a coherent vision for a geography curriculum. In a worst-case scenario, pupils could complete their geographical education considering geography to be simply a long list of case studies from around the world. What is needed here is what Bruner (1996) terms 'an interpretive narrative', that is to say an effective contextualization of what is being studied to ensure that geographical thinking, themes and skills are being continuously developed and to ensure that pupils can see linkages between the elements within their programme of study. Curriculum coherence is determined by the elements of connectivity within the curriculum and by the existence of clear threads of geographical thinking that run through the lesson sequences (Rawding 2013).

Conclusions

This chapter has identified how varying approaches to geographical knowledge have resulted in different geography curriculum documents since the introduction of the original GNC in 1991. To a large extent, political influences can be identified in determining what has been either included or left out, yet at the same time, the significant scope for teacher interpretation of the documents means that pupils experiencing the same notional curriculum may have very different geographical experiences.

Notes

1. Even where the debate prior to the production of a given curriculum document has been acrimonious and overtly political, it is usual to present the final version as a 'neutral' document.
2. The beginnings of this shift are often traced to a speech by the Prime Minister, James Callaghan, at Ruskin College in 1976 – see http://education.guardian.co.uk/thegreatdebate/story/0,9860,574645,00.html for the full script of the speech.
3. PISA is an international study that was launched by the OECD in 1997. It aims to evaluate education systems worldwide every three years by assessing 15-year-olds' competencies in the key subjects: reading, mathematics and science. To date, over 70 countries and economies have participated in PISA. http://www.oecd.org/pisa/
4. For a fuller discussion of the changing geographical content within the GNC, see Rawding (2010b).
5. The very use of the term 'traditional' is heavily value-laden – giving a supposed intellectual superiority to academic subjects that were largely developed in the final quarter of the nineteenth century and the early years of the twentieth century. On the historical origins of the secondary curriculum, see Goodson (1985); on the history of geographical education, see Ploszajska (1999).
6. See the April 1995 issue of *Teaching Geography* which was a special issue covering the introduction of the new GNC.
7. It should be pointed out here that there are dangers in over-simplifying the political categories. For instance, Sir Keith Joseph, a right-wing Thatcherite Secretary of State for Education (1981–6), argued strongly that Geography was a value-laden subject and pupils were done a disservice if values and conflicting positions were not discussed.
8. On his personal profile page at the Institute of Education, University of London http://www.ioe.ac.uk/staff/CPAT/75664.html. Accessed 27 September 2013.
9. Based on an analysis of all current GCSE and A Level syllabi, the author edited a series of texts for teachers of Geography where it became clear that the most logical approach was to produce Human, Physical and Environmental volumes (Rawding 2010a; Rawding et al. 2010; Suggitt 2010).

10. Although the government is a coalition of Conservatives and Liberal Democrats, the coalition agreement means that education policy has effectively been in the hands of the Conservatives throughout their period in office.

11. A glance at the contents of the bestselling textbook of the 1960s and early 1970s *A Course in World Geography* by Young and Lowry (1960–71) illustrates this point. Ten books were produced covering The World (four books), The British Isles (two books), Europe and the Soviet Union, North America, East Africa and Central Africa. The absence of any systematic study of either Asia or South America highlights the inadequacies of the regional approach, while the book on Europe and the Soviet Union had 75 per cent of its pages focused on Western Europe reflecting a whole range of assumptions about the relative importance of some regional geographies over other regional geographies.

12. For the original letter, see: http://www.telegraph.co.uk/comment/letters/10302844/The-Government-should-stop-intervening-in-early-education.html; for the Department of Education response, see: http://www.theguardian.com/education/2013/sep/12/early-years-schooling-damaging-wellbeing

References

Ball, S J (1994) *Education Reform: A Critical and Post-Structural Approach*. Buckingham: Open University Press.

Battersby, J (1995) Rationale for the revised curriculum. *Teaching Geography* 20(2): 57–8.

Biddulph, M (2013) Where is the curriculum created. In Lambert, D and Jones, M (eds.) *Debates in Geography Education*, pp. 129–42. Abingdon: Routledge.

Big Picture (2008) http://webarchive.nationalarchives.gov.uk/20101014180246/http://curriculum.qcda.gov.uk/uploads/BigPicture_sec_05_tcm8–15743.pdf

Bruner, J (1996) *The Culture of Education*. London: Harvard University Press.

Butt, G (1997) *An Investigation into the Dynamics of the National Curriculum Geography Working Group (1989–1990)*. Unpublished PhD thesis, University of Birmingham.

Cresswell, T (2004) *Place: A Short Introduction*. Oxford: Blackwell.

— (2013) *Geographic Thought: A Critical Introduction*. Chichester: Wiley-Blackwell.

Duncan, J S, Johnson, N C and Schein, R H (eds.) (2008) *A Companion to Cultural Geography*. Oxford: Blackwell.

Fairclough, N (1989) *Language and Power*. Longman: Harlow.

— (2003) *Analysing Discourse: Textual Analysis for Social Research*. Abingdon: Routledge.

Firth, R (2013) What constitutes knowledge in geography? In Lambert, D and Jones, M (eds.) *Debates in Geography Education*, pp. 59–74. Abingdon: Routledge.

Geographical Association (1999) Geography in the curriculum: a position statement from the GA. Published simultaneously in *Teaching Geography* 24(2): 57–9 and *Geography* 84(2): 164–7.

— (2009) *A Different View: A Manifesto from the Geographical Association*. Sheffield: Geographical Association.

— (2014) http://www.geography.org.uk/cpdevents/curriculummaking. Last accessed 5 March 2014.

Geographical Association and RGS-IBG (2011) *The Action Plan for Geography 2006–2011: Final Report and Evaluation*. Available at http://www.rgs.org/NR/rdonlyres/82F00DE8-A7A3–4411-B111-E6A3610317EF/0/APG20062011_FinalReportandEvaluation.pdf. Last accessed 5 March 2014.

Goodson, I F (ed.) (1985) *Social Histories of the Secondary Curriculum*. Barcombe: The Falmer Press.

Hall, S (2001) The spectacle of the other. In Wetherell, M, Taylor, S and Yates, S J (eds.) *Discourse Theory and Practice: A Reader*, pp. 324–44. London: Sage.

Harvey, D (1996) *Justice, Nature and the Geography of Difference*. Oxford: Blackwell.

Hickey, M and Lawson, V (2005) Beyond science? Human geography, interpretation and critique. In Castree, N, Rogers, A and Sherman, S (eds.) *Questioning Geography*, pp. 96–114. Oxford: Blackwell.

Lambert, D (2004) Geography. In White, J (ed.) *Rethinking the School Curriculum: Values, Aims and Purposes*, pp. 75–86. London: Routledge Falmer.

Lambert, D and Morgan, J (2010) *Teaching Geography 11–18: A Conceptual Approach*. Maidenhead: Open University Press.

Livingstone, D N (1992) *The Geographical Tradition*. Oxford: Blackwell.

Maton, K and Moore, R (eds.) (2010) *Social Realism, Knowledge and the Sociology of Education*. London: Continuum.

Morgan, J (2013) What do we mean by thinking geographically? In Lambert, D and Jones, M (eds.) *Debates in Geography Education*, pp. 273–81. Abingdon: Routledge.

Ploszajska, T (1999) *Geographical Education, Empire and Citizenship. Geographical Teaching and Learning in English Schools, 1870–1944*. Historical Geography Research Series, 35. London: Royal Geographical Society (with Institute of British Geographers).

Rawding, C (2010a) *Contemporary Approaches to Geography, Volume 1. Human Geography*. London: Chris Kington.

— (2010b) What are the connections between subject developments in academic and school geography? *International Research in Geographical and Environmental Education* 19(2): 119–25.

— (2013) *Effective Innovation in the Secondary Geography Curriculum: A Practical Guide*. Abingdon: Routledge.

Rawding, C, Holden, V and Worsley, A (2010) *Contemporary Approaches to Geography, Volume 3. Environmental Geography*. London: Chris Kington.

Rawling, E (2001) *Changing the Subject: The Impact of National Policy on School Geography 1980–2000*. Geographical Association: Sheffield.

Roberts, M (1995) Interpretations of the Geography National Curriculum: a common curriculum for all? *Journal of Curriculum Studies* 27(2): 187–205.

— (2010) Where's the geography? Reflections on being an external examiner. *Teaching Geography* 35(3): 112–13.

— (2013) *Geography through Enquiry: Approaches to Teaching and Learning in the Secondary School*. Sheffield: Geographical Association.

Rose, G (1997) Situating knowledges: positionality, reflexivities and other tactics. *Progress in Human Geography* 21(3): 305–20.

Sayer, A (2000) *Realism and Social Science*. London: Sage.

Standish, A (2003) Constructing a value map. *Geography* 88(2): 149–51.

— (2007) Geography used to be about maps. In Whelan, R (ed.) *The Corruption of the Curriculum*, pp. 28–57. London: Civitas.

Suggitt, S (2010) *Contemporary Approaches to Geography, Volume 2. Physical Geography*. London: Chris Kington.

Unwin, T (1992) *The Place of Geography*. Harlow: Prentice-Hall.

Young, E W and Lowry, J H (1960–71) *A Course in World Geography*. London: Edward Arnold.

What Is the Role of Theory?

Graham Butt

6

Chapter outline

The status and place of theory in educational research	83
Types of theory	83
'Grand', Empirical, Interpretivist and Critical Theories	86
New kid on the block? The rise of complexity theory	88
Theory in geography education	89
Conclusions	90

One of the key determinants of whether assessed written work is deemed to be 'at Masters level', particularly that which describes research activity, is its successful engagement with theory. The nature of this engagement can vary. Theory is often employed to provide analytical, structuring or interpretive frameworks within which ideas and research methods can be considered – towards the end of a research project the application of theory may also enable the researcher to avoid merely describing what he or she has found, opening up the possibilities for a deeper analysis of findings. Theory can therefore help in the planning of research activity and be applied during and after data collection to aid the interpretation of data. In certain situations, theory building can also occur – that is, new theory can be generated from the data, or may be 'grounded' in the findings that result (Glaser and Strauss 1967; Lincoln and Guba 1985).

The theoretical perspective within which one's research is located is usually considered *before* any data is collected. Here the role of theory may be primarily to help the researcher think about the relationships between agents and factors observed, increasing his or her understanding of the processes that link them together. Theories can be employed as explanatory devices – structured around concepts and focused on key ideas – to help construct new knowledge, or offer guidance on the causes and consequences of events, actions and activities. They can be measured or, in some cases, 'tested' against the data that is gathered; in this way, existing theory can either be supported, rejected or changed. However, it should be noted that as a result of adopting a particular theoretical position, interpretation of data may be limited by this chosen perspective (sociological, psychological, philosophical, scientific, etc., Hitchcock and Hughes 1995). There is a generally accepted requirement for researchers to base their work within existing theoretical standpoints and disciplinary traditions, mindful of the knowledge sets in which they are working. Research in educational contexts tends to operate across a range of theoretical settings, involving the application of theories from a variety of disciplines and traditions.

Educational theory has its critics. Wilf Carr (2006), cited in Thomas (2007), refers to educational theory as a term given to 'the various futile attempts that we have made over the last hundred years to stand outside our educational practices in order to explain and justify them . . . we should now bring the whole educational theory enterprise to a dignified end' (p. 137). In this context Carr, in Thomas' eyes, offers a rather narrow conception of theory (contrapositioned with practice), but presents a genuine concern about the ways in which theory can be distorted. As Thomas (2007) himself recalls, again comparing the relationship between theory and practice, 'theory seemed to act as a kind of drug – a hybrid of intoxicant, hypnotic and hallucinogen – to otherwise sensible people in education, offering delusions about practical intervention' (p. 7). He questions the centrality of theory in much educational research, has concerns about whether our confidence in theory is always justified and challenges whether educational practice should necessarily be based on theory. The alternative (according to Thomas) may be to devise simpler, less theoretically rigid, structures for enquiry – not driven by existing theories, but more reliant on clearer conceptions of values, thoughts, reflections and ideas. Indeed, in many circumstances, use of the term 'theory' is simply a conflation of what many would describe as 'critically reflecting', or simply 'thinking'. 'Thinking' is not necessarily congruent with 'theorizing'; it is therefore also wrong to assume that all forms of intellectual work can be described as 'theory-making', or that the thinking that arises from one's everyday professional practice and discourse has a clear relationship with theory (Fish 1989). Commenting on the status of different theories, Cohen et al. (2007) are also critical of educational theory (compared with, say, theories in the natural sciences) referring to them as 'only at the early stages of formulation and (are) thus characterized by great unevenness' (p. 13).

Notwithstanding such criticism, theory can provide the bedrock on which to build meaningful enquiry – highlighting areas that require deeper investigation, identifying gaps in knowledge, aiding understanding and helping researchers to predict outcomes.

The status and place of theory in educational research

Thomas (2012) notes the increasing demand for educational research to employ scientific principles, following the presumption that other forms of research offer neither robust evidence, nor reliable data (particularly when attempting to determine 'what works' in schools). In the United States, educational research is assumed by some to have 'failed', has an 'awful reputation' and 'does not generate knowledge that can inform education practice and policy' (Shavelson and Towne 2002, p. 28, cited in Thomas 2012). In the United Kingdom, similar assertions are easily found. Furlong and Oancea (2005) note a perception in government circles of the poor quality of much education research, with earlier reports by Tooley and Darby (1998) and Hillage et al. (1998) highlighting the lack of impact made by the same. Research in geography education is not exempt from such criticism (see Naish 1993; Butt 2002a, 2006; Firth and Morgan 2010). There is an underlying assumption in certain quarters that scientific methods, and the application of scientific theory, are required to ensure rigorous results that can be applied to improve teaching and learning. Thomas (2012) describes this as a conscious 'linking of research with theory and the need to replicate and to generalize across studies' (p. 27), but notes that this view of scientific method is narrow and not easily replicated within the context of education. Here 'truth' is hard won at the individual and local level, and the knowledge accrued by the social scientist is different from that of the natural scientist.

A fundamental question arises: What is the place of theory in educational research? The answer varies according to the work to which theory is put. Research driven by the postgraduate student will afford the researcher a wide choice of theories that might be applied. By contrast, use of theory in research designed simply to test the effectiveness of policies, strategies and projects may be much more restricted, or even nonexistent. Such evaluative research work is important, but the link to a funder – who may be politically driven, represent the specific interests of a funding body or have a vested interest in the findings – will influence the flexibilities and freedoms of the researcher. In such circumstances, those who should not necessarily set the research agenda and its parameters may have greater control than is perhaps advisable. We come back to the issue of whether research is truly open, being primarily driven by theory building and a desire to explore, or whether it is tightly restricted to testing the effectiveness of an initiative, project or policy. The difference is important: for the former is often emancipatory and encourages knowledge creation, whereas the latter takes theory as a set framework within which research is simply applied.

Types of theory

Defining different types of theory is not easy. Indeed, the term 'theory' has a variety of meanings. Thomas (2007), for example, notes a common view that 'theory is anything that isn't practice' – simply placing theory at the end of a supposed 'theory-practice' continuum. Schön (1991) comments on the status of theory, referring to the 'high ground of theory' being contrasted with the 'swampy lowland of practice'. There are also concerns about the uncritical, 'promiscuous' use of theory in education – to describe almost anything that is not 'practice', denote explanation, to gather personal reflections, orientate principles, aid epistemological presuppositions and to develop arguments (Thomas 2007). With admirable conciseness, Robson (1997) defines theory as 'a general statement that summarises and organises knowledge by proposing a general relationship between events' (p. 18).

In attempting to provide an overview of different types of theory, let us begin by exploring the important relationship between theory, epistemology and ontology. Epistemology refers to our theories of knowledge and how knowledge is constructed – which impacts on the theoretical perspective adopted in one's research design and the methodology selected (see Crotty 2003). It is possible to research a particular question from a variety of theoretical perspectives and along a number of different methodological lines, but some will be more suitable than others. In academic geography, until the 1970s, the preferred theoretical perspective was predominantly positivist and objective, with concomitant effects on the research methodologies employed. This is still the case in much research in physical geography, although human/social geography tends to adopt a more interpretivist, subjective stance – in much geographical study it can be argued that the two cannot be easily separated, as both the physical and social worlds exist side by side and combine (Crotty 2003; Taylor 2009). This may create tensions, simultaneously pulling the researcher in different directions. Interpretivist research covers a wide spectrum of epistemological positions – here researchers see truth as socially constructed and mobile, rather than external, fixed and awaiting discovery. As a result, some would argue that no single epistemological position can underpin educational research. In the geography education community research within the interpretivist paradigm has traditionally been strong, particularly within the United Kingdom, but debate about the contribution of theory to research in geography education has been rather limited (Butt 2002a; Gerber and Williams 2000; Williams 1999).

Within interpretivist research, theory tends to be generated as a consequence of enquiry, which Robson (1997) refers to as 'hypothesis generating' (as opposed to 'testing'). Here data collection and analysis may proceed 'hand in hand', with the latter often suggesting what new data needs to be gathered. Theory generation and refinement may be nonlinear and uncertain, with ill-defined outcomes. A mechanistic, methodologically 'tight', theory-driven piece of research may look good in terms of its design and expected results, but may not yield much valuable data. As Thomas (2012) asserts, 'we seek to capture regularity, and its encapsulation goes under the title of *theory*' (p. 31, emphasis in original), but he also points out that generalization is not always possible, or indeed the point of research in the social sciences. Too many shaky assumptions within our evidence, methods and theory – often because of the number of variables in play and the changeable conditions in which they occur – mean that generalizations, theory building and model construction can be dangerous projects in educational research. Robson (1997) notes that adopting a purist approach to the adoption of research theories and methods, from either one tradition or the other, may ultimately prove unrewarding. He suggests that a more sensible 'real world' approach may be afforded by bringing the empirical and interpretivist traditions together in some way – as achieved through the use of a mixed methods research design (see Onwuegbuzie and Leech 2005; Weis et al. 2009).

Social science tends to look at reality in different ways to scientific research. Ideas about the social world are built on assumptions – these may be defined as ontological (concerned with the essence of the social phenomena considered, whether these exist independent of the individual in the 'real world' or are a construction of one's mind) and epistemological (what knowledge is, how it is acquired and how it can be communicated). Ontology is a branch of philosophy that considers the nature of reality and the form that this takes. It employs contrasting theories, but these tend to be closely aligned to associated epistemologies. For example, according to one's view of knowledge – whether it is considered to consist of objective facts, or is subjective and personal to the individual – one's theoretical position and research approach is determined. In effect, knowledge-seeking disciplines and practices are shaped and influenced by the reality they seek to describe. Concern about what knowledge is and how it is constructed is central. It helps us to judge the validity of others' research findings (and our own) and the appropriateness of the methodology adopted to create knowledge. I believe that Crotty's (2003) definition of the theoretical perspective of any piece of research is helpful when he describes it as 'the philosophical stance lying behind a methodology' (p. 66).

Ideally, theories should be applicable – within given parameters, caveats and sets of conditions – to the majority of situations they consider; they should therefore be able to make strong claims to generalizability within their chosen context. However, theories often include rather guarded statements about their degrees of certainty – a 'strong' theory may have good predictive powers ('in these circumstances, given these factors, this will result'), making explicit links between cause and effect. 'Weaker', or more tentative, theories may not be able to make such bold and defensible assertions. However, it could be the theory's generative mechanism, rather than the theory itself, that is robust and enduring (or 'strong') and therefore observable across different contexts. Broadly, theories can be classified as being *normative* – which suggests how things should be, and what can be expected given a particular set of circumstances or interventions – or *explanatory* – which suggests how things work. Many different types of theory exist – in this chapter, 'grand' theories, empirical theories, interpretivist theories and critical theories have been selected for further discussion as they tend to describe collections of accepted theoretical positions. Discussion of other, more specific theories (such as grounded theory, socio-cultural activity theory, feminist theory, etc.), which fall within these parameters, is unfortunately curtailed by lack of space.

'Grand', Empirical, Interpretivist and Critical Theories

'Grand' theory attempts a meta-narrative of a particular theme and seeks to draw together concepts, structures and empirical findings into a defined field of study. This may involve some degree of speculation if empirical 'evidence' cannot be presented to support and illustrate all of the aspects of the theory. By their very nature, such theories are ambitious and open to criticism, as they aim to achieve all-encompassing scope.

Empirical theories aim to create deductions and generate laws, which can then be empirically tested. With repeated hypothesis testing (and rejection), confidence in such theories grows, following attempts to falsify or verify their propositions (Popper 1968). Each theory is amended, or replaced, by a better theory as knowledge grows – importantly, the types of evidence that can either confirm, or refute, aspects of the theory are made increasingly clear through this process. Exceptions to the original theory can be built into new theories, which then ameliorate or even replace this theory. New theories should be broadly compatible with those that have gone before, be empirically sound and move towards greater generalizability. There must be internal consistency in the theory; it should have explanatory and predictive power and be able to respond to anomalies (Cohen et al. 2007). In essence, positivist and empirical theories differ from those with interpretivist roots because:

> positivist and interpretive paradigms are essentially concerned with understanding phenomena through two different lenses. Positivism strives for objectivity, measurability, predictability, controllability, patterning, the construction of laws and rules of behaviour, and the ascription of causality; the interpretive paradigms strive to understand and interpret the world in terms of its actors. In the former observed phenomena are important; in the latter meanings and interpretations are paramount. (p. 26)

Interpretivist approaches allow some deviance from the 'pure' theoretical perspective, refuting the possibility of a universal truth 'out there' that is open to discovery. They therefore adopt a contrary position to positivist approaches, looking for 'culturally derived and historically situated interpretations of the social world' (Crotty 2003, p. 67). By their very nature interpretivist theories are open to a variety of readings – often within broad, context-driven, inclusive perspectives – are adept at exploring meanings and are useful in considering 'the whole' rather than the parts. The epistemological underpinnings of interpretivism highlight the differences between people and objects, with social researchers using various theories and methods in their attempt to understand the complexity and richness of human action. In conclusion, positivism aligns with scientific enquiry, and empiricism, where only observable phenomena can be accepted as knowledge – and where the gathering of 'facts' can lead to the creation of 'laws'. By contrast, the achievement of objective, unbiased research is believed to be unattainable in the social sciences (Bryman 2004).

Critical theory originating from the Frankfurt School regards the positivist and interpretivist paradigms as incomplete, for they tend to ignore the ideological and political circumstances within which social behaviours occur. Critical theorists claim that many theoretical approaches accept, rather than question, the status quo; within the educational context, this results in simply replicating the flawed systems of society and schooling, despite our research efforts. Theorists in this paradigm are working towards the creation of a more egalitarian, democratic society within which individuals are free to act and express themselves. Essentially, such research is transformative, rather than descriptive, striving to break the perpetuation and reinforcement of existing social status and process (Habermas 1988). The desire to create change towards a more just society, rather than merely *describing* a situation that currently exists, marks out critical theory as a force for emancipatory action. Originally founded on Marxist ideas, researchers who adopt a critical position in their research cannot claim to be ideologically neutral – they question (rather than accept) given research agendas, and seek to interrogate and examine how social institutions work (Kincheloe and McLaren 2005). In the context of educational research, this might include enquiry into the ways in which schools reproduce rather than mobilize social status, how they perpetuate inequalities and class divisions, and how curriculum decision making occurs. Who gains and who loses from education – often with particular reference to their class, race and gender – is a common concern, as is the consideration of the place of knowledge in education. Here researchers question the very nature of knowledge and the taken-for-granted assumptions about ways of knowing (Firth and Morgan 2010). This has become a focus for much contemporary research in geography education – driven by questions such as: whose geographical knowledge is being taught; what counts as valuable geographical knowledge; who advocates and supports such knowledge creation and transition (see Young, Lambert, Roberts, Firth)? Young's (2007) conception of 'powerful knowledge', recognizing as it does the social constructedness of knowledge and its cultural significance, has been a stimulus to recent research activity for many geography educators.

Research methodologies favoured by critical theorists (among others) include methods associated with action research, interpretivist approaches and ideological critiques. Action research tends to be undertaken by practitioners researching their own practice within its particular context (its specific place, historical setting, social dimensions, power bases, etc.) and often claims to be emancipatory and empowering (Butt 2002b). However, change may still *not* occur as a result of this research. This is the consequence of research being carried out by those who have limited power, or who are situated in very specific, local contexts – their study being restricted to individual classes, or a school, rather than impacting more widely across schools and society. The power of the individual teacher, even one who adopts action research methods, very rarely affects the real locus of power and the actions of decision makers. The extent to which engagement with critical theory research can change situations therefore requires verification. Despite its claims, has this theoretical position really led to much change? Has teacher and student agency increased and transformation occurred? The political drivers of this type of research are both a blessing and a curse – critical research seeks real change, but by taking an ideological position it is open to legitimate claims of partiality, bias and subjectivity (although researchers in this paradigm would assert that the very situatedness of other research means that it works towards maintaining the status quo and the reproduction of existing power relationships). Critical theory also implies the adoption of a critical pedagogy – where teachers refuse to teach a curriculum that simply replicates society, favouring one that is emancipatory, destroys social inequality and frees students.

New kid on the block? The rise of complexity theory

The next section of this chapter discusses a relatively new theoretical position, to geography educationists at least, which has the potential to influence future research agendas. Complexity theory breaks with simple cause-and-effect models and linear descriptions of phenomena – which largely assume their susceptibility to forensic examination – facilitating a view of the world that is organic, nonlinear and holistic. Uncertainty, along with notions of predictability and control, are carefully considered in an attempt to provide sophisticated models of real world complexity. This theory claims that behaviours in educational settings are rarely predictable, seldom being understood through the application of simplistic theories and research designs; such behaviours are therefore unwilling to reveal their complexities to positivist approaches, or even the more sophisticated interpretivist research designs.

The holistic approach is important, as complexity theory rejects the idea that dissection of situations into constituent parts will necessarily reveal greater understanding (Wood and Butt 2014). The variables are considered too numerous and too complex to submit to such enquiry. For a geographer the analogy is that of an ecosystem where the parts can only be analysed and understood as constituents of the whole. Complexity theory offers a tantalizing link between small- and large-scale research, with methodology largely taken from action research, participatory approaches and the qualitative paradigm. The range of actors and their perspectives is acknowledged as being huge, involving multiple connections between individuals, groups and society. The plethora of views of reality requires the application of numerous research methods, several views of situations and the recognition of different voices.

The origins of complexity theory arise from the natural and physical sciences. It was created to describe and explain systems which are too complex to understand, or model, through linear computation, but which are not purely random (Mitchell 2009). Such systems are difficult to predict and although they may give rise to observable patterns, they do not reflect simple cause-and-effect relationships (Johnson 2007). In the natural world there are numerous examples – ant hills and weather systems, for example – where large-scale patterns are obvious, but the small-scale behaviours from which they result appear chaotic. The term 'emergence' is used to describe ways in which small-scale interactions lead to change; this concept can also be applied to the development of new ideas and ways of working. Here the sum of the parts is greater than the whole, whereby individual traits and capacities combine to create a complex system (Boschetti et al. 2005; Davis and Sumara 2006). Complexity theory has been increasingly applied to describe and analyse phenomena in the social sciences, beginning with research into both cities (Johnson 2001) and the activities of business organizations (Stacey 2001; Fonseca 2002).

As complexity theory has advanced, a number of theoretical positions have developed. An uncomplicated typology of complexity theory is offered by Richardson and Cilliers (2001), who suggest three approaches: hard complexity, soft complexity and complexity thinking. Hard complexity theory is usually applied within the sciences, based on the application of computational modelling and quantitative analysis. Soft complexity theory is used within the social sciences, where complexity is employed as a metaphor to explain social systems. Somewhere between these two lie complexity thinking – which describes complex systems as never yielding to complete understanding due to the presence of multiple factors interacting across different scales of activity (Wood and Butt 2014). Nevertheless, Hardman (2010) is critical of the concept, believing that researchers in the social sciences often claim that the systems they work with are complex, but only offer nonempirical evidence to prove this.

Osberg and Biesta (2008, 2010) have applied complexity theory to the classroom, with a particular focus on knowledge. Here the curriculum is seen as a medium through which the subjectivity of children is shaped as they interact with knowledge, a process structured by the preconceived goals of formal education systems. As a consequence of socio-political constraints on the curriculum, often a result of the use of assessment performance targets, Osberg and Biesta (2008) argue that 'limit must be placed on the kinds of meaning that can emerge in a classroom' (p. 315). Morrison (2003) agrees, maintaining that rapid shifts in education policies and practices discount any notion that the curriculum, learning and assessment are ever predictable or secure:

> Linear, mechanistic models of curricula no longer apply, and networks and dynamical, ever-changing curricula and turbulent environments are the order of the day. . . .Gone are the simplistic views of linear causality, the ability to predict, control and manipulate, and the scientistic advancement of instrumental reason. . . (Morrison 2003, p. 286)

Theory in geography education

Morgan and Firth (2010) point out that the status of theory in geography education research is rather tenuous, indicating that it currently experiences a degree of 'anxiety' about its role. Providing an illustrative (rather than exhaustive) overview of the types of theories adopted in such research over the past 30 years, they concentrate on a number of texts that have been produced in geography education to support the application of theory. There is a keeness to point out that theories are human constructs and responses to events – that they are not easily dissociated from the people that produce them, nor the conditions within which they are produced. Particularly pertinent for Morgan and Firth (2010) is the fact that the contextual origin of much research in geography education is from within higher education institutions (HEIs), with research conducted by tutors primarily engaged in initial teacher education. The location for much of this work is the classroom, which may determine the theories that researchers choose to apply. The historical approach is a valuable one – by the end of the 1980s Morgan and Firth (2010) describe the emerging field of research in geography education as 'a gradual flowering of a variety of substantive themes underpinned by a number of theoretical perspectives' (p. 89). Two pathways for research became clear – one that focused on curriculum development and the other concerned with teacher development and pedagogy (with a lens on 'what works').

Morgan and Firth (2010) note that 'since the early 1990s, geography education as a research field has been challenged by pressures that seek to downplay the importance of theory' (p. 89). Government conceptions of initial teacher education (ITE) have derided the use of theory as irrelevant for learning how to teach, with centralized notions of 'effective teaching' and practical 'tips for teachers' always trumping the pursuit of theoretical understandings. As we have seen, the 'what works' agenda always seems to supplant any recourse to theory to inform and understand process. This has recently led to scholarship in geography education being dominated by a focus on classroom-based problems, but with little recourse to theory (Morgan and Firth 2010). Firth and Morgan (2010) assert that as a consequence the geography education community 'requires a wider range of orientations to research, concerned as we are with . . . classroom practice, policy-making and future directions for geography education' (p. 109). In the light of expectations in the United Kingdom for research to have 'impact' and to be of high quality, they pose important questions about the value attributed to theoretically informed research and about which theoretical positions are considered worthwhile. They conclude that, 'without theory our data on the experience of schooling do not get very far and are unlikely to tell us much that is not already obvious' (Firth and Morgan 2010, p. 111).

Attempts to bring theory into the classroom have had some limited success. The *Theory into Practice* series, published by the Geographical Association from 1999, was an explicit attempt to convey theory into the lives of practitioners, offering clear research and theory-driven perspectives on issues geography teachers faced. This set of short research monographs sought to provide access for busy teachers to research findings that related to their own (often classroom-based) contexts, although they were not all driven by a desire to explore 'what works' in the classroom (Butt 2002a).

Conclusions

In preparing to undertake any research activity consideration of theory is essential. Literature reviews will inevitably cover thematic issues and questions, and the findings of others. However, such reviews should also engage with the theories that underpin previous studies – which may then influence the structure, organization and analysis of future research. The dissertation you write will therefore not simply recount the 'facts' you have discovered, but will comment on the theoretical framework within which your observations sit explaining their links and relationships with your data. As we have seen, theory not only helps us explain what has been discovered, but also indicates knowledge gaps that still need to be filled and questions that have to be pursued. It may help to organize and interpret the data you have collected and point the way to new data gathering. It is certainly the case that research can be carried out without the consideration, application, or generation, of theory. This is undoubtedly quicker and easier than undertaking research that is theory informed or theory driven, but this may not constitute what is generally accepted as research enquiry and the results may not be considered as significant.

It is interesting to reflect on the developing culture of research in geography education – as Kent did at the turn of the century (Kent 2000), and Morgan and Firth did after its first decade (Morgan and Firth 2010; Firth and Morgan 2010). Dividing the growth of research activity in the discipline into three stages (incipient, intermediate and mature) Kent (2000) concluded that geography education research was still at an incipient stage – 'dominated by immediate practical issues' – rather than approaching the maturity stage, which is described as being 'dominated by universal theoretical issues'. We may conclude that research in geography education is still at a 'youthful' stage (with all the excitement and challenge one usually associates with the term!) and that with respect to its engagement with theory still has some way to go. Worryingly, Firth and Morgan (2010) go so far as to suggest that ours is a research community 'that seems to have overlooked theoretical traditions in ways of researching and analysing geography education' (p. 112). However, this problem is arguably not altogether uncommon in many other education and subject-based research communities.

References

Boschetti, F, Prokopenko, M, Macreadie, I, and Grisogono, A-M (2005). Defining and detecting emergence in complex networks. In Khosla, R, Howlett, B and Jain, L (eds.) *Knowledge-Based Intelligent Information and Engineering Systems*, 9th International Conference, KES 2005, Melbourne, Australia, 14–16 September, Proceedings, Part IV, Lecture Notes in Computer Science, 3684, pp. 573–80.

Bryman, A (2004) *Quantity and Quality in Social Research*. London: Unwin Hyman.

Butt, G (2002a) *Reflective Teaching of Geography 11–18: Continuum Studies in Reflective Practice and Theory*. London: Continuum.

— (2002b) Teachers as action researchers. In Gerber, R (ed.) *International Handbook of Geographical education*. London: Kluwer Academic Publishers.

— (2006) How should we determine research quality in geography education? In Purnell, K, Lidstone, J and Hodgson, S (eds.) *Changes in Geographical Education: Past, Present and Future*, pp. 91–5. Proceedings of the IGU- Commission on Geographical Education Symposium. Brisbane: IGU CGE.

Cohen, L, Manion, L and Morrison, K (2007) *Research Methods in Education*, 6th edition. Abingdon: Routledge.

Crotty, M (2003) *The Foundations of Social Research: Meaning and Perspective in the Research Process.* London: Sage.

Davis, B and Sumara, D (2006) *Complexity and Education: Inquiries into Learning, Teaching and Research.* Abingdon: Routledge.

Firth, R and Morgan, J (2010) What is the place of radical/critical research in geography education? *International Research in Geographical and Environmental Education* 19(2): 109–13.

Fish, S (1989) *Doing What Comes Naturally.* Oxford: Clarendon Press.

Fonseca, J (2002) *Complexity and Innovation in Organizations.* London: Routledge.

Furlong, J and Oancea, A (2005) *Assessing Quality in Applied and Practice-Based Educational Research.* Oxford: OUDES.

Gerber, R and Williams, M (2000) Overview and International Perspectives. In Kent, A (ed) *Reflective Practice in Geography Teaching.* pp. 209–218. London: Paul Chapman.

Glaser, B and Strauss, A (1967) *The Discovery of Grounded Theory.* Chicago, IL: Aldane.

Habermas, J (1988) *On the Logic of the Social Sciences.* Cambridge: Polity Press.

Hardman, M (2010) *Is Complexity Theory Useful in Describing Classroom Learning?* Paper presented at The European Conference on Educational Research. University of Helsinki.

Hillage, J, Pearson, R, Anderson, A and Tamkin, P (1998) *Excellence in Research in Schools.* London: TTA.

Hitchcock, G and Hughes, D (1995) *Research and the Teacher,* 2nd edition. London: Routledge.

Johnson, N (2007) *Simply Complexity: A Clear Guide to Complexity Theory.* Oxford: Oneworld publications.

Johnson, S (2001) *Emergence.* London: Penguin Books.

Kent, A (ed) *Reflective Practice in Geography Teaching.* London: Paul Chapman

Kincheloe, J and McLaren, P (2005) Rethinking critical theory and qualitative research. In Denzin, N and Lincoln, Y (eds.) *The Sage Handbook of Qualitative Research*, pp. 303–42. London: Sage.

Lincoln and Guba (1985) *Naturalistic Enquiry.* Newbury Park, CA: Sage.

Mitchell, M (2009) *Complexity: A Guided Tour.* Oxford: Oxford University Press.

Morgan, J and Firth, R (2010) 'By our theories shall you know us': the role of theory in geographical education. *International Research in Geographical and Environmental Education* 19(2): 87–90.

Morrison, K (2003) Complexity theory and curriculum reforms in Hong Kong. *Pedagogy, Culture and Society*, 11: 279–302.

Naish, M (1993) 'Never mind the quality – feel the width'. How shall we judge the quality of research in geographical and environmental education. *International Research in Geographical and Environmental Education* 2(1): 64–5.

Newby, P (2010) *Research Methods for Education.* Harlow: Pearson Education Limited.

Onwuegbuzie, A and Leech, N (2005) On becoming a pragmatic researcher: the importance of combining quantitative and qualitative research methodologies. *International Journal of Social Research Methodology* 8(5): 375–87.

Osberg, D and Biesta, G (2008) The emergent curriculum: navigating a complex course between unguided learning and planned enculturation. *Journal of Curriculum Studies* 40(3): 313–28.

— (2010) The end/s of education: complexity and the conundrum of the inclusive educational curriculum. *International Journal of Inclusive Education* 14(6): 593–607.

Popper, K (1968) *Conjectures and Refutations: The Growth of Scientific Knowledge.* New York: Harper and Row.

Richardson, K and Cilliers, P (2001) What is complexity science? A view from different directions. *Emergence* 3(1): 5–22.

Robson, C (1997) *Real World Research: A Resource for Social Scientists and Practitioner-Researchers.* Oxford: Blackwell.

Schön, D A (1991) *The Reflective Practitioner: How Professionals Think in Action.* Aldershot: Avebury.

Shavelson, R and Towne, L (eds.) *Scientific Research in Education*. Washington, DC: National Academies Press.

Stacey, R (2001) *Complex Responsive Processes in Organizations: Learning and Knowledge Creation*. London: Routledge.

Taylor, L (2009) *The Negotiation of Distant Place: Learning about Japan at Key Stage 3*. Unpublished PhD thesis, University of Cambridge.

Thomas, G (1997) What's the use of theory? *Harvard Educational Review* 67(1): 75–105.

— (2007) *Education and Theory: Strangers in Paradigms*. Maidenhead: Open University Press.

— (2012) Changing our landscape of inquiry for a new science of education. *Harvard Educational Review* 82(1): 26–51.

Tooley, J and Darby, D (1998) *Educational Research – A Critique*. London: OfSTED.

Weis, L, Jenkins, H and Stich, A (2009) Diminishing the divisions among us: reading and writing across difference in theory and method in the sociology of education. *Review of Educational Research* 79: 912–45.

Williams, M (1999) Research in Geographical Education. In *International Research in Geographical and Environmental Education*. 8(3): 301–4.

Wood, P and Butt, G (2014) Exploring the use of complexity theory and action research as frameworks for curriculum change. In *Journal of Curriculum Studies*. http://dx.doi.org/10.1080/00220272.2014.921840. Downloaded 26 June 2014.

Young, M (2007) *Bringing Knowledge Back In: From Social Constructivism to Social Realism in the Sociology of Education*. London: Routledge.

Discussion to Part II
Gemma Collins

Chapter outline

Constructing geographical knowledge   96
Constructing the geography curriculum   96
What is the role of theory?   97
Conclusions   97

A central theme of all three chapters in the 'Constructing' part of *MasterClass in Geography Education* is that of 'knowledge', in one form or another. In Chapter 4, Firth considers the need to understand knowledge, and 'the relation(ship) between knowledge, the curriculum and pedagogy' (p. 65). Rawding's chapter (Chapter 5) provides important context for the knowledge delivered in schools via the National Curriculum and examines not only the ways in which the geography curriculum has been shaped by changing notions of geographical knowledge, but also how geography teachers use their disciplined knowledge to interpret, design and deliver the geography curriculum. Finally, Chapter 6 from Butt elaborates on the role of theory in the creation of new knowledge and the identification of gaps in knowledge. Between them, these authors use the term 'knowledge' almost 280 times in those chapters.

For most teachers, knowledge is accepted as the 'core business' of education; in basic terms, knowledge can be seen as a commodity to be traded, transmitted from teacher to pupil, and also often exchanged between pupils (according to the theory that knowledge is, or can be, socially constructed). Schools are filled with talk of knowledge, even to the point of it being present in the everyday vocabulary of the classroom where teachers routinely refer to what pupils 'know, understand and can do' and where prescribed knowledge is set out clearly in curriculum documents, syllabi and specifications. So the idea of knowledge in education, and by extension education research, shouldn't be problematic. Yet the ideas are complex, and I foresee the need to think deeply about the content of the chapters in this part, each of which introduces ideas, arguments and discussions that prompt serious questions about the process of undertaking geography education research in order to create or examine knowledge. However, I would argue that this 'struggle' is necessary in order to fully engage with the research process at Masters level, and intend this discussion to be an encouragement to readers to embrace those serious questions that will be raised. Each chapter is considered in turn, although any links between the three distinct themes are highlighted, particularly with regard to knowledge. Finally, some conclusions are offered for the reader which it is hoped will briefly summarize the importance of an understanding of knowledge in constructing high-quality research in geography education.

Constructing geographical knowledge

Amongst many valuable points made by Firth, the idea of 'disciplined judgement' (Stemhagen et al. 2013) is perhaps one of the most pertinent for teacher-researchers. Firth writes of the importance of illustrating 'how teachers can become more epistemologically aware of their discipline and its approaches to knowledge' (p. 64); this is a process which all those engaging with research in geography education must go through. For example, most geography teachers will recognize the pedagogical tool of enquiry learning, but perhaps may not have considered enquiry learning in the context of its links to 'procedural knowledge' (Geographical Association 2011), or that one's decision to use enquiry learning might stem from what Firth describes as an 'epistemological awareness of the discipline' (p. 59). Firth makes reference to Perkins (2006) and his example that, although students may not be familiar with the term 'episteme', they deal with epistemes all the time. Arguably, there are some parallels here with the relative unfamiliarity that some readers may have with some of the terms used by Firth (and Rawding and Butt), but that they do make informed decisions about knowledge, the curriculum and pedagogy on a regular basis. Firth's chapter enables the reader to begin to understand some of the theoretical considerations behind the choices that they make in their teaching. This in turn is the key to understanding and framing their research, and indeed the key to successfully writing about it.

Constructing the geography curriculum

At a time where many geography departments, at the time of writing, will be embarking upon the delivery of a new Geography National Curriculum (GNC) from September 2014, Rawding's chapter on the changes to the GNC over time will reinforce what the majority of geography teachers know to be true; the 2014 GNC requires geography teachers to interpret and translate the document into programmes of study which reflect the geography that they believe should be taught. Implicit in this therefore is the need for geography teachers to be secure in their understanding of what Butt describes in his chapter as 'valuable geographical knowledge' (p. 87). Getting to grips with the ideas of 'powerful knowledge' (Young 2007), or the Geographical Association's (2011) distinctions between 'core', 'content' and 'procedural' knowledge is important for those embarking on geography education research, and also for those involved in curriculum making (Geographical Association 2014). There are also clear links here to the 'disciplined judgement' discussed by Firth Chapter 4. The subject specific examples that Rawding uses to illustrate his points are particularly interesting for geography teachers to reflect on, as are his questions regarding the lack of definition for phrases such as 'globally significant places' and 'the world's major countries' (Department of Education 2013). Some readers might also find themselves reflecting on the departments they work within, and whether they are (as described by Roberts 1995) *content rich*, *framework*, or *process* departments. The outcome of this might enable readers to then identify the extent to which they experience the 'regulated autonomy' in curriculum making found by Biddulph (2013), which in turn prompts reflection on the bigger questions of what geographical knowledge we value most and why.

What is the role of theory?

High-quality research should be framed by theory, and as Butt states, 'theory not only helps us explain what has been discovered, but also indicates knowledge gaps that still need to be filled and questions that have to be pursued' (p. 91). Butt's chapter (Chapter 6) is extremely helpful both in gaining a deeper understanding of the role of theory in research and for geographers to place their own research in a sound theoretical framework. It clearly sets out the current situation regarding the state of geography education research, in that it is still in its early stages of development and therefore there is some way to go in terms of its engagement with theory. This presents an opportunity for geography education researchers to take on the challenge of furthering the field, but requires an engagement with and understanding of knowledge. As Butt writes, 'According to one's view of knowledge – whether it is considered to consist of objective facts, or is subjective and personal to the individual – one's theoretical position and research approach is determined . . . Concern about what knowledge is and how it is constructed is central' (p. 85). Knowledge can be considered a major focus of current geography education research (as both Firth and Rawding also describe in Chapters 4 and 5, respectively) and the role of epistemology is made clear from the discussion in Chapter 6.

Conclusions

The construction of research in geography education, particularly by teacher-researchers, should ideally be focused on the geography that is taught and learnt in schools. Its aim should be to further the discipline, and to retain a strong focus on geographical knowledge. These chapters highlight for the reader the important aspects of knowledge that must be understood in order for the production of high-quality research to take place. Although at times the questions raised by the authors can be difficult to answer, the value of the process of trying to answer them should not be underestimated.

References

Biddulph, M (2013) Where is the curriculum created. In Lambert, D and Jones, M (eds.) *Debates in Geography Education.* Abingdon: Routledge.

Department for Education (2013) Geography programmes of study: Key stage 3. Available from https://www.gov.uk/government/uploads/system/uploads/attachment_data/file/239087/SECONDARY_national_curriculum_-_Geography.pdf. Last accessed 4 May 2014.

Geographical Association (2011) *The Geography National Curriculum: GA Curriculum Proposals and Rationale.* Sheffield: Geographical Association.

— (2014) What is curriculum making? Available from http://www.geography.org.uk/cpdevents/curriculummaking/. Llast accessed 4 May 2014.

Perkins, D (2006) Constructivism and troublesome knowledge. In Meyer, J H F and Land, R (eds.) *Overcoming Barriers to Student Understanding.* Abingdon: Routledge.

Roberts, M (1995) Interpretations of the Geography National Curriculum: a common curriculum for all? *Journal of Curriculum Studies* 27(2): 187–205.

Stemhagen, K, Reich, G and Muth, W (2013) Disciplined judgment: toward a reasonably constrained constructivism. *Journal of Curriculum and Pedagogy* 10: 55–72.

Young, M (2007) *Bringing Knowledge Back In: From Social Constructivism to Social Realism in the Sociology of Education.* London: Routledge.

Part III

Researching

Approaches to Research in Geography Education

7

Paul Weeden

Chapter outline

Why is this change being introduced now? (What's the context?)   106

Does academic performance, gender or ethnicity influence subject choice?
(Is there a relationship between variables?)   106

Why do students choose to study geography at GCSE? (What's happening here?)   107

Conclusions   110

Undertaking research in the 'real world' (Robson 2002) can be a daunting prospect because schools and classrooms are complex places where multiple social interactions make it difficult to describe and analyse experiences. This chapter illustrates some commonly used methods for identifying worthwhile research questions and clarifying your research aims. It shows how initial ideas can be developed into a research problem that is accurately defined and whose resolution is potentially achievable. The importance of familiarity with the two main research traditions (positivist/empiricist and interpretative/relativist) used in education is discussed. An argument is made for an eclectic 'mixed methods' approach where the researcher makes reasoned choices about methods from a developed philosophical position. Achieving this position requires familiarity with the place of theory and practice in approaches to research and recognizes the complexity of the social interactions within schools. It is argued that educational research has to adopt a relativist position on research that is 'generating working hypotheses rather than immutable empirical facts' (Robson 2002, p. 25). These ideas are developed through the 'stories' of two fictional teachers – Matthew and Kim – who are beginning to identify potential research areas and approaches that will lead to research questions they can investigate.

Matthew is a geography teacher working in a suburban school. He is beginning to think about research areas for his Masters dissertation, but does not have one clear idea, so spends time identifying possibilities. His 'story' shows that research ideas can come from a range of sources and have different purposes.

Matthew's first idea comes from a major change to the curriculum structure in the school. In the last two years the school has started General Certificate of Secondary Educations (GCSE) in year 9 and some students will take their geography GCSE examination at the end of year 9. He is concerned about reports in the news that students entered for GCSE in year 9 got lower grades than those entered in year 11 (BBC 2013). After teaching the year 9 course for the last two years, he is undecided whether there is enough time to teach a GCSE effectively. He is also concerned that these students will not choose geography at A-level having not studied the subject for two years. These concerns could lead to an *evaluation* of this innovation (Thomas 2009, p. 4) with the aim of identifying how successful it has been. This appears to be a potentially fruitful area that would provide easily accessible sources of data such as the school's examination results, students' work and personal experience.

The second research area Matthew considers comes from his teaching, where he has been using different strategies to help students think more for themselves and to reflect on their progress. In this case the purpose is to find out *whether a particular innovation 'what works'*. This would allow systematic testing where a strategy is used with one class and a different approach with a parallel group (Thomas 2009, p. 4).

Further potential research areas are suggested by other members of the department. The head of department is interested in knowing whether the content in the new GCSE syllabus and the move to controlled assessment is affecting student performance. This is again a potential evaluation exercise and might possibly involve development, or overlap, with the first idea.

Another member of staff suggests it would be useful for the department to have a clearer idea about whether the recent introduction of Assessment for Learning (AFL) strategies has resulted in pupils reviewing their own learning better. The purpose here is to *improve practice within the department*. Reflecting on the use of AFL as a group within the department, identifying benefits and problems as they occur is a form of action research that aims 'to change practice – for the better' (Thomas 2009, p. 4).

Matthew is now swimming in a muddy pool of different ideas, many of which are really interesting and potentially may provide insights that will be useful both for his own teaching and for the department. This 'story' has shown that generating a range of potential research areas need not be difficult. In the first instance, it is often useful to consider several different research ideas before choosing. Ideas can come from various sources, such as: the teacher's own interests, particular areas of curriculum or pedagogy, identified problems or issues in the classroom or department, newspaper reports, questions raised by educational literature and 'theory', school management priorities or students and parents (Thomas 2009, p. 3; Robson 2002, p. 47; Cohen et al. 2000, p. 73).

The next task is to choose one of these interesting topics and narrow the focus so there is an aim, a research approach and achievable research questions. Matthew decides the most interesting and currently relevant area is the introduction of a one-year GCSE course in year 9, because this major change in the school curriculum has been introduced with little evidence of its effect on student outcomes. His aim is to evaluate the benefits and costs of this innovation and to use the insights gained to promote discussion within the department and school.

At this point it is tempting to plunge straight into collecting data and conducting analysis, but before doing this it is important to have a better understanding of the different methodological approaches that can be used in research. This involves engaging with philosophical ideas and terminology that may be confusing and off-putting. Research methodology has been the subject of much debate and there are many different viewpoints and often disagreement about the meaning of different terms (Cohen et al. 2000; Robson 2002; Thomas 2009; Williams 1996). In the same way that definitions and interpretations of the terms 'geography' (Gerber 1996, p. 14) or 'geographical enquiry' (Roberts 2003) vary, it is important and useful to clarify what is being looked at (ontology) and the sort of knowledge being studied (epistemology). This allows a reasoned justification for the choice of methodological approach (Thomas 2009, pp. 86–7).

There are two main research paradigms (positivist and interpretivist) used in education, although there are sub-categories within each paradigm. One model (positivist) suggests that you should have a clear hypothesis to test before starting the research and that you collect your data before analysing it. The other (interpretivist) suggests that your design develops as you undertake your research and that data collection and analysis are intertwined (Robson 2002, p. 45). Research paradigms arise from the ways researchers think about and research the world – so a particular research approach will share ideas about enquiry, researchers 'thinking habits' and rules of procedure. However, paradigms are subject to continual scrutiny and *shift*, as the old one proves to be inappropriate (Thomas 2009, p. 73).

The positivist research paradigm originates from 'basic' science where the researcher stands outside the phenomena they are investigating and attempts to measure it in an objective, quantifiable, numerical manner (Robson 2002, p. 19; Thomas 2009, p. 71; Williams 1996, p. 6). The philosophical assumption that underpins this approach is that there are identifiable 'laws' that govern the processes and patterns observed. Even in pure science research this position is often untenable and in educational research involving social interactions these constraints are almost impossible to achieve. Even if the researcher merely observes and records, they will impact on the dynamics of the classroom.

In social situations, such as classrooms, it has proved virtually impossible to attribute outcomes to causes in a generalized manner that produces 'laws'. There are many examples in teaching where ideas or methods appear to 'work' in one context and not another. This is because of the complex factors influencing social interactions, with the result that outcomes are context dependent. For example, the same lesson taught to two different groups may result in different learning outcomes because of environmental factors such as time of day or the weather, or social factors such as the interactions between the members of the group. The alternative paradigm (interpretivist) suggests that the complex interactions in class-rooms and schools are socially constructed and that the researcher's own value position can and may influence both the process and outcomes. Research concerns are more to do with peoples' perceptions and individual stories than trying to create generalizations. Research will be only applicable to the local context and not transferable to other situations; data will often be collected using words, such that the analysis of discourse or text – rather than numerical and statistical relationships – will be paramount (Thomas 2009, p. 73; Robson 2002, p. 24; Gerber 1996, p. 12).

Most educational researchers do not adopt a strictly positivist or interpretivist approach to their research. They tend to adopt a 'mixed methods' approach, drawing on both research traditions as appropriate. Fundamentally, the researcher must be able to justify the approach adopted and recognize that the case he/she makes will be stronger if it is underpinned by an understanding of its philosophical positioning.

For example, does Matthew believe that the reasons for choosing to study geography are relatively simple and fixed so he can conduct 'experiments' where he isolates different variables and measures their effect to test or obtain a 'hypothesis' about choice (a positivist view)? Alternatively does he believe that choice is an individual decision where opportunities to exercise 'agency' (the individual's capacity to act independently and make free choices) are limited by 'structures' such as social class, religion, gender and ethnicity? An individual's choice may be further influenced by their experiences and the complex and unique social interactions operating in the school setting (an interpretivist view). These two positions are sometimes associated with the terms quantitative (involving numbers – positivist) and qualitative (words, thoughts and images – interpretivist), but this is too simplistic and can be confusing because analysis of words and numbers can and should be used in both approaches (Thomas 2009, p. 83). In reality the two positions should be seen as com-plementing each other.

For example, over the last few years the mushrooming of data collection in schools and nationally has enabled some educational research to be carried out using a two-stage 'new political arithmetic' research approach (Smith 2008, p. 44).

> In the first stage, a problem (trend, pattern or situation) is defined by a relatively large scale analysis of relevant numeric data. In the second stage, this problem (trend, pattern or situation) is examined in more depth using recognised 'qualitative' techniques with a subset of cases selected from the first stage. (Gorard 2001, p. 251)

Most educational research (and probably most scientific research) will develop in an itera-tive way and may involve going down routes that are circuitous or even dead ends. It is rarely possible to map out initial ideas using the pure scientific enquiry route. As ideas and theories are developed, they can be examined further using:

> a back and forth movement in which the investigator first operates inductively from observations to hypotheses, and then deductively from these hypotheses to their implications, in order to check their validity . . . (Mouly 1978 quoted in Cohen et al. 2000, p. 4)

Whichever methodology is adopted it is important that the research is undertaken in a systematic, sceptical and ethical manner (Robson 2002, p. 18). This means that the researcher is seeking for the 'truth' and should understand the implications, strengths and weaknesses of the different research approaches. Much of the debate in educational research is a healthy discussion about ensuring that the research is 'fit for purpose'. The different philosophical approaches to knowledge are important in shaping research because they show us that 'knowledge is construed in different ways and that there are different ways of coming to knowledge' (Thomas 2009, p. 89).

Matthew's research area contains the potential for the numerical description of patterns of entry. This is essentially a positivist approach where the researcher observes, measures and records in an objective manner, searching for relationships between variables (Thomas 2009, p. 74; Robson 2002, p. 19) and seeking to quantify the patterns. The school has data about different variables that can be analysed and compared to national data which are obtainable from a number of different sources (DfE 2013a, 2013b, 2013c; JCQ 2013; Stubbs 2011; Weeden 2013). The inferences obtained from the data for this school will either replicate or challenge national patterns. In itself this data could be useful as contextual information but may not help Matthew understand why students in his school choose to study geography. To do this he may use an interpretative approach that seeks to understand the motivations of students, recognizing that each of them will have their own particular story to tell. He can then use the reports of their experiences to seek patterns. This data is much less generalizable, but may lead to a richer view of the motivations of the students.

Having decided on the main research focus the next stage of the research process is to define the problem better and to consider what data collection is feasible. Matthew's 'story' will be used to illustrate three different types of question that are commonly asked. These questions provide different starting points, have implications for the research approach (Thomas 2009, p. 7) and involve different conceptions of 'theory' (Thomas 2009, p. 67; Robson 2002, p. 61; Cohen et al. 2000, p. 23).

Matthew's second attempt at questions to investigate include:

1. Why is this change being introduced now? (What's the context?)
2. Does academic performance, gender or ethnicity influence subject choice? (Is there a relationship between variables?)
3. Why do students choose to study geography at GCSE? (What's happening here?) (Questions in brackets adapted from Thomas 2009, p. 6)

Why is this change being introduced now? (What's the context?)

This question involves description of the context with perhaps limited opportunity for interpretation. In this example, it provides an opportunity to investigate the policy decisions that have led to the school adopting this new curriculum. Matthew discussed the research further with his head of department who reminded him that numbers taking GCSE geography increased nationally in 2012 and 2013 after a period of decline (Weeden 2013). This change appeared to be the result of government policy and the measurement of schools' performance in the English Baccalaureate (EBC) subjects. She reminds Matthew that the changes to the reporting of school performance ('school league') tables have been hotly debated in school and suggests he discusses this aspect of the research with the senior manager in charge of option choices. This discussion provides a developing theory, or hypothesis, that one contributory factor 'causing' change in entry numbers is the schools' response to national policy. This is an explanatory theory (Thomas 2009, p. 66) where previous findings are tested in this particular school context.

However, description is rarely simple, because each observer may only have a partial view of an experience. Furthermore, their beliefs and past history may influence their perception so they 'see' the event in different ways or express 'hidden beliefs' in the words they use to describe the experience. For example, describing the glass as 'half full' will present a different picture from saying it is 'half empty'. When using numerical or statistical analyses it is also possible to 'describe' the data in different ways. It is important to recognize the interpretation that is being presented and to recognize the difficulty of being a totally objective observer or analyst.

Does academic performance, gender or ethnicity influence subject choice? (Is there a relationship between variables?)

Matthew's reading of the educational literature suggests that there are structural factors (academic performance, type of school, ethnicity, gender, attainment and option systems) that have some influence on choice (Stables 1996; Weeden 2012). Some of these are beyond the scope of his research because he is restricted to his own school, but he decides that he would like to investigate the relationships between academic performance, gender and choosing to study geography.

There is always a danger when attempting to link variables that a spurious causal relationship will be identified. For example, although national data shows higher achieving students are more likely to take GCSE geography (Weeden 2012), the relationship is not causal.

It is a much more complex mix of factors that results in these students having increased opportunity and motivation to study the subject. The danger here is that the researcher will see a correlation between two relationships and propose a causal hypothesis or generalization without really thinking through the implications. The links between two variables need to be made explicit, using deductive reasoning.

Describing relationships between variables can lead to the development of new 'working theories' that can be explored further. For example over the last 20 years, at the national level, 56 per cent of entries for GCSE geography have been boys (Weeden 2012). This doesn't mean that being a boy automatically causes them to study geography but rather there may be a number of aspects of geography that predispose or interest boys more than girls. Knowing this national pattern (generalization) provides a yardstick against which local patterns can be tested. In itself this relationship may not be very significant, but the 'hard' evidence of numbers means that the researcher has moved beyond anecdote and instinct in describing what is going on. Analysing this data can result in surprising patterns being identified and reflection can lead to further questions or theories being explored. In this case, therefore, theory involves 'making links, generalising, connecting your own findings with others and having insights' (Thomas 2009, p .67).

Why do students choose to study geography at GCSE? (What's happening here?)

Matthew is most interested in trying to get inside students' heads to find out more about the reasons they choose to study geography. This type of question could be approached in two ways. He can try to define quantifiable elements that can be measured and manipulated, or he can take a different research approach (interpretive) where he is trying to understand individual(s) motivations and actions (adapted from Thomas 2009, p. 89). The researcher cannot possibly know everything that is going on inside someone else's head and the individual may only give partial or inaccurate answers. The researcher therefore has to interpret the situation as best they can, acknowledging that their own views and perceptions may influence the outcomes. It is important to reflect carefully on the interpretations made and to discuss them with others to verify findings. This may lead to further insights and different perspectives. What this type of research question is doing is to throw light on something that is not seen clearly (Thomas 2009, p. 9). Researchers using this approach do not start with a theory that they are testing but look for patterns within the data collected that provide tentative and partial explanations of the experience being observed. This is called 'grounded theory'. In reality they may have some partially formed theories derived from literature, discussions or prior research that may influence their interpretation of the evidence. As in detective work this may lead them down blind alleys and it is always important to step back and try to reflect on whether their 'personal theory' is overly influencing the analysis (Thomas 2009, p. 66).

Analysing these three questions highlights that the research approach influences how the researcher thinks about the social world, the manner in which they develop theories, the way they conduct their investigation and the research methods they use.

The second 'story' considers a different approach to developing a research question. Kim is working in an inner city school with students from many different ethnic backgrounds. She is passionate about 'green issues' and has succeeded in getting her department to introduce a module on 'futures' education into year 8. She is hopeful this will increase students' awareness of the issues and lead them to make changes in their lifestyles. An article in Teaching Geography (Hicks 2013) prompts her to consider potential dangers in teaching about futures, for example, that it can become too focused on 'doom and gloom'. The article also identifies four different dimensions to studying issues such as 'climate change', knowing, feeling, choosing and acting. Kim therefore decides her aim is to investigate how she can move beyond just teaching knowledge of the topic but also encourage students to consider their feelings about it and whether it is possible for them to take positive actions in relation to these issues.

Kim quickly recognizes this is a problematic and potentially large area to investigate. The issues being introduced are controversial, the scientific evidence (knowledge) is disputed, 'solutions' are not clear-cut, the topic arouses strong feelings in many people and actions may range in scale from individual and local to global (Hicks 2007). The research question that begins to formulate in her mind is:

> What impact will the futures module have on student knowledge, attitudes and behaviour towards climate change? (What are the consequences?)

This type of research suggests the researcher will collect some evidence before and after the innovation to see whether there are any changes taking place, but the type of evidence collected will depend on the research approach (positivist or interpretive) adopted which comes from an underpinning philosophical position. Kim is more interested in researching students' feelings and attitudes about 'futures' rather than assessing their knowledge at the end of the module, but senior management are pushing the department to improve their examination results. She realizes that this may create tensions and that she will have to find some persuasive arguments to justify her research aims. She is struck by the arguments that Hicks makes about political influences on the curriculum, such that in the early draft of the most recent national curriculum climate change was omitted (Hicks 2013, p. 94). This recognition of the political dimension has the potential to take the research into the critical research tradition (Fien and Hillcoat 1996; Robson 2002, p. 28) where the researcher is explicit about recognizing the power structures that exist and has the intention of challenging and questioning accepted traditions and norms.

She realizes this will require her to adopt a research methodology that acknowledges issues such as: Who decides what should be taught and how? How will the module's impact on students' attitudes be assessed? What influence will the teacher's personal views have upon their teaching and the students? What ethical issues are associated with teaching this topic?

In her reading (literature search) she finds that controversial issues can be defined as important to a appreciable number of people and involving value judgements so that the issue cannot be 'solved' by facts, evidence or experiment alone (Wellington quoted in Claire and Holden 2007, p. 5). Even more significant is that:

> . . . the decisions about what is seen as controversial is in itself controversial, as interest groups may work to stifle debate in order to maintain the *status quo* or, conversely bring specific issues to into the public arena in order to advance their cause. (Claire and Holden 2007, p. 5)

This highlights the importance of her decisions about the research approach she will adopt. She is committed to exploring different ideologies and political standpoints with students in the expectation that she can influence their personal actions in the future. She wants these to go beyond tokenism because of her belief that radical change is needed to combat climate change (Hicks 2007, p. 78). She begins to realize that her strong personal views about climate change will influence the way she teaches and also possibly the way she interprets the evidence collected. She will have to acknowledge this and adapt her approach as a result. She does not want to be a detached objective observer, although throughout her research she can attempt to look at the evidence from different standpoints (be sceptical) and try to unravel evidence in an inductive way.

Kim is aware that she will have to consider carefully how she approaches both the teaching of this topic and the researching of students' attitudes. Any data collected must be analysed for signs of bias (unintended or intended) and she recognizes that as a teacher she will influence students' views. She therefore has to consider questions such as whether she will take on the role of impartial referee, devil's advocate or outline her personal views. When processing data she will have to consider to what extent her views about the topic or the students have coloured or altered both her teaching and her analysis of student reactions and perceptions. She also has to consider carefully the ethical issues, discuss them with her head of department, senior management team and mentor. She will need to get ethical approval to conduct the research.

She doesn't have a 'theory' that she can test; in fact, she is not really clear about the range of knowledge, attitudes and opinions about climate change within year 8. It seems therefore that this research will be exploratory from which she will try to collect evidence and reflect on the outcomes. She has decisions to make about whether she wants to collect evidence from the whole year group, to focus on a few students or to combine both these approaches. She believes that individuals' attitudes to climate change are the result of socio-cultural factors – the influences that have formed their beliefs (ideologies) and actions (structures) as well as their own decisions (agency). Philosophically this will take her towards interpretivist and critical research methodologies.

Conclusions

This chapter has illustrated how understanding different research approaches and associated terminology can result in researchers asking better questions, developing a clearer rationale for their research design and hopefully achieving outcomes that are 'fit for purpose'. The importance of adopting a systematic, sceptical and ethical approach to tackling research (Robson 2002, p. 18) and understanding the two main approaches (positivist and interpretive) that are adopted by educational researchers has been discussed. While beginning researchers can often find the terminology and ideas difficult and confusing, it is necessary for them to demonstrate that the methods of data collection adopted have an underpinning rationale and to be able to justify these methods in terms of the two main educational research paradigms (Thomas 2009, p. 72).

The two main groups of research methods have different starting points. The positivist/empiricist approach has its origins in traditional scientific method where problems are recognized and defined, hypotheses developed and data collected in an objective manner. This data is then analysed to test the hypothesis and to develop generalizations about the phenomena studied. The interpretivist/relativist approach is based upon a view of the world that assumes there are no 'facts' that are beyond dispute and that knowledge is created by social and historical interactions. This position draws upon scientific method while recognizing the complexity of the social context. An important feature of realism is that 'observations are not the rock bottom of science, but are tenuous and always subject to reinterpretation' (Manicas and Secord 1983, quoted in Robson 2002, p. 34). The interpretivist/relativist approach views the research process 'as generating working hypotheses rather than immutable empirical facts' (Robson 2002, p. 25).

The two 'stories' have illustrated how a research topic might be considered, possible questions identified and how research approaches influence research design. However, research approaches are not mutually exclusive, so research can have a number of different strands that adopt different methodologies (a mixed method approach).

It has been suggested that the start of the research process is to identify something that is of interest that you want to understand better. The source of these research ideas can be personal interest, current issues, the desire to improve practice, evaluation of a change, an idea in the news or literature, or something suggested by other members of staff or senior management.

In summary, successful research is characterized by regular contact with others to help the continuing development of ideas and methods, timeliness in recognizing that an issue is important now, a concern for theoretical understanding and awareness that the issue is relevant to the workplace. Less successful research comes from expedience (easy, cheap, quick and convenient), starts with a method or technique and lacks theory (Robson 2002, p. 56).

References

BBC (2013) GCSEs 2013: Top Grades Fall for second year in a row [online]. http://www.bbc.co.uk/news/education-23783094. Accessed 29 October 2013.

Claire, H and Holden, C (2007) *The Challenge of Teaching Controversial Issues.* Stoke on Trent: Trentham.

Cohen, L, Manion, L and Morrison, K (2000) *Research Methods in Education.* London: Routledge Falmer.

DfE (2013a) Data: research and statistics. [online] https://www.education.gov.uk/researchandstatistics/statistics. Accessed 29 October 2013.

— (2013b) National Pupil Database. [online] http://www.education.gov.uk/researchandstatistics/national-pupil-database/b00212283/national-pupil-database. Accessed 29 October 2013.

— (2013c) Performance tables. [online] http://www.education.gov.uk/schools/performance/. Accessed 29 October 2013.

Fien, J and Hillcoat, J (1996) The critical tradition in research in geographical and environmental education research. In Williams, M (ed.) *Understanding Geographical and Environmental Education: The Role of Research.* London: Cassell.

Gerber, R (1996) Interpretive approaches to geographical and environmental education research. In Williams, M (ed.) *Understanding Geographical and Environmental Education: The Role of Research.* London: Cassell.

Gorard, S (2001) *Quantitative Methods in Educational Research.* London: Continuum.

Hicks, D (2007) Education for sustainability: how should we deal with climate change. In Claire, H and Holden, C (eds.) *The Challenge of Teaching Controversial Issues.* Stoke on Trent: Trentham.

— (2013) A post-carbon geography. *Teaching Geography* 38(3): 94–7.

JCQ (2013) Examination results. [online] http://www.jcq.org.uk/examination-results. Accessed 29 October 2013.

Ofsted/DfE (2011) RAISEonline. [online] https://www.raiseonline.org/About.aspx. Accessed 25 August 2011.

Roberts, M (2003) *Learning through Enquiry: Making Sense of Geography in the Key Stage 3 Classroom.* Sheffield: Geographical Association.

Robson, C (2002) *Real World Research.* Oxford: Blackwell.

Smith, E (2008) *Using Secondary Data in Educational and Social Research.* Maidenhead: Open University Press.

Stables, A (1996) *Subjects of Choice: The process and Management of Pupil and Student Choice.* London: Cassell.

Stubbs, B (2011) Student performance analysis. [online] http://www.bstubbs.co.uk/gcse.htm [accessed 1 August 2011]

Thomas, G (2009) *How to Do Your Research Project.* London: Sage.

Weeden, P (2012) *An Investigation of Changing Patterns of Entry for GCSE Geography: Choice, Diversity and Competition,* Birmingham University PhD thesis. [online] http://etheses.bham.ac.uk/3667/1/Weeden12PhD.pdf. Accessed 29 October 2013.

— (2013) Analysis of GCSE geography results. [online] http://www.geography.org.uk/11–19/examresults/. Accessed 29 October 2013.

Wikispaces (2012) National Pupil Database. [online] http://nationalpupildatabase.wikispaces.com/. Accessed 12 March 2012.

Williams, M (1996) Positivism and the quantitative tradition in geographical and environmental education research. In Williams, M (ed.) *Understanding Geographical and Environmental Education: The Role of Research.* London: Cassell.

Writing a Research Proposal

Mark Jones

8

Chapter outline

What makes a good research proposal?	113
Where do I begin?	116
The importance of context	117
Philosophical and theoretical considerations	118
Arriving at research questions	119
Fitness for purpose of research design	120
Research methods	122
Data collection and analysis	124

What makes a good research proposal?

One definition of a research proposal is a 'written document summarizing prior literature and describing the procedures to be used to answer the research question(s)' (Johnson and Christensen 2012, p. 87). What might at first appear to be a straightforward require-ment to communicate a step-by step plan of intended research can present significant challenges – from finding a worthwhile theme and refining this into research questions, to navigating what might seem an overwhelming array of paradigms, theoretical perspec-tives, methodologies and methods. One approach to getting started is to view this physi-cal statement of intent more conceptually as a series of interconnected choices concerning the different elements of the research design. Research traditions can suggest a sequential approach is required at the proposal stage, for example, establishing an epistemological stance before considering methodology and methods (Crotty 1998). However, those new to researching geography education may not initially conceptualize research in this way, with philosophical considerations being secondary to the practicalities of research. Drawing on discussions with geography teachers who have successfully completed small-scale research, this chapter helps the reader understand what makes a 'good' research proposal by discussing some of the many choices, challenges and potential pitfalls that this stage can present.

> I thought that it [research proposal] was just a necessary step, to get down a question to investi-
> gate and then to explain how I would gather data to answer it. . . . I now realise it was a crucial
> part of the research. (Student response A)

Those new to research might initially consult generic texts (e.g. Johnson and Christensen 2012) and practical guides (e.g. Denscombe 2012) in search of definitions, analogies and advice for successfully writing a research proposal. Additionally, where previous proposals are available, these may provide further examples of structure and approach. However, a more critical reading of these procedural texts will examine whether the authors have approached this stage with conceptual clarity and rigour. Three features of quality research proposals include clarity and connectedness; evidence of reflexivity and the extent to which the author's voice conveys the proposal as a crucial stage in the research.

Firstly, a good research proposal will provide evidence of sustained conceptual, theoretical and methodological clarity in decisions concerning the purpose of the research, research questions, methodology, methods, data collection and analysis techniques. In addition, the connectedness of these different elements will be justified to demonstrate fitness for purpose of the overall design. Secondly, the proposal should convey that the author has adopted a reflexive approach, meaning he/she has acknowledged his/her central role in this decision-making process and shown he/she has the ability to be open and ethical, and to stand back and question the underlying values and beliefs informing the choices made in the research. Thirdly, the quality of the proposal could ultimately affect whether the research is worthwhile, able to make legitimate knowledge claims and is judged as 'good'. Whilst the notion of what qualifies as 'good research' is contested and the focus of much debate (Yates 2004; Furlong and Oancea 2005), the pursuit of quality from the outset is essential. Therefore the proposal requires rigour, so that the actual research process and outcomes are more likely to stand up to internal and external scrutiny, both now and in the future. By fore-fronting these three overarching considerations, new researchers can critically engage with the proposal stage to avoid poor-quality research, which is often the result of poor research design (Butt 2006).

Finally, Figure 8.1 is intended as a backdrop to this chapter – a 'big picture' to highlight many of the different choices that are required during this stage. When deciding what to research, consideration of purpose, context and previous literature is important. Once a theme is established, the sequential research design implies that the researcher makes

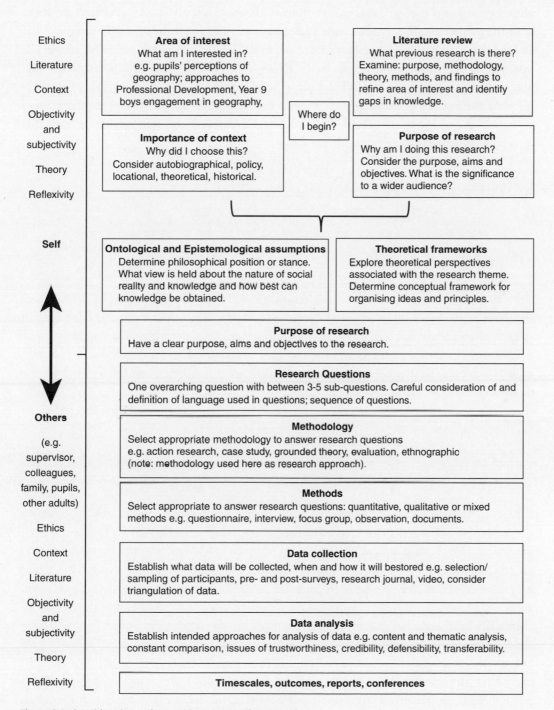

Ethics

Literature

Context

Objectivity
and
subjectivity

Theory

Reflexivity

Self

Others

(e.g.
supervisor,
colleagues,
family, pupils,
other adults)

Ethics

Context

Literature

Objectivity
and
subjectivity

Theory

Reflexivity

Area of interest
What am I interested in?
e.g. pupils' perceptions of
geography; approaches to
Professional Development, Year 9
boys engagement in geography,

Literature review
What previous research is there?
Examine: purpose, methodology,
theory, methods, and findings to
refine area of interest and identify
gaps in knowledge.

Where do
I begin?

Importance of context
Why did I choose this?
Consider autobiographical, policy,
locational, theoretical, historical.

Purpose of research
Why am I doing this research?
Consider the purpose, aims and
objectives. What is the significance
to a wider audience?

Ontological and Epistemological assumptions
Determine philosophical position or stance.
What view is held about the nature of social
reality and knowledge and how best can
knowledge be obtained.

Theoretical frameworks
Explore theoretical perspectives
associated with the research theme.
Determine conceptual framework for
organising ideas and principles.

Purpose of research
Have a clear purpose, aims and objectives to the research.

Research Questions
One overarching question with between 3-5 sub-questions. Careful consideration of and
definition of language used in questions; sequence of questions.

Methodology
Select appropriate methodology to answer research questions
e.g. action research, case study, grounded theory, evaluation, ethnographic
(note: methodology used here as research approach).

Methods
Select appropriate to answer research questions: quantitative, qualitative or mixed
methods e.g. questionnaire, interview, focus group, observation, documents.

Data collection
Establish what data will be collected, when and how it will bestored e.g. selection/
sampling of participants, pre- and post-surveys, research journal, video, consider
triangulation of data.

Data analysis
Establish intended approaches for analysis of data e.g. content and thematic analysis,
constant comparison, issues of trustworthiness, credibility, defensibility, transferability.

Timescales, outcomes, reports, conferences

Figure 8.1 Considerations when writing a research proposals

philosophical and theoretical considerations of the research questions – connecting these with the methodology, methods, data collection and analysis techniques. Throughout the decision-making process, constant attention to ethics, theory, literature and context is essential to sustaining conceptual clarity. However, Figure 8.1 can be problematized and made sense of in relation to individual contexts and concerns. It is, of course, also an over-simplification of the messy reality of research, more a maze than a linear route where many aspects of the proposed research will be revisited, reworked and refined during both this stage and the actual research.

Where do I begin?

> It needed to directly benefit my career progression . . . be relevant, contemporary . . . something I could bring up at interview and debate . . . to directly improve my teaching practice. (Student response B)

Decisions concerning what to research can originate from personal interests, professional concerns, work-based situations and career aspirations. For some researchers the area of interest may already be clear, having emerged from reading literature, wanting to evaluate a recent initiative or seeking to improve or better understand an aspect of practice. At this stage the data collection may seem some way off, but it is worth considering whether the theme selected will sustain interest and balance originality with relevance for a wider audience. Two potential pitfalls often encountered early on are the theme being too broad, or based loosely on a researcher's 'hunch' (Brooks et al. 2010).

> Student voice is of personal interest and I felt in my school it was tokenistic. I wanted to see how far students could be involved in curriculum development. (Student response C)

When approaching this first pitfall, using mind maps or concept maps can help visualize alternative potential routes for research where a broad theme such as student voice has been identified. Two techniques used in arriving at research questions, but equally valuable here, are the 'Russian doll principle' and the 'Goldilocks test'. The former helps in getting to the very essence of a theme, the latter in considering its feasibility (see Clough and Nutbrown 2007, pp. 37–43). Refining key words such as 'student voice' and 'curriculum development' eventually led the teacher researcher to focus on year 8 pupils planning pupil-led geography lessons as part of an action research cycle. Undertaking a literature review to identify gaps in knowledge of previous research findings will also support this refining process. In addition to refining the theme, critical analysis of the purpose, theory, methodology, methods and data collection of previous research will inform methodological and conceptual considerations for the intended research. Following her literature review, Kitchen (2013) identified the teacher's influence on pupils' perceptions of geography as under researched and adopted a phenomenological approach; her tabulated literature review summary is a useful starting point for beginning researchers.

> I certainly had assumptions at the beginning about what my results would show and my own beliefs about what I felt the results should be. (Student response D)

> Research was always about seeing myself in my white lab coat and testing hypotheses through repeating experiments, it was initially hard to move away from that [approach] and rephrase the questions differently. (Student response E)

The second pitfall requires researchers to adopt a more reflexive approach, particularly if the hunch has potentially ended the search for causality before it has even begun. This can be challenging if the students' prior experiences are from an empiricist background of hypothesis testing, and seeking cause and effect. Encouraging such beginning researchers to ask questions such as 'What else could influence this?' seems a simple solution but being open to different possibilities and interpretations will need constant revisiting at each stage of the research, particularly in refining the theme into specific and clear research questions.

The importance of context

> Because it was a school agenda that I felt worked well within my lessons and those I observed. (Student response F)

In order to ensure the area of interest is worth pursuing a number of interrelated considerations need to be addressed. In addition to the essential requirement of a literature review, asking 'Why have I selected this area of interest?' not only demands closer scrutiny of the relevance and significance of the theme but also encourages considering its 'importance of context' (White 1985). From a social theory perspective, Whitty (1997) has suggested that 'much educational research . . . remains decontextualized' (p. 156), where the significance of context is ignored or receives only tokenistic consideration in a small section of the completed thesis. Therefore understanding context as influencing all aspects of research should be reflected in the proposal, both implicitly and explicitly. The researcher needs to consider the extent to which they are already 'contextually loaded' – that is, situated in contexts, relationships and situations. Historical, political, locational or personal contexts should be acknowledged to keep 'the background in view', but should also be used to provoke questions concerning choices made in the research.

> At the time skills based learning was 'all the rage' in schools so I wanted to determine if it had an effect on the pupils' perception of geography. (Student response G)

Personal, locational and policy contexts can influence numerous decisions, from the researcher's choice of area of interest to their selection and understanding of a methodology. Recent government directives, policy debates and initiatives represented in the practice of schools may partly be responsible for the research focus, for example, research into skills-led learning and competency-based curricula. This is not to suggest that such 'of the moment' research is not valuable; indeed, research of this kind is essential to challenge and question initiatives that may too readily become accepted orthodoxies. The point here is that the researcher needs to adopt a reflexive attitude to contextual loading to scrutinize their rationale for selecting a research theme or methodology. For example, where a school has a community of teacher-researchers, one style of action research may have become routinized; this could potentially be problematic for the quality of research if the approach has become 'domesticated as telling stories' (McNiff 2013, p. 6). While both action research and case study are appropriate methodologies for research where practitioners are seeking to better understand or improve situations, there needs to be an appreciation of the significant variation within and between such methodologies.

This reflexive process of constant questioning will help to clarify the importance of context and the purpose of the research. Establishing the significance of the research and its wider relevance beyond personal interest and impact is also required in the justification of the research theme and methodology. In particular how will it have relevance to a wider audience, and be considered worthwhile? This is problematic, since the small-scale and context-specific nature of practitioner research restricts generalizability – something addressed later in the chapter.

Philosophical and theoretical considerations

This [establishing ontological and epistemological positions] was expected in the proposal although at the time I was less clear about the significance and how it affected my classroom based research. (Student response H)

A tenet of a good research proposal is that it makes sense philosophically, theoretically and methodologically. Philosophical positioning – what it is; when it should be established; and its relevance to the practicalities of research – is a concern of most novice researchers. At some point (when and where varies considerably) teacher-researchers examine the origins of the views they hold about the nature of reality and knowledge. From a qualitative research perspective, Savin-Baden and Howell Major (2013) have suggested five 'essential choice moments' as inhabiting a position; framing the research; choosing a research approach; collecting data and working with data (p. 38). They suggest the first essential choice of 'inhabiting a position' requires considering one's ontological and epistemological assumptions to establish a philosophical stance. Ontological assumptions are how we believe the world to be and therefore what is open to research, while epistemological assumptions concern what counts as valid knowledge of that world, in other words how we come to know about that world. Crotty (1998) provides a hierarchical distinction between epistemology, theoretical perspective, methodology and methods where the researcher's philosophical stance is established by questioning their epistemological assumptions; these subsequently inform the selection of methodology and methods. Having a section in the proposal structure requiring philosophical positioning does not guarantee reflexive engagement by the researcher and may simply lead to rehearsing philosophical perspectives rather than articulating the relationship to theoretical perspectives and methodology.

Whilst acknowledging that 'no theory can capture the full complexity of the things we study' (Maxwell 2013, p. vii), the research proposal needs to show critical engagement with theoretical perspectives relevant to the theme, since the theoretical framework situates the research theme and connects the philosophical stance to the practicalities of the research design. From a practitioner's perspective, Freeman (2010) discusses the importance of engaging with theory, in particular learning theory and curriculum theory. In learning theory, constructivist and social constructivist approaches have helped to inform classroom-based research involving pupils' development of geographical knowledge – however, theories are not to be adopted uncritically and creation of a theoretical framework requires the application of critical reasoning. 'Researcher readiness' is therefore paramount to critically engaging with and understanding philosophical and theoretical perspectives, and their relationship to methodology and methods.

Arriving at research questions

> This part was challenging. I felt I knew what I wanted to achieve, but found it difficult to put into words or be specific enough. (Student response I)

The process of translating the research theme and purpose into specific, clear, focused, well-defined research questions is central to the conceptual coherence of the research proposal. The research questions need to seek answers directly relevant to the purpose of the study for them to be considered 'fit for purpose'. This process can be challenging, but working from the original aims and objectives of the research can help.

> I found it much easier to think about what I wanted to achieve in terms of research objectives before I formulated my main research question. (Student response J)

Usually there will be one or two main questions that clearly convey the scope and focus of the research. 'What' and 'how' are open and organic questions, consistent with 'descriptive' and 'explorative' research, while 'why' questions start the search for causation consistent with 'explanatory' research. Cresswell (2003) suggests the language of research questions relates directly to emerging methodologies in qualitative design. However, data originating from good descriptive or explorative questions can also prompt and begin to answer 'why' questions, which can lead to questions being adapted. Since much practitioner research is seeking to improve a situation, 'how can' questions support research that has a transformative purpose as in this teacher's overarching research question.

> How can collaborative professional enquiry between geography teachers impact on learning and teaching? (Student response K)

Besides linking to the research purpose, the wording of questions also communicate the context of the research. Adopting a more philosophical approach to questions and research in general, Pring (2012) urges us to ask 'what do we mean' when we use words such as 'skills' or 'learning'. Such philosophical questions are helpful in opening up terms such as 'collaborative professional enquiry' by examining different interpretations and clarifying the researcher's use of 'collaborative', 'professional' and 'enquiry' in the intended research. In addition, contextual clarification can help us to make more informed choices when using words such as 'impact', 'influence' or 'effect'. Sometimes overly complex questions suggest the researcher still lacks clarity in purpose and direction; having a colleague share their understanding of a research question is useful in seeking clear and focused central and sub-questions.

> I lost count how many times I reworded these. . . . they changed regularly! (Student response L)

In support of the central research question, usually between three to five supporting or sub-questions are manageable. These sub-questions need to be able to stand alone, but must also have clear links between them to ensure they are logically sequenced and conceptually connected (Vithal and Jansen 2004). Having consistency of terms might suggest connectedness; however, the questions may still lack conceptual clarity (Pring 2012). It is also important to review how the research questions differ to questions asked in previous research and therefore how these may offer the potential for claims to new knowledge. Once established, research questions should not be viewed as fixed entities but should be open to refining as phenomena become better understood during the research. The questions therefore are continually reviewed – something that may be problematic for those coming from a quantitative research background.

Fitness for purpose of research design

> I was clear about methods from the start but was unsure of which methodology I should use, after discussing with my tutor I did eventually settle on case study and the methods I wanted to use seemed to fit well . . . Interviews and focus groups. (Student response M)

One view of research design is as a series of informing stages for planning research; the philosophical stance informs the methodology, which in turn informs the selection of specific methods used to collect data appropriate for answering the research questions. While such models have been critiqued for their predeterminedness (Maxwell 2013), research does need to be pursued systematically – with choices concerning the overall design of methodology, methods and data collection requiring conceptual clarity and connectivity. While the choice of methods may be sound and sit well within a chosen methodology, the methodological rational may be less convincing. The reality of arriving at a final fit for purpose methodology and methods may occur differently for individuals, as is clear in the quote above. This relates back to the notion of 'researcher readiness' – that is, the ability of the researcher to *critically* engage with the different considerations required at the proposal stage.

The teacher-researcher needs to carefully consider the literature on philosophical positioning and theoretical perspectives in order to justify their choice of research methodology. However, research terminologies such as 'philosophies', 'approaches' and 'methodologies' are sometimes used synonymously, which can cause confusion for novice researchers. In much practitioner research 'methodology' is used interchangeably with 'approach', Wilson (2013) suggests the methodological approaches of case study and action research as most appropriate to school-based research. Qualitative researchers such as Savin-Baden and Howell Major (2013) prefer to think of methodology as 'an analysis of the principles of research methods, rules or postulates . . . theoretical analysis of the methods and principles . . .' (p. 40). This second definition suggests methodological clarity must exist throughout the research and not just in the justification of an approach. Therefore, developing a sophisticated understanding of the significance of methodology will help ensure rigour within this aspect of the research proposal.

If we view the research design as 'an integrated statement of and justification for the technical decisions involved in planning a research project' (Blaikie 2009, p. 15), we also need to acknowledge that the research design is inherently subjective. This is the case because the researcher is intimately involved in making these decisions at every stage, decisions about methodology and methods being just two. Researchers can bring certain assumptions to the selection of research design; therefore, there is a need to stand back from the object of research, to try to seek a sense of objectivity in the research design process.

> I initially thought quantitative data was more useful as it is 'measurable and I was going to have to prove' something . . . having reworked the research questions I needed to access the views and opinions of students and teachers so I chose qualitative approaches. (Student response N)

Research designs should clarify whether data will be collected through a quantitative, qualitative or mixed methods approach. A mixed methods research design combines quantitative and qualitative approaches, data collection techniques and/or data (Jonson and Onwuegbuzie 2004). This 'mixed research' approach, since it is not just methods that may be combined, can appeal to teacher-researchers as a more practice-driven and pragmatic option than situating the research within a quantitative or qualitative paradigm. However, adopting a mixed research approach does not guarantee fitness for purpose if the design itself lacks rigour and is 'fragmented and inconsistent' (Denscombe 2008, p. 280). Morrison (2007) encourages researchers to engage with quantitative, qualitative and mixed methods approaches 'knowingly and self-consciously' (p. 33). Therefore, justifying both why and when a quantitative or qualitative component has priority is an important requirement in mixed methods research (see Cohen et al. 2011).

Robson (2002) makes the distinction between a 'fixed' and a 'flexible' research design. Fixed designs are more representative of large-scale quantitative studies where surveys have predetermined routes for the research, often seeking patterns, trends, correlations or causal connections. Not all fixed designs are like this though, and some may include more flexible data collection phases. Two approaches of experimental and non-experimental designs are discussed by Wilson (2013), whose edited volume devotes two chapters to quantitative approaches (see pp. 171–210) which are sometimes neglected in other education texts.

> After the first action research cycle I decided that I needed to respond to what they [the pupils] were saying and this meant giving more freedom on assessment and not the planned intervention I had wanted to do. (Student response M)

Flexible approaches are considered more appropriate to those researching aspects of geography education, as the research focus is often situated in complex and changing 'real life' contexts. Flexibility allows adaptation and modification to the research process affording greater freedom as new developments occur or new avenues to explore open up. This flexibility fits well with qualitative research where the researcher makes knowledge claims from a constructivist perspective, and where emerging themes are identified during the data collection and analysis phase. However, flexibility in design still requires sound methodological reasoning as one criticism of this approach is that it can be unsystematic and not founded on firm philosophical principles. As with the research design, the research proposal should not be viewed as fixed – as once research is underway there may be practical reasons why changes are required to the intended methods, size of sample or type of data being collected.

Research methods

> I wanted to use a combination of methods that would get as close to what was happening in how teachers' talk influenced the students' engagement in lessons. . . . I used video, teacher and pupils interviews. (Student response N)

While quantitative and qualitative paradigms may lay claim to particular methods, we must be careful not to establish a false dualism between paradigms that implies automatically discounting or adopting a particular approach or method. Grey (2004) sees methods as independent of methodology; however, a good research proposal requires a rationale that connects the methods to the particular purpose and context of the research and reinforces their suitability for answering the research question 'as unambiguously as possible' (de Vaus 2001, p. 9). In addition, all methods require careful ethical considerations of how participants – their identities, wellbeing and accounts – will be protected.

Whatever the purpose of the research, essentially there are three main approaches utilized within research methods: analysis of documents, (including visuals and artefacts), observing and questioning.

Documents as data sources include written materials (policies, prospectuses and plans); visual images (photographs, animations, videos) and electronic media (blogs, twitter, email). They represent 'situated' accounts written with a particular audience and purpose in mind; they occupy a particular context and can provide valuable data for socio-political or -historical research. Justifying the use of documentation beyond providing a context for the research will be required. How will analysis of the particular documents contribute to the purpose of the research and specific research questions? In addition, the researcher needs to demonstrate how the documents will be critically read for analysis – reading for meaning that is there, and not yet perceived to be there.

> I chose observation as this was part of my role in the school I was used to observing and grading teachers' lessons against criteria but I initially struggled with not making judgements about what I was seeing and noticing. (Student response O)

From a research perspective, participant and non-participant observation (like any other research method) requires justification of approach: structured or semi-structured; data type and amount: quantitative and/or qualitative; and the medium: video, checklists or reflective journal. Non-participant observation requires the researcher to be a passive observer, although their very presence may affect participants' attitudes and activities through 'the Hawthorne effect' (Landsberger 1958). Participant observation can produce 'thick descriptions' of social interaction but it also brings challenges, not least concerning ethics and questions of power. In both approaches, asking 'what else might be going on here?' will encourage questioning of subjective judgements and the recognition of multiple rather than singular realities.

Surveys, questionnaires, interviews and focus groups all involve asking questions of participants, either face to face or from a distance. While acknowledging that practical considerations of access, availability and timescale may steer researchers towards a particular method, selections must be made which are congruent with the research purpose. Methods can be presented as homogeneously distinct, each with potential benefits and drawbacks for those involved in the research. However, a good research proposal shows deeper awareness of different types of method and relates this to its purpose. For example, the purpose of a focus group might be to increase researcher understanding of an issue (exploratory focus group) or unpack participants' hidden views (clinical focus group) (Savin-Baden and Howell Major 2013). Once a method for asking questions is selected, the field questions demand the same level of scrutiny as the initial research questions both with respect to purpose (descriptive or exploratory) and type of question (open or closed) – and whether these require a quantitative or qualitative response.

Data collection and analysis

> I did not really consider it [data analysis] fully until the masses of data had been collected and I realise looking back that I should have planned the whole piece out, even with a basic mind map. (Student response P)

Practical considerations such as handling a large amount and different types of data, together with the ethical collection and storing of data, must be considered at the proposal stage. Having too much data is often the result of a lack of clarity in the research design, but equally masses of data can be generated from a single interview or focus group – this is why piloting a method is advisable to help refine the focus or questions, as well as contributing to research credibility. At the data level sometimes the terms 'quantitative' and 'qualitative' are mistakenly equated with 'objective' and 'subjective'. When applied to data the distinction is whether a number, or word, is being collected and therefore the terms should not be used synonymously as this simple example demonstrates.

> Quantitative/objective – 'What is the number of times you have been on fieldtrips'?
> Qualitative/objective – 'Have you attended fieldtrips'?
> Quantitative/subjective – 'How much do you enjoy fieldtrips'? (Likert scale 1–4)
> Qualitative/subjective – 'What do you enjoy about fieldtrips'?

In their discussion of mixed methods approaches, Symonds and Gorard (2008) have argued that in seeking quality, the main consideration is not whether one or more types of data are collected but 'the quality of our actual research techniques, the resulting data and how the data is used' (p. 17). Therefore, the proposal needs to show how the data likely to emerge from the research process is providing possible answers to the research questions. Morrison (2007) reminds us to attend to epistemological and methodological considerations and to be aware that once data is collected it does not automatically become knowledge without analysis by the researcher. Where this is acknowledged it will contribute to the rigour and quality of the research.

In seeking to ensure methodological and theoretical robustness the concept of 'trustworthiness' is fundamental (Furlong and Oancea 2005). Lincoln and Guba's (1985) concept of 'trustworthiness' is the level of confidence claimed in the data collection, analysis and research findings. As a concept it challenges positivists' concerns with the rigour of qualitative research and makes the case that findings are 'worth paying attention to' (p. 290). Some qualitative researchers are reluctant to use the 'holy trinity' of objectivity, reliability and validity as this can be considered to be positivist terminology preferring Guba's (1981) terminology of confirmability (objectivity), dependability (reliability), credibility (validity) and transferability (generalizability). Credibility refers to whether the research measures what it actually intended to; therefore, the research design requires conceptual connectivity so that findings are more likely to be viewed as 'credible' or valid by others. But credibility relies on the dependability of the research process, where dependability refers to how the research will be carried out in a reliable way. (Reliable in the sense that if it was repeated, or carried out by another researcher, the outcomes would be the same; this is key to addressing concerns of subjectivity and researcher bias). Much practitioner research is small scale and context dependent, so generalizability may not be relevant, but the concept of transferability suggests rich contextual information in the research may be helpful to others working in similar contexts. Whichever language is adopted in the proposal, what is more important is that strategies are included to ensure a more 'faithful description of the ideas, interpretations and understandings of those researched' (Howell 2013, p. 191). Shenton (2004) provides a detailed account of strategies for ensuring trustworthiness in qualitative research projects; here triangulation and reflexivity are discussed.

> I used triangulation of data from students, teachers and my reflective journal so that this increased the reliability and validity of my research. (Student response Q)

Triangulation seeks to increase the trustworthiness of research by drawing on multiple perspectives, methods or investigators. The perspectives of different participants, colleagues or observers may reveal divergence or convergence of data and emerging themes in the research. Designing two or more methods to collect the same data from a group means the strength of one method can compensate for the bias or weakness of another. The relevance of using different methods, in the context of the research questions posed, needs to be made clear. These choices must also be based on sound methodological principles. Triangulation of investigators usually refers to adult researchers, but including 'students as co-researchers' is an acceptable form of research collegiality (Fielding 2004).

> I had sixth form students act as 'co-researchers' to interview the pupils as I thought they [the pupils] would be more open and honest with the sixth formers. (Student response R)

This teacher's research made use of 'students as co-researchers' partly because the research had a strong focus on student voice; additionally she was seeking to reduce her influence on the students' responses. The sixth form students were trained to undertake a focus group and made aware of their ethical responsibilities, but issues of subjectivity still needed to be addressed. This is where building in opportunities for sharing research data with participants can help further reduce researcher bias.

> I kept a reflective log of all my thoughts and feelings. . . . It had lots of questions, drawings and doodles . . . I sometimes went around in circles. . . . I also wrote in it when I changed the research! (Student response S)

Reflexivity is a more critical approach than reflectivity; it is based on the notion that 'knowledge cannot be separated from the knower' (Steedman 1991, p. 53) and demands a researcher's commitment to constantly considering how they are positioned in the research. However, those adopting a reflexive attitude also need to be aware of the potential pitfall of 'excessive self-analysis at the expense of focusing on the research participants' (Finley 2002, p. 532).

This chapter has emphasized the research proposal as a crucial stage in the research journey which requires the researcher to adopt a reflexive approach and have a 'critical design attitude' (Clough and Nutbrown 2007, p. 35). A good research proposal clearly conveys the author's philosophical, theoretical and methodological positions in justifying the conceptual connectivity of the research questions, methodology, methods and data. In this way, the research design will lead to findings that are trusted and taken account of by others.

References

Blaikie, N (2009) *Designing Social Research*, 2nd edition. Cambridge: Polity Press.

Brooks, C, Conradi, A and Leonard, A (2010) Undertaking research and doing a dissertation. In Brooks, C (ed.) *Studying PGCE Geography at M Level: Reflection, Research and Writing for Professional Development*, pp. 152–65. Abingdon: Routledge.

Butt, G (2006) How should we determine quality in research in geography education? In Purnell, K, Lidstone, J and Hodgson, S (eds.) *Changes in Geographical Education: Past, Present and Future*. Proceedings of the International Geographical Union Commission on Geographical Education Symposium. Brisbane: IGU-CGE.

Clough, P and Nutbrown, C (2012) *A Student's Guide to Methodology*, 3rd edition. London: Sage.

Cohen, L, Manion, L and Morrison, K (2011) *Research Methods in Education*, 7th edition. London and New York: Routledge.

Creswell, J W (2003) *Research Design: Quantitative, Qualitative and Mixed Methods Approaches*, 2nd edition. Thousand Oaks, CA: Sage.

Crotty, M (1998) *The Foundations of Social Science Research: Meaning and Perspective in the Research Process*. St. Leonards, NSW: Allen and Uwin.

Denscombe, M (2008) Communities of practice A research paradigm for the mixed methods approach. *Journal of Mixed Methods Research* 2(3): 270–83.

— (2012) *Research Proposals: A Practical Guide*. Maidenhead: McGraw-Hill/Open University Press.

De Vaus, D A (2001) *Research Design in Social Research*. London: Sage.

Fielding, M (2004) Transformative approaches to student voice: theoretical underpinnings, recalcitrant realities. *British Educational Research Journal* 30: 295–311.

Finley, L. (2002) 'Outing' the researcher: the provenance, process, and practice of reflexivity. *Qualitative Health Research* 12: 531–45.

Freeman, D (2010) Engaging with theory. In Brooks, C (ed.) *Studying PGCE Geography at M Level: Reflection, Research and Writing for Professional Development*, pp. 139–51. Abingdon: Routledge.

Furlong, J and Oancea, A (2005) *Assessing Quality in Applied and Practice-Based Educational Research: A Framework for Discussion*. Oxford: OUDES.

Grey, D (2004) *Doing Research in the Real World*. London: Sage.

Guba, E G (1981) Criteria for assessing the trustworthiness of naturalistic inquiries. *Educational Communication and Technology Journal* 29: 75–91.

Howell, K E (2013) *An Introduction to the Philosophy of Methodology*. London: Sage.

Johnson, B and Christensen, L (2012) *Educational Research: Quantitative, Qualitative, and Mixed Approaches*, 4th edition. London: Sage.

Jonson, R B and Onwuegbuzie, A J (2004) Mixed methods research: a research paradigm whose time has come. *Educational Researcher* 33(7): 14–26.

Kitchen, R (2013) Student perceptions of geographical knowledge and the role of the teacher. *Geography* 98(3): 112–22.

Landsberger, H (1958) *Hawthorne Revisited: Management and the Worker: Its Critics and Developments in Human Relations in Industry*. Ithaca, NY: Cornell University.

Lincoln, Y S and Guba, E G (1985) *Naturalistic Inquiry*. Beverly Hills, CA: Sage.

Maxwell, J (2013) *Qualitative Research Design: An Interactive Approach*, 3rd edition. London: Sage.

McNiff, J (2013) *Action Research: Principles and Practice*, 3rd edition. London and New York: Routledge.

Morrison, M (2007) What do we mean by educational research? In Coleman, M and Briggs, A (eds.) *Research Methods in Educational Leadership and Management*. England: Paul Chapman Publishing.

Pring, R (2012) Importance of philosophy in the conduct of educational research. *Journal of International and Comparative Education* 1(1): 23–30.

Robson, C (2002) *Real World Research*, 2nd edition. Oxford: Blackwell.

Savin-Baden, M and Howell Major, C (2013) *Qualitative Research: The Essential Guide to Theory and Practice*. London and New York: Routledge.

Shenton, A (2004) Strategies for ensuring trustworthiness in qualitative research projects. *Education for Information* 22: 63–75.

Steedman, P (1991) On the relations between seeing, interpreting and knowing. In Steier, F (ed.) *Research and Reflexivity*, pp. 53–62. London: Sage.

Symonds, J E and Gorard, S (2008) *The Death of Mixed Methods: Research Labels and their Casualties*. Paper Presented at the British Educational Research Association Annual Conference, Heriot Watt University, Edinburgh, 3–6 September 2008.

Vithal, R and Jansen, J (2004) *Designing Your First Research Proposal*. Lansdowne: Juta.

White, R (1985) The Importance of context in educational research. *Research in Science Education* 1985: 15.

Whitty, G. (1997) Social theory and education policy: the legacy of Karl Mannheim. *British Journal of Sociology of Education* 18(2): 149–63.

Wilson, E (ed.) (2013) *School-Based Research: A Guide for Education Students*. London: Sage.

Yates, S (2004) *Doing Social Science Research*. London: Sage.

Ethical Considerations

Maggie Wilson

9

Chapter outline

The research ethics context	130
Research integrity	132
Informed consent	133
Privacy and confidentiality	137
Special considerations concerning research with children	139
After data collection	141
Conclusions	142

The growth of taught Masters and doctoral programmes during the 1990s has led to an increase in part-time study and practitioner-based research by teachers and education professionals undertaking research within their own institutions or professional networks. This poses particular ethical issues for those acting as 'insider researchers' or 'practitioner researchers', in addition to those conventionally raised in relation to the research process (Mercer 2007). Despite the undoubted advantages of insider research, practitioner researchers often have to juggle multiple roles and responsibilities. Rather than 'wearing two hats', practitioner researchers can often find that these roles fluctuate, making them difficult to disentangle. Nonetheless, ethical considerations affect all kinds of research directly involving human participants, as well as the use of personal data. Such considerations present the researcher with a series of 'moral equations' throughout the research process – from research design, to data collection, analysis and also after completion of the study (Gregory 2003; Oliver 2010).

This chapter will firstly place the development of research ethics in context and outline the main stances within the field. It will then outline ethical considerations in relation to the key concepts of informed consent, privacy and confidentiality. The particular ethical considerations involved when undertaking research with children will be identified. Lastly, the sometimes-neglected final stages of research and publication will be examined. The generic nature of the issues identified in this chapter largely negates any necessity to make reference to specific aspects of research in geography education.

The research ethics context

Ethical review of research in the United Kingdom, United States, Canada and Australia can be seen as a historical legacy of the Nuremberg Code of 1947 and Declaration of Helsinki of 1964, strengthened by public outrage over the effects of thalidomide testing in the 1960s and the retention of the organs of deceased children for research purposes, without parental knowledge or consent, in the United Kingdom in the 1990s (MacFarlane 2010; Alderson and Morrow 2011). This resulted in the 'capturing' of research ethics by the bio-medical sciences and the establishment of stringent ethical review procedures in this research domain, which required that all clinically based research projects should have ethical approval at the local level. Professional associations for other subject areas within the Humanities and Social Sciences, such as the Social Research Association (SRA) and British Education Research Association (BERA), followed, providing guidelines for self-regulation. In 2005 the Economic and Social Research Council (ESRC) required that all British institutions undertaking research in receipt of funding should have a research regulatory framework in place. By the early 2000s most British universities had established such frameworks and resultant protocols, which were based more on a model of compliance than self-regulation. They began to publish codes of conduct and lofty statements of principle to guide decision-making and instituted tiered procedures for research ethics review.

Such developments came under heavy fire from some sections of the professional research community. The appropriateness of the bio-medical research model was particularly questioned. It was argued that the risks involved in undertaking research in the social sciences were not comparable to those encountered in medical research (Hammersley 2010) and that increased regulation or 'ethicism' represented increasing surveillance and a threat to professional autonomy (Hammersley and Traianou 2012). Particular concerns were voiced by qualitative researchers who maintained that an anticipatory model based on 'technicist rules of conduct' (Pole and Morrison 2003, p. 146) were inimical to this kind of exploratory, free-flowing research, where the research journey is not necessarily mapped out in advance (Miller et al. 2012). The expertise and composition of research ethics committees were queried (Hammersley 2009) and the process of ethical review criticized as leading to a tick box mentality, which diverts attention away from the need for constant vigilance throughout the research process (Bryman 2012).

However, other writers have argued that the potential 'risks' involved in research, to both the researcher and the researched in the Humanities and Social Sciences, are not inconsiderable. These include the risk of physical harm or psychological damage, infringement of privacy or the law, and of reputational damage to the research location, participants, university or wider research community (Thomas 2009). While recognizing that some research ethics committees may be overly 'risk averse', Gorman (2007) argues for a positive, transparent and open relationship between the university research community and research ethics committee, in which research ethics procedures should ensure robustness of research but are flexible and always stress a positive way forward. Underlying her argument is a sense of public accountability and a move away from the conception of the researcher as a 'lone ranger', whether as a professional or student.

In many ways it could be argued that ethical issues have changed little since the 1960s, apart from a greater scrutiny and social awareness of such issues. However, there have been significant changes in the research landscape and its wider location, which have impacted on ethical considerations. Reflecting on changes which have occurred within the ten years between two major research studies, Miller identifies these as resulting from computer-enabled multiple sources of data gathering, digital data storage and sharing, concerns over the use of data, disclosure of information and blurring of privacy boundaries which information technology brings (Miller 2012). Commenting on revisions to the ESRC's ethical guidelines in 2010 (from the 2005 version), Bryman (2012) adds to this list an increasing concern over researcher safety, possible conflicts of interest in research, potential litigation and a greater emphasis on quality in research. The 1989 *UN Convention on the Rights of the Child* has also had a significant impact on the status and treatment of children in research, with a clearer focus on children's rights and participation in research, a change which will be explored later in this chapter (Alderson and Morrow 2011; Graham et al. 2013).

Many of the criticisms levelled at the ethics review process stem from concerns about the erosion of professional autonomy among experienced researchers. For those at the 'foothills' of research, ethical considerations are just as important, but the research ethics review process is likely to be simpler. There is no uniform pattern of review among universities, with some delegating all aspects of review to faculties or departments, some operating a centralized system and some a two-tier system. For Masters students, the process is often based on a 'screening' form, which asks similar questions to those applied to the research projects of staff and doctoral students. Such review either is delegated to dissertation supervisors, who may offer frontline support and sign off the application for the next stage, or is carried out at faculty level and can be completed more quickly. In both cases, additional documentation, such as drafts of interview schedules, is required. However, in more open-ended research, such instruments may be in a very embryonic form and can be adapted and reviewed at a later date.

Research integrity

The fundamental principles of research ethics are not in dispute. The foremost of these relates to the justification of the research and the balance between potential harm and good. Researchers should ask themselves, and be prepared to publically justify, whether the research should be undertaken and whether it is potentially worthwhile. The research should not intentionally cause harm (the principle of 'non-malificence') but should identify clear potential benefits (the principle of 'benificence'). In addition, research should be based on respect for the individual 'according to standards and values which affirm their essential humanity' (Oliver 2012, p. 12) and on justice in the treatment of individuals.

However, in practice such universalistic and seemingly static principles are often challenging to apply. The application of principles may conflict (Thomas 2009) rather than being complementary (Alderson and Morrow 2011), or may be subject to different cross-cultural understandings (Hammersley and Traianou 2012). The potential benefits of research may not be immediately tangible either in the short term, to the research participants, or in the long term, in terms of contribution to the public good. While some writers define the goal of education research to be transformative of individual lives (Gregory 2003), others champion the goal of 'worthwhile knowledge' and understanding (Hammersley and Traianou 2012).

In countering the non-negotiability of universalistic principles, various alternative positions have been proposed. In consequentialist or utilitarian ethics, decisions concerning research design and conduct can be based on a cost-benefit analysis of outcomes or judged by the consequences of actions. Such a position can, however, lead to a position where the ends come to justify the means and this has been countered by more flexible models. In situation ethics, decisions are taken on a case-by-case basis. Exceptions are only made when the end justifies the means and no other choice is available (Bryman 2012). In order to make such decisions, the 'virtues' of the researcher are of prime importance in the research process. MacFarlane (2010) defines these, among other attributes, as courage, honesty, respectfulness, humility and reflectivity. This necessarily entails careful consideration of any potential conflicts of interest and scrupulous attention to research rigour. Feminist researchers have also advanced a model based on the social value of the 'ethics of care', a model which emphasizes the primacy of relationships in research (Edwards and Mauthner 2012). This is extended in the call for 'thinking ethically' in research – defined as a contextual, situational and practice-based approach, which is reflexive and supportive and puts the participant at the heart of the research (Miller et al. 2012, p. 4). Research in this model is something which is done with, rather than on, people.

The concepts of 'virtue' in research and 'thinking ethically' have particular implications for practitioner researchers in terms of choice of research focus and accountability in the field. Professional codes of conduct drawn up by schools and employers, trade unions and local authorities offer further guidance to practitioner researchers. Increasingly research ethics reviews raise questions about the safety of both researchers and the research participants. This is often framed through questions concerning whether the study involves more risk than that normally encountered in everyday life. As practitioner researchers, teachers will be aware of the myriad decisions which inform their everyday experiences and the sometimes conflicting principles which underpin the frequent dilemmas they face. The next sections indicate guidelines for good practice in the field of research ethics, but should always be informed by continuous reflection in action.

Informed consent

Informed consent has been described as the 'lynchpin of the research relationship' (Graham et al. 2013, p. 42) and 'the bedrock of ethical procedures' (Cohen et al. 2011, p. 52). Giving participants full information about the purpose of a research study, what involvement entails and how participant data will be used, supports the trust relationships which are essential in research and which support the integrity of a research study. According to BERA Guidelines, securing informed consent before the research gets underway should be considered the 'norm' of research (BERA 2011, p. 6) and is often on two levels: that of the organizational 'gatekeeper' and that of the actual participant.

In both cases, securing informed consent is based on the assumptions that this is an explicit act, is voluntary, based on information and understanding, and is produced in written form, which is comprehensible to and can be retained by the participant or organization. It is now generally accepted by research ethics committees that participants should actively consent to take part in a study by 'opting in'. The default position of 'opting out', where participants are contacted without volunteering to take part and only excluded when they are unwilling to participate, undermines the principle of the right to freely give consent. However, this is still an area of debate, as 'opting in' can significantly affect response rates and 'opting out' may be suitable for very low risk studies (Thomas 2009). This has implications for research in schools, which will be discussed later in the chapter.

In order to make a considered decision about whether or not to take part in a study, potential participants should normally be given sufficient time in which to do so (Gregory 2003). A period of 48 hours is often suggested. The SRA Guidelines point to the fine balancing act between swamping potential participants with information and withholding information (SRA 2003). It is now accepted practice to produce participant information sheets, which outline essential information about involvement, accompanied by a consent form, with a series of tick boxes to indicate understanding and acceptance of specific items, signed by both the researcher and participant. Most universities will have templates for these on-line. Essential information to include is as follows:

- the value and purpose of the study;
- main research methods involved;
- what participation entails, including the location and expected time commitment of involvement, whether the event will be filmed or audio recorded, and how participants engage in the study;

- expected benefits of the study;
- possible risks involved in the study;
- if pupils or students are involved, an assurance that participation will have no impact on their studies;
- information about confidentiality and anonymity;
- details about data storage, length and when data will be destroyed;
- details about dissemination and publication of results;
- details about any funding for the study;
- ethics review procedures and contacts for concerns and
- the researcher's contact details.

Participant information sheets should also stress the right of the participant to withdraw at any time from the study and should, in addition, inform them about why they have been invited to take part. In many ways, the best starting point for reviewing information sheets is through empathy: what would I want to know if I (or my child) were approached to take part? Usually, consent forms are not required for questionnaires, as completion implies consent. Similarly on-line surveys will incorporate key information in an explanatory screen at the start. When particularly sensitive questions are involved in an interview, it may be advisable to send these in advance and to emphasize the participant's right to decline to answer questions. It has also now become common to offer to send a transcript of an interview for 'accuracy checking'. Flick (2011) suggests a time limit of 14 days in which participants can do so. However, this is not unproblematic, as the act of writing already involves interpretation. Oliver (2010) warns that this can often be contentious and a time-consuming process and raises questions about the extent to which transcripts remain the property of the participant or researcher. This in turn may depend on the relationship between the researcher and researched. In more participatory models of research, research participants may, for example, contribute to the analysis of findings (Miller 2012).

Participant information sheets should be written in plain English and should be readily understood by the reader. It may be necessary to translate sheets into community languages and to produce appropriate versions for different age groups of children. Particular care should be taken with those considered to be 'vulnerable' in research. These are defined as children under 16, the socially vulnerable, such as the homeless, participants whose first language differs from that of the researcher and those with limited cognitive abilities. People over the age of 80 and those with chronic conditions are also sometimes included in this group. However, Oliver (2010) warns against making unwarranted assumptions which may undermine participant dignity and underestimate capabilities. Participant information sheets are expected to include a brief statement on the possible benefits to participants in a research study. There is often the temptation to 'oversell' these in order to enhance recruitment. In practice, studies may have few or no direct or material benefits to participants and care should be taken to make this transparent (Cohen et al. 2011). However, if the study is well justified and the public benefits of the study are clear, this should help recruitment.

If an incentive to take part in research is offered, this should normally be clearly stated. Incentives can take the form of hospitality (light refreshments) or reimbursements for costs, such as travel. The BERA Guidelines state that these must be 'commensurate with good sense' and must avoid creating 'choices which in themselves may have an undesirable effect' (2011, p. 7). Although the payment of incentives could skew a sample or influence participant behaviour, by putting actual or perceived pressure on the participant to give the 'right answer', careful consideration should be given to whether the absence of incentives may also create a sample bias.

Securing 'gatekeeper permission' for research to take place within a specific location does not involve the same level of detail, but should conform to the same principles of clarity and transparency. Gatekeepers are defined as those who have managerial or organizational control, such as a Head teacher. In some cases it may be necessary to negotiate permission at several levels, such as at Departmental level as well. Requests should be made at a reasonable time, should be clear, explicit and modest in demand, and should seek to minimize the 'bureaucratic burden of research' and impact on workloads (BERA 2011, p. 7). They should include reasons for undertaking the study, the potential value of the study and possible outcomes. Offering something in return – for example, a presentation of findings to a suitable forum within the organization – is also considered to be both good practice and judicious (Oliver 2010). This is, however, not always a straightforward process. Gatekeepers can block access or exercise surveillance, put pressure on researchers to pursue certain research results or 'deliver the research goods' (Cohen et al. 2011). They may select participants in order to influence results, put pressure on less powerful members of the organization to take part in the research or assume they can give consent to participate on behalf of colleagues (Doyle 2007; Mockler 2007). Working with teachers in senior positions over many years, I have often observed that there is a tendency to underestimate the power relationships which exist in ostensibly collegial settings. Perceptions of pleasant open relationships may not be viewed in quite the same way by members of staff at less senior levels, such as teaching assistants and those in 'dependency relationships', such as pupils or students. While overall gatekeeper permission should be sought, acceptance to take part in a study should in principle be directly from the participant, rather than assuming consent.

Although ostensibly straightforward, the process of obtaining informed consent is not unproblematic. A strong criticism of the process has been expressed by MacFarlane (2010) who contests that the use of consent forms can give a spurious legality to the consent process, acts as a 'fig leaf' to real ethical considerations (p. 21) and is more to do with protecting the university than participants' rights. Indeed, the signing of a quasi-legal consent form may be regarded with suspicion by the less powerful or hard to reach groups, undermining relationships based on trust (Duncan and Watson 2010; Miller and Bell 2012). In addition, the one-off signing of consent may not be appropriate for some forms of research, particularly qualitative research, which may well entail unexpected turns and unfolding issues (Edwards and Mauthner 2012) Indeed, Hammersley and Traianou (2012) query whether giving full information about a study is ever a realistic proposition, with participant information sheets only offering spurious assurance. Although not fully addressing such concerns, the concept of renegotiated consent may be helpful here (Oliver 2010). This can be overt and at every stage of participation and in any kind of research, while not committing to a positivist 'grand plan' at the start of the study. Studies which involve stages of research with the same participants, such as in longitudinal research, should involve securing re-consent. Where a written consent form presents problems, oral consent can also be obtained by reading out the participant information sheet and clearly recording consent to questions on the form.

If a participant withdraws consent to participate, declines to answer some questions or decides to withdraw data, this can clearly be problematic for the researcher, but is a commitment which has to be honoured. The BERA Guidelines suggest that participants can be approached to re-consider their decision or discuss reasons behind it, but that this should be handled with great care.

A further complexity to the research landscape is provided by on-line research. The BERA Guidelines refer to the 'challenges' presented by social networking and other on-line activities and state that 'participants must be clearly informed that their participation and interactions are being monitored and analysed for research' (BERA 2011, p. 5). Potential research sites now include discussion fora, blogs, Facebook and e-mail exchanges. Whether explicit gatekeeper permission should be sought to use such exchanges depends on whether each item posted can be deemed to be 'owned' by its author or whether they are more akin to a published article or letter to a paper (Oliver 2010). Bryman (2012) offers some useful guidance in suggesting that explicit consent should be sought from both the site controller and individual concerned if:

- the information is not publically archived and readily accessible;
- a password is required to gain access to the site;
- material is sensitive and
- the site policy prohibits use of material

Although site users may be asked for blanket permission to use material when they sign on, they may have forgotten this or not realize the implications or assume that transactions are private. Particular care should be taken with children's contributions. The Association of Internet Researchers (AoIR) records particular hostility directed towards internet 'lurkers', but also resentment at being asked for permission to use existing material. The Association suggests using existing sites to recruit participants (always with the permission of the data controller), but creating dedicated websites for research.

Private e-mail exchanges have extended what Miller refers to as 'door knob conversations' (Miller 2012), those 'off the record' conversations which occur after the end of a formal interview after the recording device has been switched off. Retrospective consent can be obtained to include such data, provided that the participant has been fully informed about the study.

Privacy and confidentiality

The right to privacy is a key canon in educational research, whereby the anonymous and confidential treatment of participant data should be the norm (BERA 2011, p. 7). However, this right extends to other aspects of research, where complex issues can arise.

The first of these concerns research design. The SRA Guidelines warn against trivial or poorly designed studies which can waste participants' time and 'contaminate the field for future research' (SRA 2013, p. 25). In particular, poorly constructed questionnaires can be unnecessarily lengthy, ask intrusive questions and be culturally insensitive. It could be argued that no one has to complete a questionnaire, but researchers have to be on their guard to ensure that coercion or undue influence to complete is not present.

A further complexity arises in relation to the tension between the right to know and the right to privacy. This is particularly apparent in the contentious debate over covert research. The right not to be observed without fully informed consent is generally upheld in research ethics guidelines. BERA advocates the avoidance of deception 'unless the research design specifically requires it to ensure appropriate data is collected' (BERA 2011, p. 6) and the SRA defines this as a last resort, only where there is no other ethically sound way of collecting data (SRA 2003). However, this can be problematic in ethnographically based research or in studies involving control and experimental groups, where full information would skew findings. Pole and Morrison (2003) suggest seeing covert research as a matter of degree, differentiating between 'white lies' and 'whopping lies' during different research phases. A study title, for example, may refer generally to observation of teaching strategies, rather than gender differences within these. In such cases, full disclosure can be presented in the findings. However, if full covert observation can be justified, gaining consent from participants on a post hoc basis is recommended to minimize feelings of hurt and betrayal.

The demarcation between public and private spaces is also a problematic area. Permission does not have to be obtained to observe public activity in a public place. However, gatekeeper permission should be sought by researchers to carry out observation in any identifiably 'owned' space, such as schools, universities, sports grounds or playing fields. The degree to which consent can be gained from a large number of potential 'participants' in such situations is problematic. A next best option is to put up posters and hand out leaflets explaining the study taking place. A related issue concerns 'guilty knowledge' obtained from casual conversations or observations in public places, such as staffrooms, either overheard, or given as unexpected 'disclosures', sometimes referred to as 'bar-room conversations'. This is particularly pertinent in insider research, where the boundary between the roles of teacher and researcher may be blurred. It may be possible in such situations to gain fully informed consent after the event, through the usual procedures, and with a transcript of comments made. Otherwise, such data should be treated as background knowledge, rather than collected data, and should not be included in the study.

Ensuring confidentiality of data is, however, the main concern associated with the right to privacy, governed in the United Kingdom by the 1988 Data Protection Act. Although Section 33 of the Act effectively exempts personal information collected for research purposes, nonetheless data is only exempt if personal information is de-identified in publication and does not cause 'substantial damage or distress' (Bryman 2012, p. 137). Particular care needs to be taken with data which 'uniquely identifies' an individual, or is considered to be 'sensitive', including religious or political affiliation, sexuality, race or ethnic origin, and physical or mental health. One of the main points is that the law gives an entitlement to people to know how and why their personal information is stored, to what use it is being put and to whom it is being made available. Researchers must therefore seek participants' permission to disclose personal information to third parties. This has implications for obtaining consent to use individual (but not aggregated) pupil records in research. It also entitles participants to have access to personal data, whether in electronic or written form, through a Freedom of Information request.

Anonymity of participants should therefore be normally ensured in publication, unless specifically waived by participants. In some research, anonymity may be inappropriate – such as research based on interviews with key figures – or identification may be desired, for example, in showcases of good practice. However, if this is the case, care should be taken to ensure that there is no 'third party disclosure', that is, identification by association or reference in interview data, if not agreed by the person concerned. Anonymity of individuals is clearly not possible at interview, focus group or observation stage, but participants can be de-identified by the use of fictional names. Job roles and titles can also be used, but can identify individuals, if the context of the study is identifiable, and care should be taken not to identify participants by minority status, such as the only male primary teacher in a case study. Institutional contexts should also be de-identified as far as possible, by use of general labels ('a secondary school in Southern England') or pseudonyms. However, the more contextual data included, which aid depth and understanding, the easier it is to identify research locations, especially through powerful on-line search engines. Direct citations from an OfSTED report may, for example, be sufficient to identify a school. Transcripts of interviews should be coded and not bear names, with codes matching participant details kept separately in a locked filing cabinet. Electronically stored data should be password protected both in relation to the computer and individual files. If assistants are used to transcribe data, they should also complete a standard university compliance form to prevent 'leakage' of data. This can also be problematic in focus group work. Establishing a protocol with participants can mitigate this to some extent. E-mail exchanges are particularly problematic in terms of confidentiality, with few guarantees against hacking or forwarding data. Indeed, complete confidentiality can rarely be guaranteed, but all reasonable steps should be taken to try to ensure this.

Concerns about identifiablity in questionnaires are one of the most commonly expressed reasons for non-completion (Singer 2008). To guard against this, names, addresses and postcodes should not be asked, years of birth should be used rather than dates of birth and care should be taken to ensure that questions which would increase the risk of identification are avoided. Paper-based questionnaires can be returned through stamped addressed envelopes or a drop-box in a neutral location, such as a reception area, and can be coded, if matching data is sought. Again, coding should be deleted once data has been aggregated. While electronic surveys offer greater anonymity, they are more susceptible to completion by those with false identities.

Universities will have specific policies regarding data storage. Researchers are obliged to ensure confidentiality of data through safe storage, controlling access by others (including family members at home), data in transit and erasure of data after the completion of the study. It is usually recommended that files are encrypted, recordings are deleted on the request of the participant, and that back-up files are checked when deleting data (Oliver 2010). The period of data storage will be specified by the university and may be different for Doctoral than for Masters students. There is an increasing move towards data sharing through digital depositories, particularly at doctoral level. While open access to data has benefits to the research community, this also has implications for confidentiality and informed consent, and should be clearly stated in participant information documentation (Mauthner 2012).

Lastly, all research must be conducted within the remit of the law. If illegal behaviour is uncovered through research, disclosure of such behaviour to the appropriate authorities can override confidentiality assurances. Current child protection legislation in the United Kingdom and World Health Organization guidelines require that disclosure of all acts which could put children under the age of 18 at risk should be made immediately to the designated authority and that this overrides confidentiality agreements. Confidentiality of named or de-identified data is also subject to the limitations of the law in that it is possible for data to be subject to subpoena, Freedom of Information claims or mandated reporting by some professional bodies. Researchers are therefore advised to offer assurances of confidentiality, 'subject to legal limitations'.

Special considerations concerning research with children

The tenets of ethically sound research apply equally to adults and children. However, researchers are under a particular obligation to 'consider, respect and protect children's involvement in research' (Graham et al. 2013, p. 13). The 1989 UN Convention on the Rights of the Child makes no specific reference to research with children but has significant implications. Article 3 stresses that the best interests of the child should be of primary consideration, while Article 12 states that 'children who are capable of forming their own views should be granted the right to express their views freely in all matters affecting them' and that this should be 'commensurate with age and maturity' (BERA 2011, p. 6). This has led to a considerable shift in attitudes towards children, more research and consultancy with and by children and a greater range of research methods used with children (Alderson 2011). In particular, there is now a greater focus on children's competency in research. After wide international consultation, UNICEF has now published guidelines on ethical research involving children, designed to provide support for researchers and 'ensure that the dignity of children is upheld in research' (Graham et al. 2013, p. 6), while recognizing the dynamic tension which exists between protection, participation and provision.

The most contentious concern in this area is the 'age of consent'. Children are defined by the United Nations as those under 18, but the implications of the UNCRC are that children should be enabled to give their informed consent, wherever possible, and in recognition of their evolving capacity. If age or intellectual capacity limits understanding of what involvement in the research entails, the BERA Guidelines state that 'alternative ways to enable a response' should be sought, or those in a care giving or guardianship role may give consent on a child's behalf (BERA 2011, p. 6). To enable this, child-friendly information sheets or creative ways of enabling understanding can be designed (Kellet 2010; Alderson 2011). Parents also have a right to be informed about, and give consent to, research which involves their children, but this diminishes with age. For children under the age of 11 the idea of co-consent is useful, where the child acquiesces to the research with full knowledge and understanding, in addition to parental consent. For children and young people aged 12–17, much depends on the sensitivity of the topic under investigation and the methods being used. For low-risk studies, it may be appropriate for the pupil to give consent directly. However, for younger pupils in the age group it is always advisable to send an information letter to parents. Blanket consent by Head teachers on behalf of children is a dated, and arguably invalid, concept in the legal context created by the 1989 Children Act of England and Wales. Alderson and Morrow (2012) state that, 'teachers are "in *loco parentis*" but do not have parental responsibility. They can grant researchers access to children, but cannot consent to the research' (p. 105). This implies that gaining parental consent is strongly advisable, for the protection of the researcher.

The principle of 'opting in' can also be problematic for teachers conducting research within class time, whether consent is given by parents or children. If the activity the students are involved in is part of the normal curriculum, data should not be collected from those students who do not opt in. If the activity is an 'extra', then students should be allowed to slip out unobtrusively, although this could be seen to reward 'opting out' (Alderson 2011). Careful consideration should also be given to why the research is taking place within students' time and who stands to benefit from the research. If benefits are not short term or directly concern participants, this should be made clear to students (Alderson and Morrow 2011). Most pupils or students are keen to be consulted, but cynicism may set in if they do not perceive that there is 'something in it' for them. A particular problem arises with research based on control and experimental groups, for example, where a teaching method is introduced to enhance achievement levels. In such work, it may be advisable to run the experiment twice, swapping the roles of the groups, so that one group of students is not seen to gain advantage over another.

In addition to requirements concerning disclosure, children are at a particular risk of distress, humiliation, embarrassment or anxiety and this can sometimes catch researchers off-guard. For some children taking part in research can incur parental reprisals (Graham et al. 2013). To counter this, protocols for dealing with distress and a referral system, as necessary, should be clearly thought through before research commences. Children should also be invited to bring a companion to an interview, if they wish, and interviews should ideally take place in a location where participants can be observed, but not overheard. All researchers in the United Kingdom who have this level of contact with children are required to have a current Disclosure and Barring Service (formerly Criminal Records Bureau) or equivalent police check. Consent to use photographs is rarely mentioned in books or chapters on research ethics, perhaps because writers underutilize visual forms of presentation. Consent from parents and/or children should be obtained to use these, with a clear understanding of the use to which the photos will be put, or a pixelated format used. It is also advisable to check school or local authority policy concerning this.

The less powerful status of children in schools can sometimes lead to breaches of confidentiality, for example, staff 'dropping in' on focus groups, tidying cupboards in the background or reading questionnaire responses. Senior members of staff may also put pressure on researchers to release identifiable information from focus groups (Mockler 2007). Parents may also 'fish' for information from interviews. This should clearly be avoided, unless children are at risk, but can reflect the problematic blurring of role boundaries in practitioner research.

After data collection

Most textbooks on research methods pay scant attention to this final phase of the research, which can be particularly problematic for insider researchers. Pole and Morrison (2003) refer to 'getting in, getting on and getting out' in ethnography, but for the insider researcher, there is no exit door.

During the final stages of completion of the dissertation or thesis, there are some essential housekeeping duties: final checks on de-identification (including material in appendices), checking university policy on data storage and the erasure of recordings. Ensuring the integrity of the research through avoidance of distortion, falsification or exaggeration of results is also essential, along with a final check on the trustworthiness of the conclusions in relation to findings. A clear indication of dissemination of findings will have been given in the participant information sheet and, rather than expecting participants to read a lengthy thesis, a summary of findings can be offered by e-mail or through presentations to staff, pupils or parents.

However, once published, the very act of undertaking the research may well have had an effect on the 'ecology' of the school or institution. Interviews may have been used as 'confessional spaces' (Williams 2009), and although participants can retract information, the researcher still retains 'guilty knowledge'. Writers have queried whether there is not always an element of 'faking friendships' in establishing rapport in interviews and both parties have to deal with the consequences of this (Dunscombe and Jessop 2012). Possible feelings of hurt and betrayal on publication can be reduced if participants have been debriefed and involved in the research as it has progressed, but may disagree with the interpretation of data. Miller (2012) gives an example of how one participant in her research used a blog to comment (favourably) on the experience, a reflection of changed research relationships through technology. Feelings can linger for many years. In a rare article on the long-term aftermath of a research project, Beynon (2008) describes the 'snakes in the swamp' encountered 28 years after he conducted an ethnographic study of a secondary school as an external researcher. Invited back to a school anniversary reunion, he reflects on the way the research acted as a catalyst for personal and institutional change and relates that on publication of the book, a guessing game of teacher identities ensued among teachers, parents and pupils, despite careful de-identification. He questions when the researcher's ethical obligations end.

Conclusions

From this account, it is clear that 'thinking ethically' involves more than simply securing research ethics approval at the start of the research study. While an important stage in the research process, anticipatory ethical review cannot fully anticipate the twists and turns which may be encountered on the research journey. This is not to argue that being asked to consider potential ethical considerations at the start of a project is invalid. Indeed being required to be explicit about such considerations and receiving guidance from the project supervisor and research ethics personnel concentrate focus on ethical considerations right from the start. Properly done, this should integrate the concept of ethical practice into the project itself, making it an intrinsic part of the process element, rather than additional event.

No matter how modest a project, the same universalistic principles apply and should guide ethical decision making. Research does not take place in a social and cultural vacuum and its integrity depends on respect for the integrity of the people researched.

References

Alderson, P (2011). 'Ethics'. In Fraser, S, Lewis, V, Ding, S, Kellett, M and Robinson, C (eds.) *Doing Research with Children and Young People*. London: Sage.

Alderson, P and Morrow, V (2011) *The Ethics of Research with Children and Young People. A Practical Handbook*. London: Sage.

AoIR (Association of Internet Research) (2012) Ethical decision-making and Internet research. Reccommendations from the AoIR ethics working committee. Available on-line at: http://aoir.org/reports/ethics2.pdf. Last accessed on 17 July 2013.

BERA (British Education Research Association) (2011) Ethical Guidelines for educational research. Available on-line at: http://.bera.ac.uk. Last accessed on 19 June 2013.

Beynon, J (2008) Return journey: snakes in the swamp. *Ethnography and Education* 3(1): 97–113.

Bryman, A (2012) *Social Research Methods*, 4th edition. Oxford: Oxford University Press.

Cohen, L, Manion, L and Morrison K (2011) *Research Methods in Education*, 7th edition. London/New York: Routledge.

Doyle, D (2007) Transdisciplinary enquiry. Researching with, rather than on. In Campbell, A and Groundwater-Smith, S (eds.) *An Ethical Approach to Action Research: Dealing with the Issues and Dilemmas in Action Research*, pp. 75–87. London: Routledge.

Duncan, M and Watson, R (2010) Taking a stance. Socially responsible ethics and informed consent. In Savin-Baden, M and Howell Major, C (eds.) *New Approaches to Qualitative Research: Wisdom and Uncertainty*. London and New York: Routledge.

Dunscombe, J and Jessop, J (2012) 'Doing rapport' and the ethics of 'faking friendship'. In Miller, T, Birch, M, Mauthner, M and Jessop, J (eds.) *Ethics in Qualitative Research*, 2nd edition, pp. 29–42. London: Sage.

Edwards, R and Mauthner, M (2012) Ethics and feminist research: theory and practice. In Miller, T, Birch, M, Mauthner, M and Jessop, J (eds.) *Ethics in Qualitative Research*, 2nd edition. London: Sage.

Flick, U (2011) *Introducing Research Methodology*. London: Sage.

Gorman, S (2007) Managing research ethics. A head-on collision. In Campbell, A and Groundwater-Smith, S (eds.) *An Ethical Approach to Action Research: Dealing with the Issues and Dilemmas in Action Research*, pp. 8–23. London: Routledge

Graham, A, Powell, M, Taylor, N, Anderson, D and Fitzgerald, R (2013). *Ethical Research Involving Children*. Florence: UNICEF Office of Research Innocenti.

Gregory, I (2003) *Ethics in Research*. London: Continuum.

Hammersley, M (2009) Against the ethicists: on the evils of ethical regulation. *International Journal of Social Research Methodology* 12(3): 211–25.

— (2010) Creeping ethical regulation and the strangling of research. *Sociological Research Online* 15(4). Available on-line at http://www.socresonline.org.uk/15/4/16.html. Last accessed on 17 June 2013.

Hammersley, M and Traianou, A (2012) *Ethics and Educational Research*, British Educational Research Association on-line resource. Available on-line at: http://www.bera.ac.uk/resources/ethics-and-educational-research. Last accessed 18 June 2013.

Kellet, M (2010) *Rethinking Children and Research*. London: Continuum.

Macfarlane, B (2010) Values and virtues in qualitative research. In Savin-Baden, M and Howell Major, C (eds.) *New Approaches to Qualitative Research: Wisdom and Uncertainty*, pp. 19–28. London and New York: Routledge.

Mauthner, M (2012) Accounting for our part of the entangled webs we weave: ethical and moral issues in data sharing. In Miller, T, Birch, M, Mauthner, M and Jessop, J (eds.) *Ethics in Qualitative Research*, 2nd edition, pp. 157–75. London: Sage.

Mercer, J (2007) The challenges of insider research in educational institutions: wielding a double-edged sword and resolving delicate dilemmas. *Oxford Review of Education* 33(1): 1–17.

Miller, T (2012) Reconfiguring research relationships: regulation, new technologies and doing ethical research. In Miller, T, Birch, M, Mauthner, M and Jessop, J (eds.) *Ethics in Qualitative Research*, 2nd edition, pp. 29–42. London: Sage.

Miller, T and Bell, L (2012) Consenting to what? Issues of access, gate-keeping and informed consent. In Miller, T, Birch, M, Mauthner, M and Jessop, J (eds.) *Ethics in Qualitative Research*, 2nd edition, pp. 29–42. London: Sage.

Miller, T, Birch, M, Mauthner, M and Jessop, J (eds.) (2012) *Ethics in Qualitative Research*, 2nd edition. London: Sage.

Mockler, N (2007) Ethics in practitioner research. Dilemmas in the field. In Campbell, A and Groundwater-Smith, S (eds.) *An Ethical Approach to Action Research: Dealing with the Issues and Dilemmas in Action Research*, pp. 88–98. London: Routledge.

Oliver, P (2010) *The Student's Guide to Research Ethics*, 2nd edition. Maidenhead: McGraw Hill/Open University Press.

Pole, C and Morrison, M (2003) *Ethnography for Education*. Maidenhead: Open University Press.

Singer, H (2008) Ethical issues in surveys. In Dillman, D A, Hox, J J and de Leeuw, E D (eds.) *International Handbook of Survey Methodology*, pp. 78–96. London: Lawrence Erlbaum Associates.

SRA (Social Research Association) (2003) *Ethical Guidelines*. Available on-line at:

http://the-sra.org.uk/wp-content/uploads/ethics03.pdf. Last accessed on 20 July 2013.

Thomas G (2009) *How to Do Your Research Project*. London: Sage.

Williams, K F (2009) 'Guilty knowledge': ethical *aporia* emergent in the research practice of education development practitioners. *London Review of Education* 7(3): 211–21.

Discussion to Part III
John Morgan

Much research in geography education is Methodist. By this I mean that much discussion of research in geography education is subject to an ideology which encourages an overly respectful and unnecessary attention to questions of method. In turn, this promotes a minor publishing industry in research methods texts that promise to offer students (usually teacher-researchers) a step-by-step guide to going about research. There is a promise that paying attention to method will act as a recipe for success, though of course, like all recipe books, there is a clause that warns that recipes have to be adapted and made fit for purpose to the contexts (personal, social, geographical, cultural, etc.) in which the researcher works. Like all ideologies, Methodism holds power because it speaks to the needs and insecurities of those who are its targets.

Quite properly, Masters students undertaking 'research' in geography education are keen to ensure that their research is rigorous and of high quality. The problem is not identifying something worthwhile about their practice to research, but making sure that what they are doing is seen as 'research'. Methodism, with its heady mix of concepts and terms from philosophy (e.g. epistemology, ontology) and science (e.g. confidence levels, mixed methods), seems to offer a solution – rendering our hunches, observations and interpretations into something more authoritative (this may seem like an exaggeration, but it is not uncommon for highly capable and qualified geography teachers, when faced with the challenge of conducting Masters work, to inquire as to whether it is acceptable to write in the first person).

The attraction of Methodism in geography education is easily explained. Geography Education Research is a young field, with relatively low status in the academy. It suffers from 'status anxiety' about the products of its research. It tends to follow trends in education as a whole, which itself has relatively low status (if this is doubted, think about the precarious position that many Schools of Education occupy within Universities). There are few active researchers[1] in the field, many of us have only recently acquired doctorates, and a key part of that doctoral experience is to be inducted into a belief in the power of methods. In addition, because the field is populated by former schoolteachers and in universities is closely linked with teacher training, Geography Education Research has become closely geared to particular forms of practice. It is generally agreed that the goal of such research is to improve outcomes or, more generally, improve the quality of teaching and learning in classrooms. The dominance within educational studies of 'evidence-based' practice ensures that there is a search for reliable and verifiable evidence based on 'sound' methods.

I say all this because I think that the effects of Methodism on Geography Education Research are corrosive. Methodism tends to encourage conformity and a narrow focus on the types of questions that can be asked and researched. This ensures that there are few philosophical, historical or sociological studies of geographical education. As such, much research is education research rather than educational research[2] in that it seeks to 'problem-solve' rather than 'problem-pose'.

I have spoken plainly because this is a short comment intended to act as a frame for the three contributions to this part of the book. My hope is that those readers who read this prior to engaging with the three chapters will be attentive to any signs of Methodism. The chapters speak for themselves, so I will limit my comments to one substantive point about each.

Methodism is evident in all the contributions to this part of the book. Paul Weeden's chapter (Chapter 7) distils some of the advice offered in generic methods texts and shows how such advice might be applied and filtered specifically for geography teachers doing Masters level research. In reading the accounts of the two teacher-researchers described as they set about finding a question and deciding upon their methods, I wonder whether a crucial source of guidance is downplayed – that of the tutor or 'supervisor', who has the advantage of knowing and understanding the debates, arguments and questions in the field. Thus, one student reads a short article by David Hicks on futures education, and uses this as the basis for a study on year 8 pupils' views of the future, which requires the search for a suitable set of methods. In terms of my earlier comments, perhaps there is a need here to first appraise the wide range of work in Futures education, read about and reflect upon geography's possible relations to this field, and identify what it is that this research might add to the stock of knowledge in Geography Education Research. I am not suggesting that this did not happen in this case, but that this 'invisible labour' – which is central to any worthwhile research – is not evident in the reporting of this research project.

Mark Jones' chapter (Chapter 8) focuses on a particular 'technology' associated with research activity – the research proposal. He shows how this can act as a 'working document' that forms the basis of a discussion between the student and research supervisor. The categories listed by Jones should provide an aide-memoire and a rough checklist. The challenge in developing such a document is that it forms the basis of discussion and argument, rather than simply being seen as a hurdle to be jumped.

The inclusion of a chapter on research ethics reflects the rise of the Ethics Committee in many universities. There are important debates to be had on this phenomenon. In some institutions, ethics is wrapped up with the types of Methodism I have described here – as students try to guess what they have to do to satisfy a remote committee who sit in judgement. In others gaining ethics approval is seen as offering a chance to think and reflect upon important aspects of how to proceed in research. Maggie Wilson's chapter (Chapter 9) provides a useful and succinct overview of current developments. In many ways, the problem that Geography Education Research faces is captured in the second paragraph of Chapter 9: 'The generic nature of the issues identified in this chapter largely negate any necessity to make reference to specific aspects of research in geography education'. For me, this raises the question of whether research in Geography Education is simply a specialist version of education research, or whether there are specific concerns and issues related to the nature of our field. There is insufficient space to enter into this here, but in many ways this question encapsulates my overall worry about Methodism in Geography Education Research.

Notes

1. As indicated in submissions to RAE and REF exercises.
2. The distinction comes from Geoff Whitty (1974).

Part IV

Producing

Getting Underway with Your Research

Simon Catling

10

Chapter outline

Full-time or part-time	152
Preliminaries	152
Where you start: Motivation and focus	154
Initiating your research journey	155
Working with your supervisor	157
Developing your 'working rhythm'	159
Access, ethics and keeping colleagues informed	161
Being thoughtful and realistic about your research	162
The pleasures of being underway	166
Conclusions	167

You may well have come onto your Masters programme with a research topic in mind, perhaps investigating an area of your school's geography practice. Alternatively you may not have had a specific idea but have been stimulated to consider a topic during modules, or discussions with colleagues at school. Whatever your starting point, getting going on your research project requires some thought and several decisions. A number of the matters to consider (such as writing a research proposal, deciding on research methods and the place of theory) are examined in other chapters. Additional concerns which are important for you to think through include a variety of practicalities: such as how you will manage your time, where you do your research and with whom, working with your supervisor and work–life balance. You will need to recognize the possibilities and the limitations of your research. These, and related matters, are the focus of this chapter.

Full-time or part-time

Whether you are a full-time or a part-time Masters student has an impact on how you go about your research. If you are a *full-time* Masters student you can concentrate fully on your studies, though these will almost certainly involve attendance at (and assignments for) taught modules alongside working on your dissertation research – unless yours is an Masters by research only. You will need to juggle a number of commitments at the same time and balance your reading for a variety of topics, not least considering where and how you undertake your investigations. One advantage is that you can make use of the university's facilities and services. Another opportunity is that you may be in a group of full-time students, though not all may have the same subject focus as yourself, depending on the Masters course you are taking. Nevertheless, you will be able to share your experiences regularly, if you so choose, and be able to support and help each other.

> *I established a daily routine where I would be studying 8–12 and 1–5 and tried to fit some exercise into my day. . . . I also found myself part of a network of fellow researchers and their conversations about study and emotional support through the process was invaluable. I would advise anyone embarking on an Masters to seek out like minded colleagues for support.* [Sarah, a full-time geography education Masters student][1]

As a *part-time* Masters student you may well have more limited opportunities to share experiences and provide support, simply because during your dissertation year (when there may be no taught modules) you will be on campus less regularly and quite possibly at different times to many of your peers. It can be a lonely study year unless you have initiated a network of colleagues who you can email or phone, and even occasionally meet up to discuss your research. You are very likely to be working full-time and may have family commitments, so you will have personal support but also many demands on your time. There is much to ponder and plan for.

Preliminaries

> *The main limitations to the research were time and the limits of my expertise. . . . Also, despite reading and theoretically feeling comfortable with the decisions I had made, practically I felt like a novice* [Rachel]

It may be somewhat scary to embark on your geography education dissertation. It can seem quite a challenge to write 20,000 words which others may read and which says something informative and meaningful. How do you get going? You are aware of your own interest in a possible topic. You may have already read some previous research and debates in geography education, about gaps in the research, or even about research methods that have been used (see publications such as: Williams 1996; Butt 2011; Lambert and Jones 2013; Bednarz et al. 2013; Catling 2013). Having read the Masters course dissertation handbook, perhaps the next task, daunting though this is, might be to look at some previous geography dissertations – and in other subjects, depending on the nature of the Masters course you are doing – to see how they were structured and written. This can give you a number of pointers, such as what a dissertation looks like, what it contains and how it is organized. It helps to know where you are going and to create a road map through the research and writing up process.

Essentially undertaking and writing up your research is the focus of your geography education Masters dissertation project. There are some key components to your research-based dissertation, which you must acknowledge from the start. While there are variations in the way your dissertation finally be presented, you will need to cover the following (Walliman and Buckler 2008; Thomas 2009):

1. *Introduction*: The focus of your study and why it interests you; its value for yourself and others; the aims of your study and what you intend to investigate; a succinct outline of the sequence of the chapters.
2. *Literature review*: Who has debated and investigated your topic in the past, how they did this, what they found out, distilled, argued and concluded; the gaps in, shortcomings of or issues with previous research and debates; how this provides direction for your study.
3. *Research questions*: What your research focuses on; what your research questions are, and why these.
4. *Research methodology and methods*: What your research philosophy or paradigm will be; the context of your research and the subjects of your research (materials or people); the methods you will use to investigate your research questions, and why these are appropriate to use; reliability and validity in your research; ethics statement.
5. *Research findings*: What you have found out, perhaps accompanied by charts, graphs, diagrams, pictures, etc.
6. *Discussion*: What your findings indicate; the value of your findings; how these relate to the literature; implications that emerge and how these relate to practice; constraints in your research methods.
7. *Conclusion*: Conclusions you have drawn from your data and discussion, however tentative; your study's limitations; what future research might focus on.
8. *References*: The full list of sources you cited in your text.
9. *Appendices*: Other matters, not key to the text, which you consider important to include for the reader, such as questionnaires, background information or examples interview transcripts (anonymous).

Of course, your study may be philosophical or historical – such as examining the debates about geographical knowledge and their connections with a geography national curriculum – in which case you may focus fully on the literature and associated debates in your study. You might examine geography textbooks and their relevance to the curriculum, as 'desk-based' research, rather than undertake action research into aspects of your own geography teaching, or examine children's experiences or reflections on fieldwork, or enquire into the attitudes of geography teachers to the debate about climate change. The particular focus and structure of your research will reflect your interest, your preferred research and communication styles, and the expectations and requirements of the institution's course you take.

Where you start: Motivation and focus

> *I think it is really important to be clear about your motivations and make sure that your study excites and is relevant to you as well as your place of work. I was keen my dissertation would provide an evidence base for the positive impact of our Welsh residential in Year 6. However, I was keen to examine our assumptions of success and look at the reality of the experience for the participants – the challenges, constraints and opportunities. I think I had always known that I wanted to explore our residential experience, but discussions with my tutor and reading widely in a number of fields, e.g. geography, outdoor learning, spiritual education, etc, provided some background for my study and helped clarify my thinking.* [Sarah]

You may have entered your Masters course with a clear idea of what you intended to research. Perhaps this is your key motivation for taking the Masters. It is important that you are fully committed; you are going to live with this study for a year, day-in, day-out. It will be in your mind at all sorts of appropriate and inopportune times, so you need to value it highly, personally and/or professionally. It should matter to you as a contribution to the geography education community, especially if it will have an impact on your colleagues or pupils. Sometimes it takes a while to decide on a topic (Furseth and Everett 2013). This may come to you serendipitously and indirectly, rather than through wide reading and a clinical decision.

> *I found it very difficult to focus on a topic. I was very confused as to where to start. I was determined not to focus on the classroom environment, as I wanted something different to my day-to-day role of school improvement. Additionally I did not want to investigate my own subject area, or age specialism. In conversation with a colleague, the topic of Forest School was suggested; this was a new initiative within the local authority for early years and I really enjoyed the taster session I had experienced. I love the outdoors and realised I could use my research to spend time outside. This made the decision for me!* [Toni]

A major difficulty when deciding on what to research is that students often have a tendency to select something which is all-encompassing. For instance, perhaps you want to get to grips with key stage 3 assessment in geography or the variety of ways in which fieldwork with children in key stage 1 can engender geographical learning. An early requirement will be to refine and focus your study to one that is sharp and do-able (Walliman and Buckler 2008; Lambert 2012). The value for you is that you have the chance to research what you want to study, investigate and write about; it is your dissertation. The best advice is to reflect carefully on whether your topic really is what you want to research – but do not take too long on this!

Initiating your research journey

Many Masters' research journeys begin with the taught components of the course. If you are taking an Masters in geography education, you will be able to read around a number of aspects of the subject. Alternatively, you may be doing a more general Masters in education focusing on aspects of primary or secondary education; here the research module may well provide you with the chance to draft a research proposal for the geography topic you want to pursue, which you will need to refine when you meet your supervisor (Denscombe 2012). You are underway.

> *Before I started on my dissertation I had to prepare a 3,000 word proposal which outlined the rationale and context, literature review, research approach, design and schedule, highlighted ethical issues and concluded with a reflective commentary. This meant that before I embarked on the dissertation, I had a fairly clear idea of what I was aiming to do and how I needed to expand each section.* [Rachel]

This will have enabled you to start reading around your topic. From researching your module assignments you will already know your way around the library and be aware of its strengths and limitations, and of the support the librarians can provide. You are likely to be conversant with the online services you can use for e-journals and e-books, and you may well have undertaken an early article search using a search engine. At this point you still need to be fairly eclectic, seeking out and reading widely about what you think may have some bearing on your study. It will be as your research journey develops during your literature review that you start to refine your investigation.

By this point you will need to have a clear sense of the educational focus of your study. Potential areas for investigation in education are numerous (Lambert 2012) and all apply to geographical education research (Williams 1996). They include:

- *Policy and practice*: In what ways, why and with what effect does government influence the geography curriculum in schools in the education system?
- *Curriculum*: How is national curriculum geography reflected in your school's geography scheme or syllabus, and why is it in this way?

- *Organization*: How are responsibilities organized for geography teaching in your school? What impact does this have, on whom and why?
- *Teaching*: What is the variety of teaching methods used in your geography department? Do teaching approaches differ with age groups or subject requirements, and why is this? What would be the effect of changing practice?
- *Learning*: How effective is the use of gaming on students' learning in your geography lessons?
- *Resources*: In what ways are mobile devices extending or constraining access to geographical information, debates and other resources for your teaching? What influences opportunities to use these?
- *Other matters*: What is the status of geography in your school, why is this and how does it reflect and/or affect the ways in which colleagues value the subject?

An initial discussion with your dissertation supervisor will be about the educational context of your research. Which of the above are you interested in and/or focused on? Are you simply wanting to find out something, or is there a concern or problem you really want to look at? This is important, since it affects how you approach your study. It concerns the nature of your critical engagement with your topic. A descriptive study will be informative but it may provide limited insights. An early decision should be to take the role of a critical investigator, of the 'detective' who wants to dig, delve and worry about what is being researched. It is about getting 'under the skin' of your topic, since this way you are likely to develop an understanding of what is really going on, why this happens, whether there are ways forward and what they might be.

The next step is to begin work on your literature review (Thomas 2009; Lambert 2012; Furseth and Everett 2013). This means critiquing what you read as well as connecting, or seeing the dissonances between, different views and previous studies (Locke et al. 2010). Your role is to describe and relate what you read, as well as to be quizzical of the literature. If you have a research question in mind, this will help you to consider your reading more deeply and to sharpen, modify or replace your question. If you have not yet clarified your focus, your literature survey will enable you to identify a number of questions from which you can select your final research focus. This will be a key matter for discussion with your supervisor.

When considering writing your draft research proposal, it is important to get underway. Your first steps might be to describe your topic of study and to justify it, then to outline what you may have to do to complete this research. You may have a proposal assignment you can use as a starting point. To start to populate the blank screen you can do three things:

- First, using the outline of the dissertation sections above, set up each of the chapters and the reference list. This gives you an initial structure.
- Second, cut and paste relevant section of your proposal assignment to the relevant chapter headings. You may replace or rewrite these sections in time; that is normal, but they have started you off. Your literature chapter is likely to be the first you will develop and redraft.
- Third, begin to list your reading in the Bibliography or References section. This might include references which in the end you do not refer to; they can be deleted later.

It is surprising how good this simple start to writing can make you feel. You have captured some words, even if at the end of the dissertation you have replaced almost every one! This can be comforting and help to engender confidence, since, for both full- and part-time students, you are likely to feel daunted about writing at such length. You are building on what you already can do from your past assignments. What will surprise you nearer the end – possibly earlier – is how few 20,000 words are to account for all the elements in your study!

Working with your supervisor

The most crucial relationship you will have during your dissertation studies is with your supervisor (Walliman and Buckler 2008). Your first meeting is important since it often establishes the tone of your tutorials. You can help to set this up positively. It is normal for supervisors to be allocated to dissertation students, perhaps on the basis of their research proposal. S/he may be someone you do not know. If this is the case it makes sense to find out something about them, whether through the university's website or by talking to your fellow students. You may be nervous at this first meeting but it is normally the case that your concerns are allayed and a strong relationship develops, built on trust and openness. This is grounded in having confidence in each other, that you are serious about your research and that your supervisor is able to help and guide you to succeed.

> I did not know my supervisor, so had a quick look on the university website and read a couple of articles that he had written. I then contacted him to arrange our first meeting. I wasn't sure what to expect from our first supervision meeting and had not had a huge amount of sleep the night before (due to the children rather than nerves!). [Rachel]

For your first meeting it is essential to go prepared. This seems obvious but it does not always happen. It is important because what you will discuss is *your* dissertation, your ideas and the thinking you have already given to what you want to research. The focus, therefore, needs to be on the matters you want to raise to help you get properly underway. A good way to start is by introducing yourself and explaining something of your background, job, context and responsibilities. Then continue the conversation by explaining what it is you want to do and why. Your supervisor may have already read a draft of your proposal, so this will give you a chance to update her/him about your thinking. In the early stages, it is likely to involve reconstructing your proposal with their guidance (Denscombe 2012).

So, what should you be looking for in your supervisor? You will, hopefully, gain a sense quite quickly of their knowledge about and interest in your research topic. You are in a power relationship in which s/he has the upper hand, since they are likely to be one of the markers of your final submission and they will read and comment on your drafts along the way. You can make good use of their knowledge, understanding and skills by doing three things:

- E-mail in a chapter draft or a particular topic paper for discussion at each tutorial in good time beforehand, so that your supervisor can read it. Hopefully, s/he will have made some notes for themselves or even give you written feedback. This facilitates informed discussion. At your first tutorial set this pattern up by booking the next date and agreeing what you will do, send in and how feedback will be provided.

- Come to your second and subsequent tutorials with an agenda, particular points to raise and questions to ask, such as about aspects of work completed or pending and about appropriate literature to read for the next stage in your work.

- Take an approach in your tutorials that fosters a critical discussion of what you are doing. It should include support for what you have done, and it will provide guidance on what to do next. This is about enabling you to improve your work. Ideally, you will leave your tutorial more clear-headed and with an improved sense of direction, even when some of your work clearly needs to be changed.

> *I am quite independent and happy to go off on my own, yet I also need reassurance at fairly regular intervals that I am on the right track. My supervisor would suggest points along the research journey for us to meet and I would produce a draft in advance for these meetings so that he could read my work and provide feedback. As most of the feedback was written, this meant that we could spend significant proportions of the supervisions discussing issues in more depth which gave me a clearer understanding of the context of my research topic within the broader literature. I was keen to hear suggestions which would improve my research from someone with great experience. Again, I felt the balance was good between me having ownership of the research and making key decisions regarding it, but also being guided and flexible. I believe that the relationship between student and supervisor is crucial.* [Rachel]

Unfortunately, it is not always the case that the supervisor you work with is right for you. There can be difficulties in the power relationship between supervisor and student, though the example below is an extreme case. The point to take from it is that if you feel after a couple of meetings that you are not getting on with your supervisor, you should discuss this with the course leader. You need to be wary of mistaking a critique of your work for criticism of you. It can certainly feel uncomfortable but this may be a temporary emotional response rather than a deep-seated personality clash. A poor relationship – or none at all because you rarely meet – can be a real hindrance to researching and writing an effective dissertation.

> *I knew my supervisor but she was allocated to me; I did not choose her. I am a member of staff and so is she. She had a powerful position in my institution; that was a problem. She knew nothing on my specific topic and that was a problem. We had a difficult relationship. She had very fixed ideas about research. She was determined to put her stamp on the way I worked. In hindsight, I should have called it quits and asked for a different supervisor, but it was awkward. I did not have a relationship with my supervisor whereby I could go and ask for help or ask her to show me/teach me things. I would advise anyone to find a supervisor who they feel will be a critical friend, not just critical, but who is also willing to pass on knowledge about research and teach you.* [Erin]

Remember that the purpose of your tutorials is to enable you to seek advice on your literature reading, the research question(s), your research methods, your data and what emerges from it, and on expressing your conclusions. Working with your supervisor develops as you get to know each other through the tutorial experience. This is a good reason for ensuring that you have regular meetings. They need to be sensibly spaced out so that you can complete tasks but also take account of both of your commitments. Your supervisor has only a limited time allowance allocated for you, though they will often give more; this includes reading your work, not just meeting you. Before meetings it is vital to check and confirm arrangements. Remember that your supervisor has a variety of responsibilities, including teaching, management, their own research and supervising other research students. S/he may also work part-time.

> I think the supervisor–researcher partnership is very important; it needs to be based in an honest and open relationship. I remember looking forward to my tutorials as I knew that they would move my study forward, but they were challenging as they were one-to-one, so there was nowhere to hide. At times I felt daunted and anxious about my lack of research experience in the face of the 'knowledgeable expert'. I think these tutorials made me realise that there was not a right or wrong answer when you are creating/researching an aspect of professional practice. I also felt that through his tutorial style my supervisor gave me full ownership of the study and this meant I felt I could be creative. I found this motivating and it helped sustain me when the process became challenging at times. [Sarah]

Developing your 'working rhythm'

There are four important matters to ponder as you begin work on your dissertation. One is that this is not your whole life, but that it is an important part of it for a year or so. Another is about resolving how you work best, and the other concerns your time management. First, though, reflect on your attitude to your research; are you determined to enjoy it, or is it just a large assignment you have to do? Remember you are human: you will feel more motivated some of the time and less at others.

> I think it is very important to maintain a work-life balance. I found it is often in the 'down times' when swimming a length of the pool or out for a walk when the 'eureka moments' came to help to move the study forward. [Sarah]

Your work–life balance is important. While for a few students researching and writing might be viewed as a 'leisure activity', for many it is a second area of work. You need to retain a social life. Clearly, your 'day job' as a teacher, lecturer or advisor, perhaps, will take up the bulk of your working day; there are all the usual and some unexpected things to do.

It is essential to set aside time for your research studies. You will need to discuss your studies with family and friends and make decisions about how you manage the balance between them. This will vary during the year, with deadlines for drafts demanding more time for study to be set aside, while you may retain your regular involvement with a local sport's team or orchestra, for instance. It may be that unless something urgent occurs you keep your weekly commitments in your schedule. You need time to relax, and you will benefit periodically from taking a complete break from your analysis and writing (for a week or so). You need to plan for this, not leave it to chance.

> *I gave up a few things and devoted weekends to it. I was very well supported at home and had an on-the-spot proof reader who proved invaluable.* [Erin]

Knowing how you work best will enable you to plan. One approach is to draw up a chart that includes elements of your study and the times you think they will take; mark these on a monthly calendar, so that you can see how you expect this to work out across the year (Thomas 2009). It is self-discipline and self-motivation which will enable you to work to this timetable. You already have a good sense of your working rhythms, whether you are a morning or evening person, where you like to work in and outside home, whether you like absolute quiet or to have music on low in the background, and for how long you feel comfortable working on a task or a problem – remember to take breaks! Establish routines which enable you to integrate your research with your working and domestic lives. Remember that your best-laid plans can be upset and you may have to re-plan your timings at set points. If you find that your way of working is not going well, talk it through with peers or your tutor to see how you might make changes that benefit you.

> *I tended to focus on deadlines – I was not very good at the 'little and often' approach. I needed the pressure of handing in work to galvanise me into action! I continued with my sporting activities throughout the research (unless deadlines were looming).* [Toni]

You need to be focused in setting time aside and managing it (Walliman and Buckler 2008). It helps to set targets for yourself, which tutorials may influence. These might focus on reading one or more articles or chapters and making notes, or be for drawing your thoughts together on what you have read or researched so far. You can use a range of approaches when doing this, since variety helps in thinking matters through and in enabling concentration. Use brainstorming, listing key points, creating charts and drawing mind maps to help you. You can arrange to discuss your reading or research methods with others; think through a problem, letting it gel for a few days; make notes on what emerges. You can return to your records and highlight key ideas, edit, revise or delete points later. For some people doing such activities little and often, daily perhaps, for 30–45 minutes works very well, while for others devoting 3–4 hours on particular days or longer at weekends and in holidays is their preference. If you need to negotiate set times weekly and blocks of days ensure that family and friends know why you need this time; they will appreciate you are serious and will be supportive.

Access, ethics and keeping colleagues informed

You may well have received workplace support to undertake your Masters, possibly with both time and funds being made available. There are a number of reasons why the support of your leadership team and colleagues is important. One concerns permissions and ethics. If you are investigating your own or colleagues' teaching practices or pupils' geographical learning, it is important that they know and appreciate what you are doing. Not least you will need their agreement, which might also include parents being informed or asked to agree. Gaining informed consent is crucial for ethical reasons (see Chapter 9). Normally there will be no issue about your research with other people, but you must check this with your supervisor and possibly the ethics tutor in the university's department. Almost certainly you will need to submit an ethics approval form with your dissertation. This is best done as early as possible in your research programme. Its purpose is to safeguard both you and your subjects from any suspicion of exploitative relationships, particularly researching with children you teach (Walliman and Buckler 2008). Chapter 9 provides detailed advice about the ethics of research.

> *I worked with students who I had access to on a regular basis. There are ethical issues with this and I had to explore these carefully in terms of power and agency in my work but I made sure I was very transparent and shared all the findings with the students. I had to gain the consent of every student taking part and I had to share my research intentions with them all. They were all given the option to not take part.* [Erin]

The support of your workplace leadership team may well enable you to access documents and other information that might not readily be available. Perhaps data held centrally would be informative to your analysis. Being able to access this and use it responsibly, so that for instance identities remain anonymous, might help you to explain influences on the topic you study or on those who have been the subject of your research. One example might be data related to assessment outcomes in internal school geography tests or public examinations. Another might concern children's access to and engagement in field trips, whether linked to family financial constraints or to behavioural matters. It can mean that you receive information when normally you might not expect to.

> *I was supported by the Head teacher and staff for my research. Many of the staff showed an interest in the study as they could see that what I was doing would hopefully impact on school practice as I hoped not only to review existing provision but make suggestions for future developments in our residential practices.* [Sarah]

If you research your own and/or colleagues' practices – perhaps you want to investigate the effectiveness of curriculum development in a geography department or across a primary school – they will be more likely to support you and engage with your research if they are informed and understand the reasons for your study. An early need, therefore, is to explain to colleagues what you are doing, why and how they can help you. This might be at a departmental or staff meeting. You may find colleagues are both interested and more forthcoming, which would provide deeper insights for your research. Sending interviewees copies of the questions before you meet, so that they give them some thought and even make some notes, enables you to probe more fully into their responses, thus gaining richer data. You can set up such opportunities from the start of your studies by outlining to others what you hope to do and updating them as you make progress. It can help you to maintain deadlines for your research agenda if you agree early on provisional dates for classroom observations and interviews, or arrange for a colleague to cover for you while you visit another site.

Informing workplace colleagues can also provide you with one of your support networks. While they may not be directly involved, since your study does not involve them, they may well be interested and possibly able to offer help. Discussions, of your initial proposals or aspects of your research journey, can be supported by outsiders asking questions and giving reflections. Others may provide insights which you may miss because of your proximity to the research. This network can be an invaluable sounding board to enable you to test your ideas – even vent your frustrations – from time to time, alongside your discussions with your supervisor.

Being thoughtful and realistic about your research

There is much to consider in undertaking a research study, which Chapters 7, 9 and 11 provide you with the background to do. Walliman and Buckler (2008, 57–8) identify six features of your dissertation research to be clear about. The first has been noted already, but the rest are equally important.

- It should be of great interest to you;
- The problem should be significant;
- It should be delineated;
- You should be able to obtain the information required;

- You should be able to draw conclusions related to the problem;
- You should be able to state the problem clearly and concisely.

Your research must be manageable. Remember that time is short. You may not really begin until October, when you have had your first supervision. You are likely to have to submit at the start of the following September. If you have a holiday in August, how do you ensure that your penultimate draft is ready for checking when you come back? You need to use common sense in selecting a topic, and consider whether your study is fit for purpose, robustly researched and useful – rather than simply completing your qualification requirements.

> *It was difficult to take a neutral stance as the Local Authority was promoting the initiative (Forest School), and the setting supervisor was very enthusiastic about the project. This could have been a source of tension.* [Toni]

- Validity needs to be true to the type of research, that is, in qualitative and quantitative studies it does not mean the same thing.
- Valid research is deemed to have some or many of these qualities: rigour, authenticity, replicability, disinterestedness, controllability, objectivity and richness.
- Interpretations of the data must follow from the data, being consistent and defensible.
- It requires the 'measuring instrument' to measure what it says it does.
- *Construct validity*: the methods used are appropriate to the matter under investigation.
- *Internal validity*: establishing, describing and explaining causal relationships.
- *External validity*: relating the findings to similar studies to consider generalizability.
- Be wary of attributing causation without very clear, indeed irrefutable evidence – social science research involves people, so there can be many factors to take into account, some of which cannot be catered for. Irrefutable evidence is very hard to come by.
- There are challenges the role of various 'terms' considered useful in judging validity, for example, plausibility, credibility, relevance, significance, comprehensiveness, confirmability, auditability . . . (Thomas 2011, pp. 64–5). Be wary of your understandings, meanings and uses of these terms as 'criteria'. Judgements and preferences are inevitably involved.

Figure 10.1 Some aspects of validity (see Thomas 2009; Newby 2010; Cohen et al. 2011; Robson 2011; Arthur et al. 2012)

It is argued that a research study will only be of value if it is as objective as possible and if the researcher is evidently neutral. The situated nature of research, such as in a particular school or geography class, raises questions about the meanings of objectivity and neutrality. It is usually asked of a piece of research how *valid* and *reliable* it is. These are reasonable questions, but the answers can depend on the interpretations of these terms. Thomas (2009, 2011) challenges the over-emphasis on validity and reliability and criticizes research students for becoming hung up about them. While these concepts are undoubtedly important, he argues that they are not the be-all and end-all of research. Discuss how rigidly or openly your tutor and yourself conceive of them. In effect, agree on the ways in which the research should be consistent (reliable), well-grounded, properly and formally carried out, acceptable and defensible (valid), so that it can be trusted and seem to be informative and helpful (see Figures 10.1 and 10.2). This is about the accountability of your research (Denscombe 2002). Newby (2010) argues that it concerns convincing others that what is found out is worthwhile knowing. He sees validity and reliability as the 'corner stones' of research. These two constructs help you to ensure that your research conclusions are credible and trustworthy.

- 'The extent to which a test or procedure produces similar results under similar conditions on all occasions' (Bell 2010, p. 119).
- Reliability can be seen as a precondition for validity.
- Reliability provides sound and consistent quality that can be relied on.
- Some of the qualities of reliable studies include: consistency, replicability, accuracy, dependability, stability, equivalence, comparability, transparency and best fit.
- The research 'instrument' should do what is required of it.
- Another researcher doing a comparable study in a similar way should be likely to obtain similar results. Thus, if the same methods are used but different results appear each time, the measure is probably unreliable.
- *Test–test reliability*: 'the same test given by different people to the same group would produce very similar results each time' (Thomas 2009, p. 105).
- *Inter-rater reliability*: knowing that 'the measure you are using is accurately assessing the feature or activity on which you are focusing' (Thomas 2009, p. 106).
- *Quantitative research* largely relies on reliability, with consistency in data collection for statistical comparisons.
- *Interpretivist research* concerns itself with identifying suitable methods for a study, where reliability is about such matters as insight.
- In singular studies, such as case studies, reliability may have little relevance since the study is a 'one-off', but inter-rater reliability can remain important.
- Be wary of such matters as bias and errors, which are matters of evaluation not of the research 'instrument' used. They concern how it was applied.
- In qualitative studies interpretation and 'subject' engagement may have an influence and impact. This need not mean that a study is not reliable. It requires that the researcher's 'position' or 'situatedness' is explicit, as is the focus of the study. It can mean, quite fairly, that reliability is not material to the study.

Figure 10.2 Some aspects of reliability (see Thomas 2009; Newby 2010; Cohen et al. 2011; Robson 2011; Arthur et al. 2012)

Perhaps the test of good and useful research rests in its truthfulness? Given that any particular research with a set of students or teachers cannot be replicated directly – since these are individual case studies – it may well be that what is found out provides insights and understandings which are of value to others and might be similarly investigated in other contexts. What is most important is that those who read, and even replicate, a research approach have trust in what has been done and sense its veracity – its reliability and validity – even though there may be different outcomes. What this may tell the researcher and reader is that this is a complex area of study, and that since it involves human subjects, it is not simply repeatable in the way a specific scientific experiment might be. If validity and reliability are interpreted more liberally, linked to trustworthiness and truthfulness, as Figures 10.1 and 10.2 indicate, they can be invaluable to 'test' the worthiness of research. You can help yourself by being explicit about your stance and perspectives at an early stage in developing your research questions, considering your methodological position and in selecting and constructing your methods of research. It will be important to remain consistent throughout your dissertation study and writing.

> *As it was an interpretive study I was more concerned about truthfulness, and I ensured I was as robust as possible in this area by asking the students to read their own interview transcripts and to validate them. My stance in the research was situated. Essentially I wanted to discover where I fitted into the students' geographical picture and whether I had any effect on their perceptions of geography. It was quite challenging to be part of the study and yet stand back to see the larger picture.* [Rachel]

Be wary of having too closed an approach to your research topic by thinking you should be clear from the start about exactly what you want to find out, as though all you have to do is indentify the correct literature and methods to answer your research question. Hopefully your supervisor will disabuse you of this at an early point. Having a good sense of your research question is vital, but you need to read the literature as widely as practicable so that you can refine your question – by which point it may well not be quite what you first thought. Once a reasonable question has been agreed, you can consider your methodology and the methods of investigation you will use. It can be tempting to decide the methods you will use at a very early stage, but this rushed approach leads to poor research and a problematic outcome. The advice is not to start gathering your data until you have understood your methodology and which methods are best to use.

> *I undertook semi-structured interviews on two separate occasions with the six case study students and embarked on this by first reading generic literature regarding research methods and then more specific literature regarding interviews. This helped me to clarify in my own mind and justify the decisions that I made. Having read a bit I initially felt that these decisions were fairly straightforward, but then I would read something else that cast doubt or was critical of these decisions. I made sure that I piloted my interview schedule before I embarked on the research and this allayed my fears somewhat.* [Rachel]

Self-discipline and an ordered approach help you to achieve a much stronger study in the long run. Part of this concerns your approach to reading both the literature and methodology/methods texts. From the start you should make notes and organize these so that you can find things readily. These may be in files on your hard drive or, as some still do, in a card index. Keep noting questions about what you read, about other literature you need to read and identify gaps into which your study might fit. If you read a challenging text – and you will come across these, probably in your methodology/methods reading – read and re-read until you can explain it to yourself. A good way to see what you have understood is to write it in your own words! This way you will become conversant with what a case study is, or participant observation, or how to draft questionnaires or construct observation schedules. In doing this, make full records of your references, using a file such as Endnote, to ensure you do not have to go searching for titles or the page numbers for quotations at the last minute.

> *As a result of my proposal I already had a fairly clear idea of what I needed to read and I felt it was important that the research was grounded clearly in the literature. When I embarked on the dissertation itself I started with the literature review. Once I had a fairly good literature review in place I started on the methodology. However, I continued to read and refine the literature review throughout the process. I think it can be quite tempting to launch straight into the data collection phase but I think it is very important to get the foundations in the literature and methodology literature right first.* [Rachel]

> *As a participant observer I was aware that I had to be clear about the purposes of my research, the nature of my data collection and the ethics with the teacher leading the residential and also with the participants. I had just one week to complete the data collection so I had to be prepared. As it was a study of one residential visit there was no opportunity to collect more data as a return to the site with the participants was not possible. So the data collection procedures had to be well planned and thought through.* [Sarah]

Some challenges which you might encounter can be overcome by doing such things as booking a session with the education librarian to learn how to make the most of the library services available or by asking for help from computer services staff. This can seem obvious in that perhaps you have used the library for assignment reading, but there is likely to be more use which you can make of it for dissertation research purposes. Problems like book access (where there is no e-book version) can be overcome by reserving books and working to the deadline you have them for, since these are likely to be popular! Internet searches are another way to enhance your access to resources (Ó Dochartaigh 2012).

The pleasures of being underway

> *Probably the most enjoyable aspect of my research project was the feeling of being a student again, the feeling of scholarship. I would go to the university library and spend several hours reading which, firstly, gave me some time out from my rather hectic life and, secondly, made me reminisce about my days as an undergraduate. I also realised how much I enjoy and how much I missed writing.* [Rachel]

Getting underway with research, while challenging, brings pleasures too. One might be that you have given yourself permission to return to study – to do something which you enjoyed either recently, or a while back. You might also feel gratified that you are undertaking a study in a topic which is important to your work professionally as a geography teacher, or teacher educator. It can be invaluable to give yourself time to sit and read theoretical and practical texts in geography, geography education and wider educational studies, to spend time in the library or online searching for new reading, or making time to discuss what you are doing with your course peers, work colleagues or friends. You make the time to think more deeply about a matter you value, (re)considering questions you may have set aside and which can open up areas of your practice to self-scrutiny. You may find informative links in your research to your teaching, even from your earliest reading. It may be that as you start to write you find that you enjoy not just the 'mark making' but trying to distil your reading of the literature into your own text, or making sense of a research paradigm, or constructing the questions for an interview and piloting them successfully.

> *I thoroughly enjoyed the reading aspect of the research – exploring the field and developing my understanding. The best part, however, was the contact with people – interviewing staff and observing the children respond to the woodland environment.* [Toni]

Conclusions

This chapter has focused on the practicalities of starting on your research journey, not by giving you a simple set of rules by which to undertake your Masters dissertation but through considering some of the matters to be aware of and offering a variety of ways in which you might respond to these. It has been intentionally discursive, since these matters interleave and no lengthy list of 'dos' and don'ts' provides a straightforward overview that will resolve the range of matters you need to consider from the start of your journey to completing a successful dissertation.

In conclusion, it is worth leaving the last word to those past successful Masters students who have provided the vignettes that have appeared through this chapter. They are informative and borne out of experience. There are three pieces of advice to note first:

- Be committed, that is, be serious about your research, be organized and value what you do.
- Be proactive with your supervisor; it is your study, so maintain control of it through doing the thinking, preparation and enquiring in tutorials.
- Read methodically and thoroughly; you cannot beat knowing your topic as fully as you can.

- *Choose a topic you are passionate about. You will be more likely to enjoy the process and, if you enjoy it, it won't seem like such hard work.*
- *Once you have a clearly defined topic, it is worth being systematic.*
- *Above all, read widely. You don't necessarily need to read, deconstruct and critique everything but you need to know how your research fits into the wider literature landscape and you need to be able to critique a few main papers.*
- *Try to engage your supervisor in a way which suits the way that you work.*
- *Read the literature on methodology as thoroughly as you read the literature of your literature review. It is vital that you structure and justify your methodological decisions from the beginning.*
- *Save everything in at least two places.*
- *Read a range of dissertations, good and bad. I began to appreciate the features that made a good piece of work and tried to incorporate these into my writing. I could see things that didn't work quite so well and tried to avoid these.*
- *Work little and often.* [Rachel]

- *Everything takes longer than you think – each stage needs realistic time planning.*
- *Be meticulous in your reference keeping. I lost the page number for one quote and it took me several hours to find the correct citation.*
- *Maintain a network of family and friends; their support will be invaluable when times are challenging.* [Sarah]

- *Listen to your supervisor's advice on reading and approaches – they will (probably) have supervised many previous students and know the way things work. A good supervisor will provide structured support and clear guidance about how to go about your research.*
- *Use online databases to find relevant journal articles.*
- *Keep your mind open to additional avenues to explore.*
- *Consider carefully how your position will influence people participating in your research: no relationship is ever neutral.*
- *Plan your work carefully and stick to it. Keep reviewing your progress against your timetable and make adjustments as you go. Do keep to deadlines set by your supervisor. . .They need time to read your drafts. Leave plenty of time for writing up – its always takes longer than you anticipated!* [Toni]

And the last word:

I knew that I wanted to do something around my subject, geography, rather than something which was generic. Partly this is because it is the love of my subject which motivates me, but also because I wanted something to say to the geographical education community. I did some initial reading and stumbled across Hopwood (2009), probably more by luck than judgement! I started to read more about student perspectives of geography and had a 'light bulb moment' when I knew that this was the area which I wanted to research. I realised I wanted to focus on perspectives of geographical knowledge, mainly because I realised I would find this interesting but also because there were significant gaps in the literature. [Rachel]

Note

1. This chapter draws on the experience of dissertation research by four successful Masters students, three of them geographers and one a scientist fascinated by the outdoors. They are identified only by pseudonyms. One was a full-time Masters student, who took secondment from school; the others worked in school or teacher education while undertaking their studies part-time. Two have primary and two have secondary backgrounds. I appreciate very much and am most grateful to them for providing their case studies, which reflect on the initial and early stages of their research journeys. All of them have gone on to further postgraduate study! Chapter 12 provides accounts of case studies of research journeys which complement this chapter.

References

Arthur, J, Waring, M, Coe, R and Hedges, L (eds.) (2012) *Research Methods and Methodologies in Education*. London: Sage.

Bednarz, S, Heffron, S and Huynh, N (eds.) (2013) *A Road Map for 21st Century Geography Education: Geography Education Research*, A Report from the Geography Education Research Committee of the Road Map for 21st Century Geography Education Project. Washington, DC: Association of American Geographers. http://natgeoed. org/roadmap. Accessed 22 May 2013.

Bell, J (2010) *Doing Your Research Project*. Maidenhead: McGraw-Hill.

Brooks, C (ed.) (2010) *Studying PGCE Geography at M Level: Reflection, Research and Writing for Professional Development*. Abingdon: Routledge.

Butt, G (ed.) (2011) *Geography, Education and the Future*. London: Continuum.

Catling, S (2013) Editorial: the need to develop research into primary children's and schools' geography. *International Research in Geographical and Environmental Education* 22(3): 177–82.

Cohen, L, Manion, L and Morrison, K (2011) *Research Methods in Education*. Abingdon: Routledge.

Denscombe, M (2002) *Ground Rules for Good Research*. Maidenhead: Open University Press.

— (2012) *Research Proposals: A Practical Guide*. Maidenhead: Open University Press.

Furseth, I and Everatt, E (2013) *Doing Your Master's Dissertation: From Start to Finish*. London: Sage.

Hooley, T, Kulej, M, Edwards, C and Mahoney, K (2009) *Understanding the Part-Time Researcher Experience*. Cambridge: Vitae.

Hopwood, N (2009). UK high school pupils' conceptions of geography: research findings and methodological implications. *International Research in Geographical and Environmental Education* 18(3): 185–97.

Lambert, D and Jones, M (eds.) (2013) *Debates in Geography Education*. Abingdon: Routledge.

Lambert, M (2012) *A Beginner's Guide to Doing Your Education Research Project*. London: Sage.

Locke, L, Silverman, S and Spirduso, W (2010) *Reading and Understanding Research*. Thousand Oaks: Sage.

Newby, P (2010) *Research Methods for Education*. Harlow: Pearson.

Ó Dochartaigh, N (2012) *Internet Research Skills*. London: Sage.

Robson, C (2011) *Real World Research*. Chichester: Wiley.

Thomas, G (2009) *How to Do Your Research Project*. London: Sage.

— (2011) *How to Do Your Case Study*. London: Sage.

Williams, M (ed.) (1996) *Understanding Geographical and Environmental Education: The Role of Research*. London: Cassell.

Walliman, N and Buckler, S (2008) *Your Dissertation in Education*. London: Sage.

Doing Your Research Project 11

Liz Taylor

Chapter outline

The project in practice: Ensuring a consistent approach	171
Reviewing literature: Locating your work in the research landscape	173
Data collection: Finding out	176
Data analysis: Sorting out	180
Communicating findings: Creating a story	182

Chapters 8 and 10 in this volume explore the process of writing a proposal and getting underway with the research project. This chapter addresses the practicalities of carrying out a project: ensuring a consistent approach through all elements of your research; locating your project in the literature; selecting and using appropriate techniques of data collection and analysis; and establishing your findings. In each section, there will be an overview of key issues for consideration then suggested readings to enable you to explore each element in more detail.

The project in practice: Ensuring a consistent approach

The research project is most likely to be both manageable and useful if it flows naturally from your teaching concerns and interests. For example, if part of your current role involved designing and teaching a new scheme of work on meteorology, then you might choose to focus your research on an aspect of that process (such as planning for medium-term progression, identifying and addressing subject knowledge misconceptions or integrating effective assessment techniques). A project which arises from your work is also likely to be under your direct control, which aids the smooth implementation of the research process.

When planning the detail of your project, the research questions are important as a basis for organizing your whole approach. Well-planned research ensures congruence between research questions, theoretical lens (or paradigm), research strategy (methodology) and practical methods of data collection and analysis. Careful consideration of each choice at planning stage, and then as the project progresses, will reduce the likelihood of inconsistencies in the final thesis. For example, there would be inconsistency if a researcher claimed they had taken an interpretivist theoretical approach (concerned with gaining a deep understanding of meaning in a complex situation) but then the data collection and analysis appeared to be informed by post-positivism (concerned with pursing objectivity and seeking to eliminate bias through an experimental approach).

The choice and wording of the research questions therefore becomes crucial, as everything in your data collection, analysis and findings should flow from them (Figure 11.1). For example, in Megan Brook's study of year 13 students' learning about development over a scheme of work informed by university-level geography (Brooks 2013), the empirical research questions she chose meant that a particular theoretical perspective, methodology and methods were appropriate (Figure 11.2).

Read on to: Chapter 1 of Crotty (2003) or Creswell (2013) to inform your thinking on research approaches suitable for different purposes and how each element of the research can fit together.

As the research progresses, it is not uncommon to reach a point where you sense some disjunction between the research questions and the data you are starting to generate. When this happens, either the questions or your methods need to be adjusted. It may be that the wording of a particular question needs to be refined to reflect more fully your initial meaning, or maybe a method needs adjustment to ensure you will gain the data needed to answer the question. Your supervisor will be able to advise further with this process.

As you plan and undertake your research, it is important to keep a careful record of your decisions, reasoning and progress. A research diary is often used for this purpose. A range

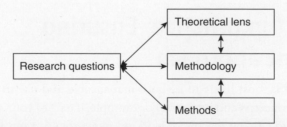

Figure 11.1 Relationship between research questions and theory, methods and methodology

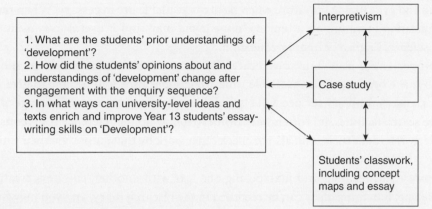

1. What are the students' prior understandings of 'development'?
2. How did the students' opinions about and understandings of 'development' change after engagement with the enquiry sequence?
3. In what ways can university-level ideas and texts enrich and improve Year 13 students' essay-writing skills on 'Development'?

Interpretivism

Case study

Students' classwork, including concept maps and essay

Figure 11.2 Example of research questions and their link to theoretical perspectives, methods and methodology

of formats for the diary can be effective (digital or manual; full written notes or jottings and diagrams). It can be used to remind yourself of questions for your supervisor, to make notes from discussions with them and to record important insights from your work in school or from your reading. For example, notes there can remind you about your choice of participants, or the impact on your planning of a particularly relevant reading.

Read on to: Chapter 2 of Altrichter et al. (2008) includes useful ideas and advice for creating a research diary.

Reviewing literature: Locating your work in the research landscape

The literature review stage has two main purposes in terms of the emerging research project. Firstly, it is clearly wise to acquaint yourself with what has already been written in your chosen field so that you can learn from previous practice. Secondly, a survey of existing literature will show where there is a need for further work and will suggest what form this might take. Often writers will highlight further needs in the conclusions of their own work. Small-scale research does not need to be completely novel; understanding of a topic can be moved on by trying out someone else's practice in a different context. Whatever the aim of your project, you need to locate it in the landscape of prior research.

To undertake the review, you will need skills of locating and accessing appropriate literature. Journal articles (on-line or hard-copy) and books are likely to be your main sources, but you may also need to draw on reports, conference papers or audio-visual sources. For some topics, for example, research on the role of gender in education, the potential set of available literature is very large. For other topics, for example, young people's understandings of coastal processes, it is small. Skills of searching out literature on more obscure topics, or sifting and prioritizing literature when plenty is available are necessary. When the geography education literature on a topic is limited, you may find it useful to consult similar work in science, English or history education.

It is important to plan your search carefully, using your initial research questions as a guide, to make best use of the available time. Your supervisor will be able to give further guidance, and your library service will also be able to help you to access the range of online literature search facilities. It is often worthwhile to follow up the reference sources used by a particularly relevant article, and also to check other work by that author via their university web page, if they have one.

The process of reading, and juxtaposing one text with another, can be a creative and enjoyable one. Emerging ideas can be recorded in the research diary, and you may find that initial research questions need amendment as a result of your reading. It is also important to keep careful records of literature as you read, including references and page numbers for potential quotations. An article record form can be helpful in disciplining this process (see example in Figure 11.3). Such records can also speed up the process of ordering and grouping literature when writing the final review. Additionally, some students like to keep their own electronic or hard copies of journal articles to avoid lengthy trips to check details later on (your library will be able to advise on copyright restrictions).

In a Masters thesis, the literature review should demonstrate familiarity with the field (but not necessarily exhaustive coverage of larger fields) and a sound understanding of the key terms and ideas. Critical engagement with previous research methods and outcomes is very important. For each article you read, you should ensure that you are noticing key details of the research including when it was carried out (this may be some time before the

Article reference:	
What was the research trying to achieve?	
When and where was the research undertaken?	
Who was being researched? (number of pupils, their ages, types of schools etc.)	
What methods of data collection were used in the research? (e.g. interviews, questionnaires etc.) Any issues with these?	
What methods of data analysis were used in the research? (e.g. statistical analysis of attainment changes, thematic analysis of participants' accounts etc.)	
What are the main conclusions that the report draws? Are the levels of generalisation appropriate from the evidence generated?	

Figure 11.3 Example of an article record form

article was published), where it was undertaken (which country? In how many schools? What were their characteristics?) and what methods of data collection and analysis were used. Also consider who did the research and what you know about their affiliation or employment (sometimes articles have a few lines about this at the end). This type of basic information is needed for you to evaluate the work and to consider how easy it is to relate to your own context.

Limitations of space in your final thesis mean that you will not be able to discuss all references to the same level of detail. Instead, you should provide an overview of the key areas under consideration and the main groupings of researchers working within them (breadth) and illustrate these by detailed critical analysis of a small number of sources which are particularly relevant or significant to your own project (depth).

In the same way that in your own research the methodology and methods should be congruent with the aims (Figure 11.1), each literature source that you engage with should also be internally consistent. Different types of empirical research studies (e.g. small-scale case study or large-scale survey) should then be evaluated against their stated aims. It is not appropriate to criticize the findings from a single case study for not being representative of the country as a whole when this was never intended. However, if an author seems to be making a wider or more definite claim than can be justified from their evidence, then it is fair to draw attention to this. Theoretical articles, which set out an argument based on logical reasoning and use of prior literature, need a different set of criteria for their evaluation than empirical work. In addition, authors will tailor the account of their research according to the audience for which they are publishing and the constraints of that type of publication. For example, there are different expectations of an article in a professional magazine than compared to one in an academic journal, as appropriate for the needs of the audience and the format.

The final literature review should link back to your own context. What have you learnt which will inform your own practice in the substantive area? What gaps are evident in current understandings of the topic? How might your research make a modest contribution to filling those gaps? What practice can you draw on, or learn from, when planning your own research methods? The literature review can be one of the most challenging parts of the Masters thesis to assemble and write, but it will play an important role in developing your understanding and practice in your chosen area.

Read on to: Hart (1998) gives a detailed guide to undertaking a literature review at Masters and PhD level. Chapter 1 and Appendix 2 of Poulson and Wallace (2004) give detailed guidance on critical engagement with previous research.

Choosing a research strategy

As discussed above, it is important that the chosen research strategy, also known as the methodology, fits well with the overall aims and research questions (Figure 11.1). There are a range of possible strategies, but two common ones for small-scale studies, such as the Masters thesis, are action research and case study. Both strategies focus in depth on a particular situation or element of practice, both are naturalistic (looking at phenomena in their usual context), both can involve qualitative and quantitative data collection (though an emphasis on qualitative is more common) and both can work with more than one theoretical perspective. However, the focus in action research is on generating and evaluating a *change* of practice in response to an identified issue or challenge, whilst this need not be the situation for case study research. Also, action research has to involve the practitioner reflecting on their own practice (possibly with outside support), whilst case study can be carried out purely by someone from outside the context.

Each methodology has its own particular issues, conventions and points to think about. For example, case study should involve consideration of how the case is chosen and bounded, whilst action research is structured around a series of cycles, comprising identification of the issue, response and evaluation. Over time, most methodologies have developed a spectrum of traditions within them, for example, action research encompasses positivist and critical emancipatory approaches. It's important to read a range of sources on whichever methodology you choose, then to explain and justify how your project is positioned within this spectrum.

Whatever methodology you choose, you will need to engage with issues of rigour and generalization (see Chapter 8). These concepts are framed differently within different approaches, so it is important to ensure that the terms you use (e.g. validity, reliability, bias, trustworthiness, credibility, defensibility) are appropriate and consistent with your choice of strategy. A combination of methods is one approach to triangulation, a popular way of aiming for rigour in qualitative research (Flick 2000).

Read on to: Bassey (1999) or Yin (2009) are good starting points for using case study methodology. Altrichter et al. (2008) or Kemmis and McTaggart (2005) are good ways in to action research. Chapter 5 of Cohen et al. (2011) or Chapter 11 of Silverman (2011) discuss ways of ensuring rigour in research.

Data collection: Finding out

At the data collection stage, the challenge is to select a suitable combination of methods from the wide range available (Figure 11.4) to suit your particular research questions and context. Some research methods involve collecting naturally generated data (e.g. students' classwork); others are introduced for the purposes of the research, though they may not be so different from normal school activities (e.g. focus groups). Most Masters projects combine a small number of different techniques to give different angles on the research problem. Whatever techniques you select, you should pay careful attention to good ethical practice (see Chapter 9).

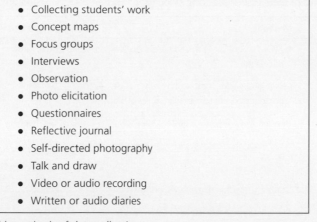

- Collecting students' work
- Concept maps
- Focus groups
- Interviews
- Observation
- Photo elicitation
- Questionnaires
- Reflective journal
- Self-directed photography
- Talk and draw
- Video or audio recording
- Written or audio diaries

Figure 11.4 Some possible methods of data collection

Each data collection technique has its own strengths and pitfalls, so it is important to prepare yourself thoroughly by reading the methods literature. For example, the way in which you structure and present a questionnaire will constrain the ways in which the resulting data can be analysed. In addition, each technique works best for particular aims and in certain contexts, so you should think carefully about which you deploy. For example, focus groups are good for encouraging peer interaction and generating ideas, but it can be difficult to attribute responses to named individuals later on. Conversely, there is no problem in attributing the data from a one-to-one interview, but some young people find this situation awkward and this can limit their responses.

It is normal to use a few complementary approaches, as relying on just one could yield an unnecessarily one-dimensional result. For example, if a researcher was interested in young peoples' representations of the United States, but only gave each young person the opportunity to write down five words they associated with the United States, it would not be surprising if the research outcomes showed they had stereotyped views. More nuanced understandings might well be demonstrated when findings from three or four data collection methods are put together.

Read on to: Cohen et al. (2011) give helpful advice on a range of data collection techniques There are plenty of good reference sources on mainstream educational research methods such as interviews, questionnaires, focus groups and observation. Slightly less common are sources which address how to explore children and young people's understandings of geographical ideas and concepts through classwork or visual methods (see Table 11.1). Young people's oral and written classwork is, of course, an excellent source of evidence regarding their understandings and skills in geography. Data collection involves considering a suitable method for recording oral responses (notes, audio or video recording; digital or analogue; placing of equipment and microphones; balancing precision in recording with possible

Table 11.1 Examples of methods for accessing students' understandings of geographical topics

Source	Methods	Geographical topic	Age group
Béneker et al. (2010)	Drawing a view out of a window, directed writing, word association	Urban areas	11–17
Hopwood (2009)	Lesson observation, post-lesson interviews, self-directed photography, photo elicitation, concept maps	Geography	13–14
Kitchen (2013)	Directed writing, stimulus posters, interviews	Geography	11–12
Mackintosh (2004)	Word association, drawing, concept mapping, interviews	Rivers	9–10
Picton (2010)	Concept mapping	Globalization	13–14
Strommen (1995)	Drawings, structured interviews, picture sorting	Forests	6–7
Taylor (2009, 2011)	Talk and draw, photo elicitation, interview, analysis of classwork	Japan	13–14
Walshe (2013a, 2013b)	Dialogic diaries, semi-structured interviews	Sustainability	14–15

distraction caused by equipment) and for collecting written responses (original or photo-copied; sample or whole class; immediately at the end of the lesson or subsequently). This requires some thought beforehand and then discipline in collecting and ordering results, but it is not usually difficult to collect a substantial data set.

Visual methods have a lot of potential for use in researching children and young people's understandings of aspects of geography. They can provide concrete 'ways in' to more abstract ideas and are likely to give a more rounded representation of the students' understandings than interview or questionnaire alone. If used in an interview situation, they also break eye contact, which can help pupils relax and communicate more. Common visual approaches include concept mapping (generally more structured), mind-mapping (generally less structured), talk and draw (students explain to you what they are drawing in response to a task you set and you can ask questions) and photo elicitation (discussing photographs). Other approaches include pupils taking photos or videos themselves (good for local area work) or making maps of their experiences.

Read on to: White and Gunstone (1992) give strategies for exploring children's understandings in science, most of which are easily transferrable to geography Banks (1995), Hazel (1995), Hurworth (2003) and Meier (2007) introduce use of a range of methods in the social sciences, many of which adapt easily to geography education. Chapter 2 of King (2000) includes various classroom observation strategies.

The data collection methods should be carefully linked to your research questions to ensure that you maintain focus. It is important to avoid the temptation to collect material which does not relate to your research questions just because it is interesting, although as mentioned previously, you should be open to consider whether you need to change your research questions as your plans unfold. To ensure that you keep an appropriate focus, it

Table 11.2 Empirical research questions mapped to methods in Claire Kennedy's MEd research

Research question	Data collection methods
1. What were pupils' initial representations of Egypt?	Drawing out of a window in Egypt Written work on initial perceptions of Egypt
2a. To what extent was my teaching effective in broadening pupils' views? 2b. How have their views become more nuanced over time?	Three pieces of written work over the sequence of lessons Lesson observations and notes Lesson plans and evaluations Focus group with six students at end of sequence
3. How might this inform planning in the future?	Reflection on teaching and learning Focus group

might be useful to construct a table matching your research questions to your data collection methods. For example, when researching young people's changing understandings of Egypt, Claire Kennedy matched her research questions and data collection methods as shown in Table 11.2 (2009, 2011).

Unless the group of students on which you choose to focus is very small (e.g. a small sixth form class), you are likely to need some form of selection to avoid the data set becoming unmanageable to analyse. Each project will call for a different method of selection, depending on its aims, theoretical perspective and methodology. For example, in a project informed by a post-positivist theoretical perspective where the teacher-researcher aims to use a mixture of questionnaire and interviews to establish how attitude to geography varies with pupil age across an 11–16 school, sampling techniques using standard principles for ensuring accurate generalization to the school population would be necessary. However, for an interpretive case study of the process of students' learning about glacial environments during a residential fieldtrip, it would be possible to focus successfully on the learning of just two or three carefully selected students at a detailed level over time. The researcher could then generalize to theory, but could not generalize to a wider population of young people. As always, there is a need to consider the appropriate balance of breadth and depth of data collection for the particular project being undertaken.

It is important to ensure that all selection choices can be justified in relation to the aims of your project and established practice in literature: why did you choose to focus on six pupils, not thirty, or two? How did you choose those pupils (random sampling, purposive selection, etc)? In small-scale teacher-practitioner research, some choices will inevitably be pragmatic, for example, to research a particular year 9 class because that is the only one you teach. This type of justification is not problematic so long as it is consistent with aims regarding generalization, but the choices should still be explained.

Once the programme of data collection is underway, it is important to keep careful records of the data collected. For example, for copies of students' classwork, ensure that each example is named and that you have a record of the task, any guidance material, the lesson plan and which students were present. Whilst you may not use all of this information in the final report, it is very hard to reconstruct such records in hindsight. Of course, the nature of teaching in schools is that unexpected events happen, for example, a lesson is cancelled or not all pupils turn up for a focus group. It may be possible to make alternative arrangements, but if it is not, then note down the situation and explanation. In your final report you will need to critically evaluate the processes of your data collection, and this is exactly the type of incident which you can discuss, with suggestions of how you might wish to refine or to improve the situation if you were engaging in this type of research in the future.

Data analysis: Sorting out

The first stage in analysing a data set is to prepare it. For some materials, such as students' work, this will just involve making sure that you know what you have and that it is well labelled and in order. For other materials, for example, audio recordings, more work will be necessary. If you need to work with audio material at a detailed level, then the time commitment involved in transcription will be worthwhile. However, for some purposes, it may be enough to listen to a recording a number of times and to transcribe only a few key quotations. If you do choose to transcribe in full, you should consider whether you are only interested in the content of what was said or whether tone and expression are relevant. There are systems available for noting the latter, but the time commitment is inevitably increased. Foot pedals are available for controlling both tape and digital audio sources (the latter also requires some simple software). These are a significant convenience when transcribing large amounts of data, and it may be possible to borrow them from your institution if needed.

Dey (1993) suggests that qualitative analysis is a circular process in which the researcher passes through successive stages of describing, classifying and connecting data (Figure 11.5).

Although the methods will be different, the underlying aim is the same in quantitative analysis as qualitative analysis. In both cases the researcher is striving to understand their data set in its breadth and depth, and to identify trends, unusual instances, patterns and

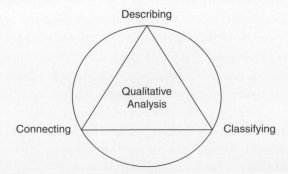

Figure 11.5 Processes of qualitative analysis (after Dey 1993)

connections in the data. In both cases there are also established methods of analysis which, if chosen, need to be carried out carefully and thoroughly, but an element of intuition and creativity is also needed. In this way, data analysis is similar to the work of a good detective as they attempt to solve a crime (at least as this is portrayed on television!). There is a certain amount of methodical sorting, sifting and noting, but the ability to ask pertinent questions and to follow leads or hunches is also necessary.

Initially it is important to invest time in getting to know your data – listening to recordings, reading work repeatedly and so on. The researcher then starts to establish similarities and differences between elements of the data (Dey's classifying), then moves to identify links and connections, looking for patterns, trends and exceptions. These stages are necessarily recursive and can be blurred in practice.

At every point, the analysis should be governed by the research questions, and any subquestions contained in them, otherwise it is easy to veer off onto aspects of analysis which may be interesting but are not relevant to the overall project. It is also important to keep noting down any thoughts, questions, impressions or ideas which occur when you work with your data. Some will inevitably turn out to be dead ends, or not substantiated in the wider data set, others will turn out to be productive.

If you intend to follow a well-established method of analysis such as content or discourse analysis, then you should ensure that you read fully about its conventions and expectations, also ensure that it is consistent with the theoretical perspective of your project. For example, a researcher using discourse analysis seeks to uncover structures of power inherent in the data, which fits well with a critical theoretical perspective, but is not in sympathy with a post-positivist perspective.

For qualitative data, some form of coding is commonly used in the categorization stage. This enables the researcher to identify themes across the data set. Codes can be established inductively (arising from the data) or deductively (decided in advance), or sometimes a mixed system is used. For example, in her work on year 8 students' understandings of sustainability, Walshe (2008) initially analysed students' concepts used an inductive method of coding, and then applied a deductive set of codes based on another sustainable development research project. This enabled her to gain familiarity with the data set first before comparing it with findings from another researcher. Sometimes, a single coding system can be established across all formats of data and research questions in a project, whilst in other projects, different approaches may be needed for different formats or questions. However, it is clearly sensible to keep the system as straightforward as possible. It is also important to keep careful records of your system and any alterations made to it.

The methods of analysis for visual data are broadly similar to those for written or verbal data, but they tend to have less prominence in the education research literature. However, there are a range of established methods used in other disciplines, such as geography and cultural studies. Some types of analysis of students' drawings are very detailed and specific to particular circumstances (e.g. psychoanalytic approaches in considering aspects of children's mental health).

With visual data, as with other data formats, the tension in analysis between breadth and depth, holism and potential fragmentation needs to be addressed. Different researchers resolve this in different ways. For example, in analysing a set of young people's drawings of a view 'out of a window in a city', Béneker et al. (2010) used a four-stage system based on a method used by the anthropologists (Collier and Collier 1986, pp. 178–9). In taking this approach, they aimed to balance a holistic approach with detailed and methodical engagement with the drawings.

Analysis of quantitative data is likely to involve the use of software, such as Excel for basic functions or SPSS for more advanced statistics. For qualitative data, you may find a package such as NVivo or AtlasTi helpful if you need to handle and code large amounts of data, or you may prefer to work by hand. Your supervisor and IT department will be able to advise on options available to you.

Read on to: McLellan (2009) gives an introduction to quantitative analysis. Dey (1992), a guide to qualitative analysis; Evans (2009) introduces coding and Chapter 2 of Boyatzis (1998) gives a detailed guide to coding practices. Chapters 1 and 2 of Rose (2007) are a good introduction to the analysis of visual sources, though note that it is a geography rather than geography education text.

Communicating findings: Creating a story

The process of data collection, analysis and presentation of findings is rarely easy to divide into clean stages, even if many researchers' finished reports make it look otherwise. Prospective findings are often identified quite early in the process, then tested out as the researcher continues to work with the data. Writing up is often consecutive with analysis, at least to some extent, and it is worth taking the opportunity to present early findings to your colleagues for feedback.

It is important to balance breadth and depth when engaging with the data and reporting findings. You will need to give a sense of the data set as a whole to provide context and to avoid any suspicion of 'cherry picking' elements which support your preconceived ideas, but in most projects you will also need to focus on particularly useful elements in depth. By the time that you are ready to present findings more formally, it is important to check that you have a firm evidence base at all points. Altrichter et al. (2008, pp. 178–80) suggest that a useful activity at this stage is to write findings statements on index cards then to match them against the available data. Again, the research questions form a helpful framework for ensuring that you keep to the point when presenting your findings.

Your thesis as a whole needs to present a clear line of argument (see Chapter 12). To construct this argument, it may be stronger to answer each research question with two or three headline points, backed up with data from a number of sources, rather than going through each source in turn, which can easily become descriptive. It is also important to make links back to your literature review to compare and contrast your findings with earlier research. Your supervisor will be able to give further guidance on this. The aim is to have a clear and consistent 'story' about your research throughout the thesis from introduction to conclusion. It is also important to ensure a clear strand of critical engagement throughout thesis, with respect to key concepts, existing research and your own methods. As you write, you will need to phrase assertions in an appropriate way to fit with the way that your project addresses generalizability. Ensure that you do not generalize to wider populations (the whole class, year group or school) unless your project was set up in a way that makes this possible.

Carrying out a research project is a demanding process. You are likely to find that it stretches your skills of engagement with literature, understanding of methodology, critical evaluation, organization and time management. However, despite finding the process challenging along the way, most Masters students find that their projects have enabled them to improve their practice, and they value having taken the time to read and research a topic in depth.

References

Altricher, H, Feldman, A, Posch, P and Somekh, B (2008) *Teachers Investigate Their Work: A Guide to Action Research across the Professions*, 2nd edition. London: Routledge.

Banks, M (1995) Visual research methods. *Social Research Update*, 11. Available online at: http://sru.soc.surrey.ac.uk/

Bassey, M (1999) *Case Study Research in Educational Settings*. Buckingham, England: Open University Press.

Béneker, T, Sanders, R, Tani, S, Taylor, L and Van der Vaart, R (2007) Teaching the geographies of urban areas: views and visions. *International Research in Geographical and Environmental Education* 16(3): 250–67.

Brook, M (2013) Development: contested, complex and diverse. *Teaching Geography* 38(1): 22–3.

Boyatzis, R (1998) *Transforming Qualitative Information*. Thousand Oaks, CA: Sage.

Cohen, L, Manion, L and Morrison, K (2011) *Research Methods in Education*, 7th edition. London: Routledge.

Collier, J and Collier, M (1986) *Visual Anthropology: Photography as a Research Method*. Albuquerque: University of New Mexico Press.

Creswell, J (2013) *Qualitative Inquiry and Research Design: Choosing among Five Approaches*, 3rd edition. Thousand Oaks, CA: Sage.

Crotty, M (2003) *The Foundations of Social Research: Meaning and Perspective in the Research Process*. London: Sage.

Dey, I (1993) *Qualitative Data Analysis: A User-Friendly Guide for Social Scientists*. Abingdon, UK: Routledge.

Evans, M (2009) Analysing qualitative data. In Wilson, E (ed.) *School-Based Research: A Guide for Education Students*, pp. 125–36. London: Sage.

Flick, U (2000/2004) Triangulation in qualitative research. In Flick, U, von Kardorff, E, and Steinke, I (eds.) *A Companion to Qualitative Research*, pp. 178–83. London: Sage.

Hart, C (1998) *Doing a Literature Review: Releasing the Social Science Research Imagination*. London: Sage.

Hazel, N (1995) Elicitation techniques with young people. *Social Research Update*, 12. Available online at: http://sru.soc.surrey.ac.uk/

Hopwood, N (2009) UK high school pupils' conceptions of geography: research findings and methodological implications. *International Research in Geographical and Environmental Education* 18(3): 185–97.

Hurworth, R (2003) Photo-interviewing for research. *Social Research Update*, 40. Available online at: http://sru.soc.surrey.ac.uk/

Kemmis, S and McTaggart, R (2005) Participatory action research. In Denzin, N and Lincoln, Y (eds.) *The Sage Handbook of Qualitative Research*, 3rd edition, pp. 559–604. London: Sage.

Kennedy, C (2009) *Imagining Distant Places: A Critical Analysis of How Students' Representations of Egypt Change over a Scheme of Lessons*. Unpublished MEd thesis, University of Cambridge, Cambridge.

— (2011) Imagining distant places: changing representations of Egypt. *Teaching Geography* 36(2): 52–4.

King, S (2000) *Into the Black Box: Observing Classrooms*. Sheffield, UK: Geographical Association.

Kitchen, R (2013) What is geography? The view from Year 7. *Teaching Geography* 38(1): 17–19.

Mackintosh, M (2004) Children's understanding of rivers: is there need for more constructivist research in primary geography? In Catling, S and Martin, F (eds) *Researching Primary Geography (Register of Researching Primary Geography Special Publication No. 1)*, pp. 55–63. London: Register of Research in Primary Geography.

McLellan, R (2009) Analysing quantitative data. In Wilson, E (ed.) *School-Based Research: A Guide for Education Students*, pp. 154–70. London: Sage.

Meier, P (2007) Mind-mapping: a tool for eliciting and representing knowledge held by diverse informants. *Social Research Update*, 52. Available online at: http://sru.soc.surrey.ac.uk/

Picton, O (2010) Shrinking world? Globalisation at key stage 3. *Teaching Geography* 35(1): 10–17.

Poulson, L and Wallace, M (eds.) (2004) *Learning to read critically in teaching and learning*. London: Sage.

Rose, G (2007) *Visual Methodologies*, 2nd edition. London: Sage.

Silverman, D (2011) *Interpreting Qualitative Data*, 4th edition. London: Sage.

Strommen, E (1995) Lions and tigers and bears, oh my! Children's conceptions of forests and their inhabitants. *Journal of Research in Science Teaching* 32(7): 683–98.

Taylor, L (2009) Children constructing Japan: material practices and relational learning. *Children's Geographies* 7(2): 173–89.

— (2011) Investigating change in young people's understandings of Japan: a study of learning about a distant place. *British Educational Research Journal* 37(6): 1033–54.

Tierney, M (2011) *Encouraging an Exploration of the Contested, Complex and Diverse Nature of 'Development': A Case Study Investigating the Impacts of Introducing University-Level Ideas about International Development into A-Level Geography Teaching and Learning*. Unpublished Med thesis, University of Cambridge, Cambridge.

Walshe, N (2008) Understanding students' conceptions of sustainability. *Environmental Education* 14(5): 537–58.

— (2013a) Exploring and developing student understandings of sustainable development. *Curriculum Journal* 24(2): 224–49.

— (2013b) Exploring and developing children's understandings of sustainable development with dialogic diaries. *Children's Geographies* 11(1): 132–54.

White, R and Gunstone, R (1992) *Probing Understanding*. London: The Falmer Press.

Yin, R (2009) *Case Study Research: Design and Methods*, 4th edition. London: Sage.

Striving for a Conclusion 12

Gemma Collins

Chapter outline

Case study: Ross Martin   186

The pitfalls and practicalities of writing up   186

Techniques and regimes for writing up   188

Effective use of the dissertation supervisor   190

Producing work on time and to the correct standards   192

Approaches to completing assignments (at PGDipEd level) and dissertations
  (at MEd level)   193

The next 'chapter' for Ross Martin   195

This chapter concerns the production of high-quality research, in particular a recognizable 'end product' in the form of a completed Masters dissertation. It does not therefore dwell on the practicalities of 'getting going', integrating research into your working/domestic life, establishing good research habits or setting realistic boundaries for research. This chapter is also not about data collection or analysis. However, in considering one's personal 'research journey', it is likely that all of these prior considerations will have an impact on the final piece of research, and therefore allusions are made to these aspects with the aim of building on other chapters rather than repeating their content. The chapter is written with a great deal of input from, and collaboration with, one particular Masters student who has shared his own ultimately successful research journey in order to illustrate and inform others' search for a conclusion. The quotes within this chapter, unless otherwise attributed, are his words. This chapter is by its very nature a largely anecdotal account, but reference to scholarly and academic work has been made to provide a context for the case study provided. It is hoped that the shared experience of one Masters student and his dissertation supervisor will offer an informative insight into the production of high-quality research in geography education.

Case study: Ross Martin

Ross Martin trained as a geography teacher at the University of Birmingham, successfully completing the Postgraduate Diploma in Education (PGDipEd) in 2008. This course offers 120 credits and, along with teaching practice, the assessed component comprises five assignments written at Masters level with a requirement to engage with existing research and to conduct one's own. This is a common route for many students embarking upon Masters level research in geography education, whereby becoming research active alongside reflective classroom practice is an immediate requirement. At this particular institution, returning at some stage after the Newly Qualified Teacher (NQT) year to complete a dissertation for a full MEd in Teaching Studies is a popular choice, and a significant proportion of geographers (by which is meant those who have completed the PGDipEd (QTS) Secondary Geography qualification) do so within the first five years of teaching. Ross chose to complete the MEd in his third year of teaching at Nicholas Chamberlaine Technology College in Warwickshire, by which time he had also obtained a pastoral role managing a Student Behavioural Support Centre in the school. His justification for the timing of his application is representative of the majority of students opting for this route; Ross felt that he wanted to take advantage of the 120 credits gained through his PGDipEd as a way of completing the full Masters degree, and while he still felt connected to academic work. Given that students completing the MEd Teaching Studies do so alongside full time teaching, Ross, like many, also felt the need to give it his full commitment before taking on too many extra responsibilities and before he became 'too busy with work to be able to do it properly'. This is a practical and realistic approach and one which recognizes the significant time and effort which Masters level research will require. An understanding of these professional demands as well as the personal demands on his time was the first step for Ross in ultimately enabling himself to produce high-quality research.

Ross' reflections on his Masters experience, and my reflections on that experience from the position of his dissertation supervisor, have been drawn out into themes which are intended to guide others through the write-up of a Masters dissertation. The additional preparation Ross gained through the production of Masters level writing for the PGDipEd has also been taken into account, although it is recognized that not all Masters students will have experienced this same academic background.

The pitfalls and practicalities of writing up

Many of the potential pitfalls of writing up can be avoided through the adoption of effective working practices from the start of the research. Previous chapters have illustrated many of these 'good habits', and to a certain extent writing up owes its success or failure to the ways in which the research has been conducted throughout. However, the experience of Ross is useful in demonstrating some of the minor pitfalls which can be easily avoided in the writing-up stage, and in highlighting some of the practicalities which should be taken into consideration.

Firstly, it is important to recognize that although inevitably building on existing knowledge and skills, a Masters dissertation can and should be seen as a unique piece of work. Ross describes his own positive experience of this:

> My dissertation was largely unrelated to the previous [PGDipEd] assignments. As such, it felt like I was starting a new project that wasn't going to be held back by previous lack of experience or know-how. The MEd was a chance to show what I had done and become since finishing my teacher training. In this sense it was far more than a mere addendum; it was unique.

There is a balance to be achieved between using prior experience of writing at Masters level (e.g. through a PGDipEd), or of engaging with academic literature (e.g. through an undergraduate degree), and embarking upon an original piece of research which has its own aims, its own clear focus and is conducted in the context of an increased personal level of experience and understanding of education. Those students who fail to significantly move beyond their prior knowledge, for example, those who might choose a research aim which is very closely aligned with previous Masters level assignments, tend to struggle with writing up. Once they are in the position of having to articulate their findings and conclusions, students who have not significantly challenged themselves or successfully identified a gap in research or literature often realize that it can be very difficult to draw together their work into something meaningful which contributes to their field.

Secondly, the use of data and the search for concrete conclusions can be a common pitfall. Masters students, who are geography teachers, are still (whether they identify themselves as such or not) also geographers and as such should be used to dealing with the discipline's 'grey areas'. However, these students can, in focusing on the 'education' element of their research, forget the skills that geographers use to draw generalizations and may become defeated by the number of variables inherent in education research. In Ross' case, he found that 'data can be daunting, even for teachers. Having someone to talk it through with and provide a different perspective was extremely useful'. In his context, the different perspective that Ross needed in order to avoid the pitfall of over-thinking the quantitative element of his research was that data doesn't necessarily provide all the answers. A reminder that much of geography education research exists somewhere on a continuum between qualitative and quantitative methods (Butt 2010) was something that Ross needed, as a reassurance that his professional judgements and day-to-day experiences with the pupils in question were potentially just as valid as a set of quantitative data.

Finally, Ross has some advice for others conducting geography education research, given from the valuable position of someone who has had the opportunity to reflect back on his experience. He describes here a pitfall which, to his great credit, he avoided but needed to remind himself of as he undertook further research:

> There are some exciting themes and ideas developing in the world of education but some of those themes, though tempting, should be avoided if they lead to a frivolous chase of the ethereal instead of the pursuit of performance that is excellence every day.

First and foremost, Masters research in geography education is often focused on the enhancement of the ways in which children and young people experience the subject. By the time students have moved from PGDipEd to MEd, with at least one year of teaching in between, they can have a heightened awareness of where their own discipline (geography, and more narrowly geography education) lies within the hierarchy of research. They are aware of limitations and criticisms, and in turn can be highly critical of their own work; however, geography education research is important, and it does matter (see Lambert 2010). It is useful for students to be reminded of this, and to maintain this as a prominent idea throughout their research.

Techniques and regimes for writing up

By the point at which an individual is in a position to undertake academic research and complete a Masters degree, it can be assumed that they have a good grasp of the ways in which they work best. However, for most, completing this level of academic work alongside full-time employment, in a condensed time frame of one academic year, will present significant challenges to what may have previously been very effective working practices. A practical approach is vital, as is the setting of realistic and achievable targets and deadlines. The ways in which this approach can be negotiated with a dissertation supervisor, and the role that the supervisor might play in organizing one's time effectively, are discussed in more detail below. Regardless of the support that supervision can offer, it is important for students to develop their own techniques and regimes for writing up, in order that the production of the final dissertation is a manageable task.

Ross recognized the need to organize his time efficiently from the start of the process. A full-time teaching career combined with a young family required that Ross was particularly organized and disciplined in his approach to further study, and particularly to writing up. What worked for Ross may not work for other individuals; each student must develop their own techniques, regimes, habits and routines which relate to their own challenges and demands. In Ross' case, setting aside a block of time each Saturday afternoon was the most manageable way of ensuring he had time to focus on research and writing. As well as manageable, this routine was realistic for him: 'Having relatively short blocks of time helped by allowing me to have enough time to really get into what I was writing, without becoming fatigued and inefficient'. It is likely that weekends and school holidays will become 'co-opted' to some extent for research and writing. Setting out realistic time frames for research will make the writing up more achievable; being honest about time intended for research and time for holidays, extra-curricular demands (including fieldwork in and out of school time) and other social activities is crucial, as is planning other responsibilities and activities into a writing schedule. Ross found it achievable to write during his working week:

> I also had a weeknight regime of writing on a Wednesday or Thursday for an hour or so. By having Monday and Tuesday to get school work done, such as marking, It meant that I could have a go at getting some ideas down mid-week and therefore maintain the flow of ideas from the weekend.

In contrast to Ross, many students struggle with this kind of approach and find it difficult to combine writing with focusing on teaching. In light of his own experience, Ross offers the following advice:

> It probably wouldn't hurt MEd students to get home from school early occasionally in order to get some writing done in the afternoon. Teachers, in particular, can be very good at being very busy in and around the department without actually getting anything worthwhile done. Trying to write late at night, especially after a busy day in the classroom, is not always effective or efficient. By being home a bit earlier than normal it would reduce the stress of sitting down to write as there would still be time to mark books and so forth later in the evening.

There is certainly no 'one size fits all' approach to time management, and few dissertation supervisors will be rigid in their expectations or demands, beyond a request for students to be honest, realistic and (to some extent) to work with the supervisor's own workload and schedule, as outlined below.

The majority of schools are rightly supportive of their staff members undertaking further qualifications in order to develop and strengthen their practice. Fortunate students may find this support extends to protected periods on timetables, 'research' afternoons which can be spent in the University, part (or whole) funding of tuition fees, or the provision of an 'in-school mentor' to support and coach Masters students. Every one of these approaches by schools has been reported by some of the students I have supervised, and such support has certainly been much appreciated by the individual in question. However, other alternatives can be sought out, should students find themselves without this level of explicit support from their school; during his Masters, Ross felt well supported by his school, but also found that:

> Another way to help the process of writing up relates to using school systems more effectively. A lot of teachers, let alone those completing Masters studies, still fail to use the support and skills of administrative staff. Meeting notes, CPD notes and so forth can, and should, be typed up by an administrative member of staff. Masters students should get into the habit of delegating work where possible and appropriate. This feels a bit awkward at first, but in reality the more time saved doing odd jobs, the more time and energy available for the dissertation.

Along with a clear writing schedule, a realistic, and perhaps regular, time frame for writing, and appropriate delegation of some aspects of workload, effective use of the allocated time for supervision can be incorporated into the techniques and regimes used for writing up. When reflecting on one particular face-to-face meeting between us, Ross recalls that 'although this session went on longer than had been allocated for the meeting, I think I ended up using less than the total time available to me because of the confidence I had been given from being able to talk through my ideas'. As will be outlined below, effective use of the dissertation supervisor can be a powerful tool in completing a dissertation.

Effective use of the dissertation supervisor

Subject-specific guidance from a dissertation supervisor can be used in a number of ways, and is a professional relationship worth carefully considering and clearly outlining at the start of your research as the role the dissertation supervisor plays in the write-up can be very important. Some key texts regarding the completion of a research project are particularly helpful in outlining the role of the dissertation supervisor (see, e.g., Thomas 2009 or Bell 2010). With particular reference to 'striving for a conclusion', some students have reported what they later realized to be a misguided belief that asking their dissertation supervisor for help might be seen by others as a sign of weakness. Perhaps to some extent this misconception might arise due to the knowledge that the dissertation supervisor will be, in most cases, the first marker of the final work. It could be felt that 'exposing' weaknesses in the process of writing up might somehow count against the final dissertation. In Ross' case, it was more a case of wanting to do things himself:

> On reflection I think I could have been more willing to go and discuss some of the difficulties with my supervisor earlier on. There is always an element of wanting to do things independently in order to prove to yourself that you can do it. However, it pays dividends to be willing to ask for help from the right person early enough for that help to make a difference. . . . If I were to change one thing, it would be to send off drafts earlier. This would have given me more time to make the changes that I needed to make.

Many dissertation supervisors try to pre-empt this misconception through an open and supportive working relationship. This relationship works best when both parties are clear on expectations, rights and responsibilities. In many cases, students will already have an existing relationship with the supervisor, where they have previously acted as the university tutor on a PGDipEd course. Even so, as a Masters student, this relationship needs to be re-contextualized, to take into account the change in dynamic (and power) from 'student-tutor' on a PGDipEd course, to something more akin to 'researcher-supervisor' or even 'colleague-colleague'.

Ross' experience can be used to further examine the potential of the role of the dissertation supervisor.

> The chapter that I made the most use of my supervisor for was the data analysis. I was fortunate to have a supervisor that understood the importance of being able to analyse large amounts of data for my project. We had a meeting where I talked through my findings from start to finish in order to see the big picture. After this I had my supervisor go through and ask questions and pick out parts of the data that were unclear. Finally, we talked about which information should be kept and which, though useful, was unnecessary for the completion of my project.

In this case, the supervisor is performing a number of functions: firstly, confirming the student's choice of data collection and analysis, and offering alternatives where appropriate; secondly, examining the data through 'fresh eyes' and highlighting any clarification needed; thirdly, helping the student to begin the editing process, which in this case involved a discussion about which data to discard. Researchers can become very familiar with their own data, and can need the more detached view of another person in order to see where explanation is required. They can also become very attached to data, having invested time and effort in its collection; establishing which data may be interesting yet not relevant is often easiest done by someone 'outside' the process. In both cases, dissertation supervisors are well placed to perform this role.

Establishing an effective working relationship with a dissertation supervisor will allow students to make full use of their services at the writing-up stage. It is important that the supervisor is aware of the techniques and regimes students have set for themselves. These must also realistically work alongside the workload of the supervisor, through the agreement of reasonable response times for example, or allowing a specified number of working days to read and comment on each thousand words of text. Amongst the methods available to facilitate this relationship might be: a combination of group meetings, where students can exchange ideas and support each other; individual face-to-face meetings between the student and supervisor at key stages of the write-up; and regular communication via e-mail (or increasingly other technology, such as Skype, use of a virtual learning environment (VLE) or social media). Ross reports considerable success with electronic feedback at certain stages of the write-up:

> Most of the support I received in completing my first draft was via e-mail. By sending chapters this way I was able to receive detailed feedback in Microsoft Word via the 'Balloons' options. This was helpful as I was then able to use this feedback immediately and within the same document to improve my work.

For many Masters students, this will not be the final chapter in their own research story, and it is possible that a productive and mutually beneficial professional relationship may be developed through the student–supervisor relationship.

Producing work on time and to the correct standards

The final stages of writing up will be concerned with the overall quality of the dissertation, and the deadline by which it must be completed. 'Will it be good enough?' and 'Will I get it finished on time?' are common themes of many of the e-mails I receive from Masters students as the deadline approaches.

If students have past work written at Masters level, for example, PGDipEd assignments, these can be used to support dissertation writing to the correct standards. They do not necessarily need to be seen as separate entities, although beware the pitfalls of over-reliance on the common topics they address, as outlined earlier in this chapter. Ross found that his PGDipEd assignments were useful at the start of the process, with a view to the eventual write-up of the dissertation:

> At the start of my MEd year I had a cursory look at my assignments to remind myself of the M-Level marking criteria. I also wanted to remind myself of how to reference properly. Occasionally I would look at sections of my work to find good ways to express ideas. . . . I looked quite closely at the marking feedback, particularly at comments on phrasing and grammar. I wanted to make sure I didn't repeat any bad habits.

Students are also given a variety of course materials to support them in writing up to the correct standards, and these can be used to check important aspects of writing such as referencing, chapter content and structure. Ross found these materials reassuring, in particular the 'peace of mind to be found from going over your work and comparing it to the materials given, even if no major changes need to be made'. The opportunity to look over previous Masters dissertations can be useful for students, as a rough gauge of quality, length and structure. This should be done with care, to avoid the misconception that there is an absolute 'right' way to conduct research or to write up a dissertation, and without denying students the valuable process of thinking through their original ideas, and rejecting or modifying those ideas as their own research takes shape. By reading and engaging with academic literature in their field, Masters students are constantly exposing themselves to writing which is of the required academic standards, and many find that extensive reading improves their ability to replicate that standard of writing themselves.

Other than the formal submission deadline set by the institution, other informal deadlines can be negotiated between student and supervisor. Although these may be flexible, students should be encouraged not to avoid them completely. Planning these deadlines early allows students to integrate them into any writing schedule and to incorporate them into the techniques and regimes of writing. Ross clearly outlines the benefits of being set informal, interim deadlines:

Having already completed much of the work early on I was able to focus on refining it rather than trying to produce thousands of words in one go. I think that this had a positive effect on me psychologically in the sense that I felt I had already achieved a lot and, therefore, felt able to cope with the stress and pressure that came later on when trying to write-up my dissertation fully. Even though some of the work submitted for early on changed dramatically it was easier to edit something already made rather than trying to start from scratch.

Sufficient time must be allowed before submission for the often time-consuming business of formatting, checking referencing and other presentational considerations. Other chapters in this book will, I am sure, reinforce the value of adopting efficient strategies and 'good habits' for the accurate recording of references and quotes, for example, the use of software such as Microsoft OneNote, which can make the final stage of writing up much less stressful than it might otherwise be.

Approaches to completing assignments (at PGDipEd level) and dissertations (at Masters level)

As acknowledged at the beginning of this chapter, not all Masters students completing a dissertation in geography education will have progressed through a PGDipEd where they have already written at Masters level. However, for those who have, there are considerable advantages which should determine their approach. As a PGDipEd student, Ross discovered that 'being good at researching and writing clearly was insufficient to ensure success . . . a different set of skills had to be learned'. Reflecting back on the PGDipEd as preparation for further Masters level research, many students will recognize that the skills of critical reflection and engagement with education research which were ingrained from their early formative experiences as beginning teachers enabled them to 'get to grips' with a Masters dissertation with greater ease. Ross states that the PGDipEd 'paved the way for me . . . to become a reflective practitioner'. A course such as the PGDipEd which is based on reflective practice will expose students to strategies and methods which enable them to approach a Masters dissertation with confidence, particularly regarding the effective use of feedback to improve writing at all stages, not just through a final draft. Feedback (both verbal and written) from dissertation supervisors has been discussed further above. However, most Masters students will have an extended support network in the form of their peers who are completing dissertations at the same time. Although often to some extent teachers can become used to working independently in the isolation of their own classroom, they also have considerable experience of working collegiately in departments or faculties. In a similar way, Masters students might consider setting up a network of 'critical friends'. A critical friend, as defined by Costa and Kallick (1993, p. 50), can be seen as 'a trusted person who asks provocative questions, provides data to be examined through another lens, and offers critiques of a person's work as a friend'. They go on to suggest that 'a critical friend takes the time to fully understand the context of the work presented' (ibid.), something which might easily be achieved by a student undertaking a similar endeavour himself/herself. In another way, the dissertation supervisor acts also as a critical friend, the difference perhaps being the benefit of more distance from the process than another Masters student may have, and a greater degree of confidence and experience with Masters level research. Using peers on an MEd course in this way, for example, by looking over each other's work, can improve a researcher's understanding of their own work. Through generic research methods training and subject-specific group supervision, Ross was able to make use of such a network and reports that 'by giving and receiving feedback I was able to identify good examples to follow and more clearly see weaknesses in my own writing'.

To a great extent, the preceding chapters of this book are about the 'bigger picture' of high-quality education research, and this chapter focuses on the smaller details, practicalities, tips and techniques. However, it was clear that for Ross, and for the majority of other Masters level students, seeing their own research as part of this 'bigger picture' was not only natural and necessary, but almost impossible to avoid. Striving for a conclusion becomes all the more difficult if there seems to be no justification for the research itself. There was a marked difference for Ross between the ways in which he approached Masters level writing for his PGDipEd assignments, and for his MEd dissertation. When completing the PGDipEd assignments, Ross felt that 'some of the grand ideas of education, such as constructivism, seemed too far removed from everyday life at the chalk face. It was also difficult to see the whole picture sometimes as placements, however long, provide only a snapshot of life in the classroom'. Masters students who are working full time, in permanent positions, in schools they have been employed by for at least one year but often two or more, are likely to experience the same transition as Ross; the process of completing the Masters dissertation allowed him to make sense of his own research, and is best described in his own words.

> I feel able to evaluate my own practice in a way that is both rigorous and meaningful. There is still the odd occasion where I wonder how some of the very theoretical aspects of my studies fit in day to day. However, I realise that as a teacher much of what we do fits into a longer term narrative and some of the theoretical aspects of education can have a place at different scales and levels, for instance at a departmental or whole school level. My studies have allowed me to gain an insight into the part that I play in a complex system and provide a context for the part that I play.

The transition in attitude and understanding that Ross and others have undergone from PGDipEd to Masters highlights a successful approach to completing Masters level research. Teachers work within a largely evidence-driven community and can struggle with the production of work that, albeit legitimately, does not 'answer a question'. When engaging with Masters level research from the outset of their teaching careers, those who train as teachers through the PGDipEd also see themselves as researchers. By seeing the small-scale, practitioner-based research produced through a PGDipEd or Masters for what it is, along with its accompanying criticisms of scale and scope, researchers may find it easier to come to terms with Bassey's (2001) notion of 'fuzzy generalizations' and in turn may find that elusive conclusion easier to reach. Or as Ross advises: 'Try to avoid epic academic adventures and querulous political quests. Make the dissertation about your practice, your students and your teaching, rather than trying to engage with everything and overcome all'.

The next 'chapter' for Ross Martin

In offering his story as a case study of a successful Masters student, it seems appropriate to outline where Ross' Masters degree has taken him. He feels that the completion of a Masters has had a significant impact on his professional development, in a number of ways. Ross has obtained a promotion, making the move from his pastoral responsibilities to taking on a Head of Department role outside of his subject specialism. The skills and knowledge gained through his dissertation have enabled Ross to deliver training sessions at a national level with a major continuing professional development (CPD) provider. He believes his Masters has been key to giving him the confidence to take on these challenges:

> I have the ability not only to share my knowledge, but do so confidently because my experiences have, in a sense, been validated and authenticated by the MEd process and qualification.

Ross has also recently embarked upon a medium-scale action research study into pupil engagement in Geography, and hopes to start an EdD programme in the near future. His decision to continue research, and his reasons for doing so, offers a wonderful justification for the process of undertaking a Masters' dissertation:

> Having finished my MEd and taken some time to focus on my classroom practice I felt a strong desire to get back into researching again. I was encouraged to do this by my dissertation supervisor as a way of improving my practice and achieving better outcomes for my students. Having seen the power of focusing on an idea and pursuing it deliberately and robustly, I felt that it would be wasteful not to use the skills I had learnt to benefit my students.

References

Bassey, M (2001) A solution to the problem of generalisation in educational research. *Oxford Review of Education* 27(1): 5–22.

Bell, J (2010) *Doing Your Research Project*. Maidenhead: Open University Press.

Butt, G (2010) Which methods are best suited to the production of high-quality research in geography education? *International Research in Geographical and Environmental Education* 19(2): 103–7.

Costa, A and Kallick, B (1993) Through the lens of a critical friend. *Educational Leadership* 51(2): 49–51.

Lambert, D (2010) Geography education research and why it matters. *International Research in Geographical and Environmental Education* 19(2): 83–6.

Thomas, G (2009) *How to Do Your Research Project*. London: Sage.

Discussion to Part IV

Graham Butt

Chapter outline

Work–life balance   198
Importance of being a 'geographer first'   201
Conclusions   202

The final three chapters, which comprise the 'Producing' part of *MasterClass in Geography Education*, take a markedly practical turn – but still retain a strong connection with the theoretical and conceptual considerations that should always be central to any Masters-level work. It is significant that when describing how to get underway with your research, how to accomplish your research project and then strive for a conclusion, each of the authors makes closes reference to their practical experiences of working with Masters students. This is often expressed through the inclusion of quoted material, sourced directly from past students.

Catling takes us through a logical sequence of work, both describing the necessary steps that students should take when 'getting started' and outlining the expectations that they should have of their supervisor (and *vice-versa!*). There is a vibrancy afforded by the first-person accounts of the four students – each of whom describes their particular experiences of undertaking dissertation-based research. It is interesting to note that they are a diverse bunch (which helps the reader appreciate how the experience of undertaking research can vary according to individual circumstances): three of them are geographers and one a scientist, who is fascinated by the outdoors. One contributor was a full-time MA student, who took secondment from school to complete her studies, while the others continued working in schools (or teacher education) carrying out their studies part-time. Two have primary and two have secondary school backgrounds. Their case studies reflect on the initial and early stages of their research journeys, all of which were successful – indeed all of these students progressed to further postgraduate study. Catling's chapter (Chapter 10) establishes a foundation from which Taylor's and Collins's chapters (Chapters 11 and 12) can logically follow. Taylor successfully positions her chapter's contents within the practicalities of carrying out a research project, helpfully suggesting readings along the way to support this work. Although the focus for research is primarily drawn on one's personal teaching interests, the possibilities for extension beyond such boundaries are apparent – with very sound advice being given about the structure and congruence of the research process. Here sensible, organizational suggestions are given to help the reader deliver on his or her research aims and questions in a timely fashion (with additional support being accessible through the extended readings). Similarly, Collins's contribution (Chapter 12) takes us to the end of the research process, offering pragmatic, prudent and practical advice on the eventual production of a high-quality research dissertation through the 'writing-up' phase.

Work–life balance

Each of the contributors to this part, particularly the Masters students who have offered their thoughts, makes reference to the need to strike an appropriate work–life balance when completing a postgraduate dissertation. Although they do not make direct reference to the law of diminishing returns, this is pertinent to the situation most students find themselves in. This law states that there comes a point at which making more and more effort, on any given task, does not correspond to achieving markedly better performance and/or productivity. In essence this describes a situation where working harder only has a negligible effect on outcomes. To complete and submit assignments, or a dissertation, while at the same time avoiding a decline in the standards of their day-to-day work, students need to be honest about the ways they organize their time and consider the best ways to shift the focus of their efforts. As a full-time teacher 'spare time' is always in short supply, even more so when you have commitments to complete coursework for an award bearing course. This underpins comments from authors in the 'Producing' part about achieving a working rhythm that will take you through the stages of completing an assignment, or a dissertation, without undue stress or negative impacts on your daily commitments. Catling outlines the importance of recognizing that Masters work is not your 'whole life', but is nonetheless a *significant part* of it for a year or so, and that completing a large piece of research and writing requires the honest recognition that one will not always be motivated and energized to fulfil the task. Planning is essential – there will inevitably be 'pinch points', times when work commitments and academic deadlines draw together, requiring detailed planning and reserves of endurance. As Catling states, 'You need to plan for this, not leave it to chance' (p. 160). Collins's chapter (Chapter 12), with its focused case study of one of her ex students, Ross Martin, reveals similar pressures and helpfully points to potential solutions. Ross clearly describes how engaging in data collection and analysis is only half the task – with writing up also presenting a significant hurdle in terms of organization and commitment. Although the way in which you choose to organize your writing time is largely an individual decision, there are some notable similarities in the advice given by Catling and Collins about time management across the whole project – from initial planning to final completion. Collins, for example, refers to the necessity of adopting 'effective working practices from the start of the research' (p. 186), with Ross's observations pointing out the particular pitfalls he faced; these may become familiar to you or may be something unique to his individual experience. There is certainly something different about completing a Masters dissertation, even though it may involve many elements that you have experienced before (such as carrying out a literature review, undertaking research for an extended essay or small undergraduate dissertation, considering ethical issues, etc.).

Just as there is a certain rhythm to successful teaching (Butt 2008), so too is there a rhythm to conducting fruitful research and 'writing up' to a defined workplan. Teachers' time is precious – at the start of the millennium the UK government was concerned about teacher workload and work–life balance, commissioning research to identify the scale of the problem, its effects on teachers' lives and the possible solutions to resolving the key issues identified. This concern owed as much to the realization that the teaching workforce was now an ageing population, with some 45 per cent of teachers in England expected to retire or leave the profession in the following 15 years, as to whether the job was enjoyable, manageable and satisfying (Thomas et al. 2004). With reports of rising stress levels, teacher 'burn out', poor work–life balance and high workloads forcing teachers out of their chosen profession a crisis was looming. Research conducted almost a decade ago (at the time of writing) indicated that secondary school teachers worked an average of 53 hours each week, with primary and special school teachers reporting similar figures (some Headteachers regularly worked 70 hours each week, with deputy heads and heads of department having similarly inflated workloads) (Butt and Lance 2005). This situation has not radically improved, despite subsequent legislation which outlined the administrative and bureaucratic tasks that teachers should not normally be required to undertake (DfES 2003). Breaking down the (secondary school) teacher's working day into its constituent parts reveals that the bulk of teachers' time is used as follows: around 45 per cent of the day is spent teaching, with 20 per cent 'supporting teaching' (lesson planning, marking, keeping records, etc.) and 13 per cent on 'other pupil contact'. The rest of the day is classified as involving school/staff management, general administration and other duties. These are challenging commitments which do not, on initial consideration, appear to afford much time for research and writing. However, it is noticeable that the axiom about 'busy people getting the job done' is often right – whilst some teachers work long hours, but rather ineffectively, others who have high workloads still somehow manage to deliver, to high standards and within tight deadlines. This is an important consideration when you take on the extra work that completing a Masters degree inevitably involves.

Reminding ourselves about the practical advice given to new teachers on how to use their time effectively is helpful here (Tolley et al. 1996; Butt 2008). In an abridged form, this advice is repeated below:

Do:

- Be content to do things as well as you can in the circumstances
- Be realistic about what you can manage to do
- Decide what your priorities are and review them regularly in the light of changing circumstances
- Make a firm decision about how much marking and preparation you need to do and can manage in the time available each week
- Establish some realistic ground rules for marking and preparation
- Try to do as much work as you can in school
- Try to arrive at school early when it is at its quietest so that you can get on with your work reasonably undisturbed
- Try to allocate regular times each week for preparation and marking, make it dedicated time and stick to it
- Make optimum use of existing teaching resources
- Try to ensure that you are as well rested as you can be
- Get involved in some regular 'stress busting' activities such as relaxation exercises or physical recreation
- Try to stay calm

Don't:

- Try to be a perfectionist
- Spend too much time on preparing lessons and marking students' work
- Try to work when you are overtired
- Try to set and mark too much work
- Take unnecessary amounts of work home to intrude on your domestic life and possibly impair your personal relationships
- Waste time on idle chit chat
- Be so intent on work that you don't spend some time each day on social conversation with your colleagues
- Waste time duplicating the efforts of others by creating new teaching resources when perfectly adequate materials are already available
- Overreact – in most circumstances it will not help matters and the chances are that it will only make things work (after Tolley et al. 1996).

It may appear that some of this advice is either counter-intuitive or irrelevant, for a full-time student studying for a Masters degree. Surely if one wishes to be a highly professional, competent and respected teacher you should not look to 'cut corners', even if this means you are more assured of completing your qualification successfully. The point is that such advice is not intended to lower standards, but to allow enough time and space for you to take on the additional workload that Masters study involves. All students have to find their own ways to work – this is clear in the preceding chapters – but there are ways of working that can also support the completion of academic tasks. Each of the contributions from Catling, Taylor and Collins state this. You will need to have self-knowledge and a clear perception of your strengths and weaknesses with respect to meeting targets; armed with this the bullet-pointed advice above can be applied. Honesty is the key – do you over-prepare? Do you spend too much time chatting to colleagues? Is your Masters work the last priority each day, and therefore always at risk of never getting completed? – find the day-to-day activities that are taking most time and be realistic about how these tasks may be simplified, alleviated or removed. This may not be a long-term strategy; just something you do during the time you have planned to complete your Masters projects. It may be that some of the pinch points that occur are not within your power to change. Such hurdles need to be crossed, rather than becoming permanent obstructions to your research.

Importance of being a 'geographer first'

The majority of people reading this text will probably have studied at some point for a geography, or geography-related, degree as an undergraduate. This does convey some advantages for completing a geography education dissertation, or assignments that contain elements of research. Most geography graduates, by dint of the geography education they have experienced at school and university, have not only learnt many 'core elements' of geography content but have also gathered a range of competences and skills commonly associated with learning the subject. Therefore, when completing a Masters assignment or dissertation, most geographers are reasonably comfortable with handling both quantitative and qualitative data, understand the reasons for collecting data in these forms, and comprehend the research methods that are applied to gather such data. Experience of being involved in fieldwork enquiry, undergraduate dissertation research and writing, decision-making exercises and handling statistical data (for example) all help the Masters student in geography education complete their tasks. This is not necessarily so for students in (say) English education, or Modern Foreign Languages education – these students may not have much, or indeed any, experience of primary data collection and analysis of the sort that geographers regularly engage with. There are obvious disadvantages if you have never designed a questionnaire, undertaken an enquiry or considered a case study – as many geographers will have done, as part and parcel of their educational journey – when it comes to doing similar tasks as a researcher in education.

But this point goes further than a surface consideration of geographical content and methods. Lambert and Jones (2013), with reference to the work of Wooldridge and East (1951), point out the important relationship between 'the discipline and those who learn, teach and research geography' (p. 11). This observation may appear self-evident, but bears closer inspection. Lambert (2010), and others (Marsden 1997; Standish 2009, 2013; Roberts

2010), have previously commented on the dangers of geography and geography education becoming increasingly disconnected. This situation is of concern in the production of geography education dissertations and assignments – specifically, that the generic nature of educational research may subvert the importance of keeping a focus on 'the geography' (or, as Lambert (2010) asserts, that geography education research represents a specialist field of study and is not simply 'education research with a geographical hue' (p. 84)). This is an anxiety reflected in a number of texts published in the last few years (see Lambert and Morgan 2010; Butt 2011; Morgan 2011; Lambert and Jones 2013) – an unease that translates directly to the themes chosen for research by geography educationists and Masters students in geography education. Underlying this is a further dilemma – that we may be starting from a point where we have not yet successfully achieved a conceptual handle on what geography actually *is* (see Bonnett 2008; Morgan 2013; Matthews and Herbert 2008).

Conclusions

Catling begins the concluding section of this book by highlighting concerns that Masters students may have at the forefront of their minds when starting their research. He notes areas that students need to think about when getting underway: 'how you will manage your time, where you do your research and with whom, working with your supervisor, and work-life balance'. The chapters by Taylor and Collins (Chapters 11 and 12) provide a logical progression into considerations of the next steps – concerned with doing the project and then writing it up (although 'Striving for a conclusion' perhaps implies something more significant than simply producing the text). Each, in their own way, highlights the necessary qualities of motivation, energy, focus, determination, tenacity and engagement that M level students require to be successful.

My contribution in this final Discussion part has sought to point out two further considerations: firstly, not only to recognize again that most students will be undertaking their studies as an adjunct to 'the day job', but also to realize that success will necessitate the adoption of various strategies to ensure standards of professional work don't slip and sanity can be maintained. Secondly, that the focus of research should take seriously the *geographical* nature of the work being undertaken – that a Masters in geography education must engage fully with the subject that is at the core of the teaching, learning and research process.

References

Bonnett, A (2008) *What Is Geography?* London: Sage.

Butt, G (2008) *Lesson Planning*, 3rd edition. London: Continuum.

— (ed.) (2011) *Geography, Education and the Future*. London: Continuum.

Butt, G and Lance, A (2005) Secondary teacher workload and job satisfaction: do successful strategies for change exist? *Educational Management Administration and Leadership* 33(4): 401–22.

DfES (2003) *Raising Standards and Tackling Workload: A National Agreement.* London: DfES.

Lambert, D (2010) Geography education research and why it matters. *International Research in Geographical and Environmental Education* 19(2): 83–6.

Lambert, D and Jones, M (2013) Introduction: geography education questions and choices. In Lambert, D and Jones, M (eds.) *Debates in Geography Education*, pp. 1–14. London: Routledge.

Lambert, D and Morgan, J (2010) *Teaching Geography 11–18: A Conceptual Approach.* Maidenhead: Open University Press.

Marsden, W (1997) On taking the geography out of geography education: some historical pointers. *Geography* 82(3): 241–52.

Matthews, J and Herbert, D (2008) *Geography: A Very Short Introduction.* Cambridge: Cambridge University Press.

Morgan, J (2011) *Teaching Secondary Geography as if the Planet Matters.* Oxford: David Fulton.

— (2013) What do we mean by thinking geographically? In Lambert, D and Jones, M (eds.) *Debates in Geography Education*, pp. 273–81. London: Routledge.

Roberts, M (2010) Where's the geography? Reflections on being an external examiner. *Teaching Geography* 35(3): 112–13.

Standish, A (2009) *Global Perspectives in the Geography Curriculum: Reviewing the Moral Case for Geography.* London: Routledge.

— (2013) What does geography contribute to global learning? In Lambert, D and Jones, M (eds.) *Debates in Geography Education*, pp. 244–56. London: Routledge.

Thomas, H, Butt, G, Fielding, A, Foster, J, Gunter, H, Lance, A, Lock, R, Pilkington, R, Potts, E, Powers, S, Rayner, S, Rutherford, D, Selwood, I and Soares, A (2004) *The Evaluation of the Transforming the School Workforce Pathfinder Project. Research Report 541.* London: DfES.

Tolley, H, Biddulph, M and Fisher, T (1996) *The First Year of Teaching: Workbook 5.* Cambridge: Chris Kington Publishing.

Wooldridge, S and East, W (1951) *The Spirit and Purpose of Geography.* London: Hutchinson.

Conclusions 13

Graham Butt

Chapter outline

The current research context in initial teacher education (ITE) and beyond   206

Quality in geography education research   207

Aiming higher – advanced conceptions of Research Quality   209

In this concluding section[1] I will attempt to draw together some of the key themes of the proceeding chapters by focusing on the issue of *quality* in research in geography education. Notwithstanding the advice, and assessment criteria, provided by the institution at which you are completing your Masters degree, a focus on quality should help you to judge the appropriateness of both the processes and products of your work. This brief chapter will also raise some questions about the demands of achieving high-quality research in geography education, given recent changes in initial teacher education in the United Kingdom and the knock-on effects this may have on research at Masters and Doctoral level.

Defining what we mean by the quality of educational research is not straightforward. In universities and higher education institutions (HEIs) in the United Kingdom an established measure of quality is generated through the research excellence framework (REF) (previously research assessment exercise (RAE)). This operation, conducted every five or six years, calculates the quality of the research environment, research-driven publications and their impact compared with international standards of excellence – in part to enable the higher education funding bodies to distribute public funds appropriately to research-led institutions. Other national jurisdictions also carry out similar exercises in attempts to measure, in both quantifiable and qualitative ways, the comparability of their institutions' research outputs. However, there are always issues surrounding our understanding of the concepts of 'quality' and 'excellence' within the education research community. But what has this got to do with research and writing at Masters level, you may ask? The simple answer is that the current determinants and criteria for research quality applied within academia have some purchase on our assessment of the work produced by (research) students – specifically when we consider the significance, originality and rigour of their outputs. These three terms, which are currently central to considerations of the quality of research publications in the United Kingdom, can be described in various ways. *Significance* can be best understood with respect to whether an important and meaningful problem, or question, is being researched. You might consider whether the theme chosen for your research is relevant at the small scale (just you, and your classroom practice), or at a much larger scale (a 'universal' problem considered by geography education researchers, or indeed across other disciplines). Is the significance of the research increased because it investigates a problem that has relevance to *other* subject areas (and is this made explicit?) or to educationists *in general*? Put crudely, someone weighing up the significance of your research might ask 'Why should I care about this?', or 'Is this a problem that is really noteworthy and important?', or indeed 'So what?'. *Rigour* is usually considered to be a measure of the thoroughness, precision and accuracy of your research method, methodologies and presentation – one might ask whether there is an intellectual meticulousness, robustness and appropriateness to your work? Does the research display integrity, coherence and consistency? Lastly, we might introduce a consideration of the *originality* of your research – does it provide new (empirical) material or insights? Does it seek to develop innovative research methods, or methodologies, or analytical techniques? Or has it successfully employed already established research techniques? Is there a possibility of generating new theory? These are quite challenging criteria which arguably take us beyond those normally applied at Masters level. Nonetheless, they do present valid questions which can be considered whenever the quality of any research work is assessed.

The current research context in initial teacher education (ITE) and beyond

The foundations of good-quality educational research at Masters level in the United Kingdom have traditionally been built on the bedrock of good teacher preparation in ITE. ITE has previously established the principles of teaching, and teacher education, being at least partly driven by research – indeed, Hargreaves (1996) has referred to teaching as a 'research-based profession' – containing strong elements of research-informed and research-generating practice. A paper on policy and practice in ITE recently commissioned by BERA RSA (Beauchamp et al. 2013) reported on the relationships between the revised teacher Standards (competencies/competences) (DfE 2013) and research-informed teacher education provision across the four jurisdictions of the United Kingdom. Using a phrase from Furlong (2013), they considered the 'turn or (re)turn to the practical' in teacher education.

Beauchamp et al.'s (2013) paper is important as it outlines a distinct direction of travel for ITE, which has become increasingly school based and craft (rather than research) driven of late. As such, those now undertaking Masters research – often building on a research foundation they laid in ITE – might represent a rather threatened and dwindling cohort. Especially within England, which was recognized as something of an 'outlier' in terms of student teachers' experiences of ITE in the United Kingdom, the researchers highlighted policy declarations, changes in practice and the effects of 'discourse(s) of relevance' – all of which chartered the steady removal of research from ITE programmes. Indeed, the UK Coalition Government's education policy from 2010 onwards indicates a decisive shift away from the idea of teaching as a research-based profession towards a model of ITE that lionizes practical performance and experiential knowledge over 'theoretical, pedagogical and subject knowledge' (Beauchamp et al. 2013, p. 2).

With the place of research-informed provision of teacher education diminishing, the role of research in teacher preparation and development has been increasingly sidelined. There is clearly a desire within government to remove research (and indeed the major involvement of HEIs) from teacher preparation. The principal focus in terms of the knowledge base for teaching is the possession of 'good subject and curriculum knowledge', with little explicit reference being made to teachers' engagement with (and in) research and curriculum enquiry. This echoes observations on earlier iterations of teaching Standards which described them as regulatory, rather than developmental, in intent (Mahony and Hextall 2000).

Quality in geography education research

Within geography education the debate about quality of research has been rather piecemeal and spasmodic. Back in 1993 the then recently launched journal *International Research in Geographical and Environmental Education* contained a 'Forum' on exactly this question: 'How shall we judge the quality of research in geographical and environmental education?' The six respondents offered sensible advice, much of which parallels that provided in this book, but arguably failed to capture the essence of what constitutes high-quality research outputs in geography education. We have seen that although large-scale, generously funded, research projects exist in education, these are not the norm. Indeed, 'non core' subjects (such as geography) attract only limited research money, often for smaller-scale, practitioner-based, research – which the government has traditionally seen as a means of providing professional development for teachers, rather than generating cost-effective, high-quality research. Such research *may* be of high quality, but invariably lacks significant long-term impact. Indeed, applied and practice-based research – which has re-conceptualized the links between research, practice and policy – has different measures of quality compared with larger-scale research projects (Furlong and Oancea 2005).

Educational researchers have often stressed the importance of teachers maintaining an awareness of current educational research and its implications for their classroom practice,

With reference to the United Kingdom, the community of researchers in geography education has regularly made efforts to both involve teachers in research and bring to their attention-pertinent research findings – professional journals such as *Teaching Geography*, and academic journals such as *Geography* (which now champions aspects of geography education through its commissioned articles), carry accounts of research that have direct relevance to the classroom. Similarly subject associations, such as the *Geographical Association*, have sought to convey research findings to classroom practitioners, for example, through its previous *'Theory into Practice'* series. Internationally, academic journals such as *International Research in Geographical and Environmental Education* and the Commission for Geography Education of the IGU have also worked hard to spread good practice through articles, publications and conferences. Michael Naish (1993) previously noted that many teachers, politicians and their advisors had a poor regard for educational research, with the former tending to see research as having little relevance to their day-to-day problems of classroom practice – indeed, 'teachers sometimes claim that research tells them what they already know' (Naish 1993, p. 64). Nothing much has changed in the past 20 years. This immediately raises 'quality' questions – for research which lacks wider relevance tends to be considered as invalid, unreliable and non-generalizable. In pursuit of definitions of quality indicators for research in geography education, McElroy (1993) claimed that all research should be based on a clear set of principles. These connect to the particular research problem, the paradigm in which the research is conducted, and whether the research will generate knowledge for a community of scholars – driven primarily by a 'need to know' (p. 66). Quality is partly determined by the principles adopted for conducting research, which must be clear before the research is started. The researcher should make clear *what* was intended (which influences the research paradigm chosen), *why* the research was carried out and *how* it was conducted. These principles led McElroy (1993) to state that a 'lucid' research report should:

- state the research problem clearly;
- explain and justify the study approach;
- locate the investigation (within a current body of knowledge/paradigm);
- plainly portray the context in which the research is set;
- report and justify the research design, methodology, instruments and means of analysis;
- state its limitations;
- acknowledge the amount and kind of researcher involvement;
- concede the interests that are inherent in the study and
- show how ethical considerations were handled.

This requires the researcher (and reader) to possess a reasonable overview of research paradigms, of theory and practice within research, and of research methods and methodologies. Purnell (1993) concurs, adding that high-quality research should also include a succinct writing style using appropriate language (gender inclusive, non-racist); an abstract providing an overview of what was researched, how this was done and major findings/recommendations;

a review of related literature; findings and discussion based on these; conclusions and recommendations; and suggestions for possible future research. It is apparent that different researchers in geography education will offer different appreciations of research quality (both in terms of process and products) from their own theoretical, methodological and philosophical perspectives. Therefore the emphasis on, say, specific theoretical foundations, use of research instruments, documentation of findings, and emphasis on quantitative or qualitative methods may vary according to the researcher.

Aiming higher – advanced conceptions of Research Quality

It is worthwhile shifting the focus to briefly consider how large-scale research organizations view quality. This almost certainly has implications for how the geography education community – and individual researchers working on their own Masters or Doctoral theses – evaluate their practices and outputs. We obviously must remain mindful of the scale and the levels of funding that may be associated with prestigious research projects. Here considerations of research quality extend beyond the usual methodological and theoretical issues to embrace: (i) user engagement for relevance and quality; (ii) knowledge generation by project teams; (iii) knowledge synthesis through thematic activities; (iv) knowledge transformation for impact; (v) capacity building for professional development and (vi) partnerships for sustainability (Pollard 2005). These quality indicators are hard, if not impossible, for a single researcher working at Masters level to address – they go far beyond the expectations of a Masters-level student; but they are revealing in terms of the aims and purposes of large-scale, high-quality research projects. They provide a yardstick. Ask yourself the following: if I was called upon to justify the research I'm doing for my Masters degree how would this measure up against the criteria outlined above? It is certainly valid to ask of any small-scale research, conducted by one or two researchers, whether others might want to use their findings? Whether the data gathered can help us to generate new knowledge? Whether the results draw together a particular theme or knowledge stream in an interesting way? And whether there might be some tangible impact from the findings?

Furlong and Oancea (2005) also note that 'research quality' is no longer solely defined within theoretical, ideological or methodological parameters, but by multidimensional criteria. This is a consequence of the wider interest in, involvement with, and dissemination of research findings in education. They choose to define four major dimensions – and numerous sub dimensions – of research quality:

(i) Epistemic – traditional theoretical and methodological robustness. These are usually most visible in research reports and are the key dimensions of quality that are used in assessing social research. Subdimensions: trustworthiness, contribution to knowledge, explicitness in designing and reporting, propriety, paradigm-dependent criteria.

(ii) Technological – provision of facts, evidence, new ideas. Subdimensions: timeliness, purposivity, specificity and accessibility, impact, flexibility and operationalizability.

(iii) Capacity building and value for people – collective and personal growth, changing people through collaboration and partnership, increasing receptiveness, moral and ethical growth. Subdimensions: partnership, collaboration and engagement; plausibility; reflection and criticism; receptiveness; personal growth.

(iv) Economic – whether the money invested in a research project is well spent, or adds value. Subdimensions: cost-effectiveness; marketability and competitiveness, auditability; feasibility; originality; value efficiency.

These quality indicators are illustrative, rather than prescriptive, and do not suggest any parameters for their application. However, they are thought provoking and may suggest the possibilities for furthering one's research beyond the immediate achievement of Masters certification – maybe through extending your original research, starting a new project, publishing some of your findings, joining others in a research endeavour, or possibly taking on a PhD or EdD. Evaluation of research quality is dependent on the purposes, intended audiences and aims of the research – factors which vary according to the type and scale of the research undertaken, but which can and should be considered for any research project (from GCSE to postdoctoral level).

Note

1   This concluding section is based on a paper previously presented at the IGU CGE conference in Brisbane in 2006, titled 'How should we determine research quality in geography education' (Butt 2006).

References

Beauchamp, G, Clarke, L, Hulme, M and Murray, J (2013) *Policy and Practice within the United Kingdom: Research and Teacher Education: The BERA RSA Enquiry.* London: BERA RSA.

Butt, G (2006) How should we determine research quality in geography education? In Purnell, K, Lidstone, J and Hodgson, S (eds.) *Changes in Geographical Education: Past, Present and Future.* Proceedings of the International Geographical Union Commission on Geographical Education Symposium. Brisbane, Australia: IGU-CGE.

— (2010) Which methods are best suited to the production of high-quality research in geography education? *International Research in Geographical and Environmental Education* 19(2): 103–7.

Department for Education (DfE) (2013) Teachers' Standards. http://media.education.gov.uk/assets/files/pdf/t/teachers%20standards%20information.pdf.

Furlong, J (2013) *Education: An Anatomy of the Discipline.* London: Routledge.

Furlong, J and Oancea, A (2005) *Assessing Quality in Applied and Practice-based Educational Research.* Oxford: OUDES.

Hargreaves, D (1996) *Teaching as a Research-Based Profession: Possibilities and Prospects.* London: TTA.

Mahony, P and Hextall, I (2000) *Reconstructing Teaching: Standards, Performance and Accountability.* London: Routledge Falmer.

McElroy, B (1993) How can one be sure? Ground rules for judging research quality. *International Research in Geographical and Environmental Education* 2(1): 66–9.

Naish, M (1993) 'Never mind the quality – feel the width' – how shall we judge the quality of research in geographical and environmental education? *International Research in Geographical and Environmental Education* 2(1): 64–5.

Pollard, A (2005) Taking the initiative? TLRP and Educational Research. *Educational Review Guest Lecture.* 12 October 2005. University of Birmingham.

Index

Page numbers in **bold** refer to figures/tables.

Abbott, A. 32, 42
academic geography 4, 8, 49, 73, 84
accountability 6, 32, 46, 48, 131, 132, 164
The Action Plan for Geography 73
active learning 25, 60, 63
activist professionals 32, 41
Alderson, P. 130, 131, 132, 140
Altrichter, H. 173, 176, 182
anti intellectualism 12
Arthur, J. 163, 164
article record form **174**
assignments and dissertations *see also* research
    project in practice; research-based
    dissertation
  approaches to completing 193–5
Association of Internet Researchers
    (AoIR) 136

Balderstone, D. 18, 19
Ball, S. J. 46, 70
Banks, M. 178
Barrett Hacking, E. 33
Bassey, M. 176, 195
Battersby, J. 70
Beauchamp, G. 206, 207
Beck, J. 4, 33
Bednarz, S. W. 18, 21, 22, 35, 48, 153
Bell, J. 5, 135, 190
Béneker, T. 182
Bennetts, T. 22, 24
Beynon, J. 142
Biddulph, M. 22, 69, 70, 97
Bielaczyc, K. 62
Biesta, G. 89
Blaikie, N. 121
Blaut, J. 25
Boardman, D. 25
Boghossian, P. 59
Bonnett, A. 21, 202
Boschetti, F. 89
Boyatzis, R. 182

British Education Research Association
    (BERA) 130, 133, 135, 136, 137, 140, 206
Broadhead, P. 57
Brooks, C. 5, 7, 10, 15, 33, 42, 46, 47, 116, 172
Bruner, J. 76
Bryan, H. 5
Bryman, A. 86, 130, 132, 136, 138
Buckler, S. 153, 155, 157, 160, 161, 162
Bull, B. 33
Bustin, R. 39
Butt, G. 4, 7, 8, 10, 11, 12, 18, 21, 24, 46, 48, 68, 83,
    84, 87, 88, 89, 90, 95, 96, 97, 114, 153, 187,
    199, 200, 210n. 1

Carr, W. 50, 82
case study research 18, 49, 176
Catling, S. 11, 22, 153, 197, 198, 199, 201, 202
Children Act of England and Wales (1989) 140
Christensen, L. 9, 113, 114
Cilliers, P. 89
cities, study of,
    particularity of place context, the 17
Civitas 73, 74
Claire, H. 109
Clough, P. 116, 126
Cochran-Smith, M. 36, 40
Cohen, L. 39, 82, 86, 102, 103, 105, 122, 133, 134,
    135, 163, 164, 176, 177
Collier, J. 182
Collier, M. 182
Collins, G. 10, 11, 12, 198, 199, 201, 202
complexity theory 88–9
  three approaches 89
    complexity thinking 89
    hard complexity theory 89
    soft complexity theory 89
confirmability 125, 163 *see also* credibility;
    dependability; reflexivity; reliability
consequential validity 26, 37–8
constructivism 54–7 *see also* social constructivism
  influence on knowledge 59–60

content knowledge 32, 58 *see also* knowledge
continuing professional development (CPD) 10, 195
core knowledge 54, 56, 58 *see also* knowledge
Corney, G. 33
Costa, A. 193
credibility **115**, 124, 125, 163, 176
    see also confirmability; dependability;
    reflexivity; reliability
Cresswell, T. 21, 73, 75, 119, 172
critical realist 38
critical theory 86–8
Crotty, M. 84, 85, 114, 119, 172
curriculum development 39, 47, 73, 90, 116, 162
    see also GNC
curriculum discourse 69
  influence of the geography community on **71**
curriculum making 23, 25, 33, 49, 73, 97

Daniels, H. 64
Darby, D. 6, 83
data collection 124–6, 176–80
  methods **177**
  research questions mapped to methods **179**
Data Protection Act of 1988 138
Davies, P. 24
Davis, B. 89
DCSF 45
De Vaus, D. A. 123
Declaration of Helsinki of 1964, the 130
Denby, N. 5
Denscombe, M. 114, 122, 155, 157, 164
dependability 125, 164 *see also* confirmability;
    credibility; reflexivity; reliability
Derry, J. 61
Dey, I. 180, 181, 182
DfE 206
discourse analysis 10, 67–9, 72, 181
door knob conversations 136
Doyle, D. 135
Duncan, J. S. 73
Duncan, M. 135
Dunphy, A. 22
Dunscombe, J. 142

East, W. 201
Economic and Social Research Council
    (ESRC) 130, 131
Edelson, D. C. 24
education,
  as a field of scholarship 17

Education Reform Act of 1988 69
educational research (at Masters level),
    characteristics of 7–9
Edwards, R. 132, 135
Elliott, J. 39, 40
empirical theory 85–6
enquiry learning 58–9, 96
environmentalism 72
episteme(s) 61–2, 96
  definition 62
epistemic, the,
  importance of, the 61–2
Eraut, M. 36
ethicism 130
Evans, M. 182
Everett, E. 154, 156
evidence-led practice 16
evidence-led rhetoric 17

Fair Trade 73
Fairclough, N. 67, 68, 75
Fairgrieve, J. 24
Fargher, M. 22
feminist researchers 132
Fielding, M. 125
Fien, J. 108
Finley, L. 126
Finney, J. 7
Firth, R. 10, 21, 22, 74, 83, 87, 89, 90, 91, 95,
    96, 97
Fish, S. 82
Flick, U. 134, 176
Fonseca, J. 89
Ford, M. J. 57, 60, 62, 63
Foskett, N. 20
Frankfurt School, the 87
Freeman, D. 119
Freire, P. 60
Furlong, J. 7, 41, 48, 83, 114, 124, 206, 207, 209
Furseth, I. 154, 156

Geographical Association (GA) 20, 33, 54, 56, 57,
    58, 59, 62, 63, 71, 73, 74, 90, 96, 97, 208
  'Geography Curriculum Consultation Full
    Report' 63
  'Thinking Geographically' 59
geographer 17, 22, 23, 49, 53, 70, 72, 73, 75, 76, 88,
    97, 186, 187, 197
  importance of being a, the 201–2
  and the significance of the ideographic 17

geographic advantage 21–2
geographical enquiry 58–9, 72, 103
geographical knowledge 10, 21, 23, 24, 25, 26, 38,
    53–65, 67, 69, 71, 72, 77, 87, 95–8, 119, 153,
    168 *see* knowledge
geographical thought 21–2, 75
Geography 19, 208
geography education,
    issues in 61
    research in 15–26 *see also* GER
geography education research (GER) 17, 18, 20, 22,
    24, 35, 48–50, 145, 146, 147
    approaches to 101–10
    exemplary curricula 25
    fieldwork 25
    priorities 24–5
    quality in 207–9
Geography Education Research Committee
    (GERC) 18, 22, 23, 24
Geography National Curriculum (GNC) 10,
    67–77, 77nn. 4, 6, 96–7
    1995 GNC, the 70–1
    1999 GNC, the 71–2
    2008 GNC, the 72–4
    2014 GNC, the 74–7, 96
geography teachers 3, 10, 31, 35, 36, 39, 41, 49,
    90, 95, 96, 97, 114, 120, 145, 146, 154,
    167, 187
    professional knowledge of 32–3
geoscience 72
GER *see* geography education research
Gerber, R. 21, 84, 103, 104
GERC *see* Geography Education Research
    Committee
Gersmehl, C. 18, 25
Gersmehl, P. 18, 25
Glaser, B. 81
global citizenship 71, 72
GNC *see* Geography National Curriculum
golden age of curriculum thinking, the 25
Goldilocks test, the 116
Golding, C. 60
Golledge, R. 21
Gorard, S. 104, 124
Gorman, S. 131
Graham, A. 131, 133, 139, 140, 141
grand theory 86
Graves, N. 25
Gregory, I. 129, 132, 133
Grey, D. 123

Grossman, P. 42
Guba, E. G. 81, 124, 125
Gunstone, R. 178
Gunter, H. 4

Habermas, J. 87
Hall, S. 76
Hammersley, M. 35, 36, 130, 132, 135
Hanson, S. 21, 22
Hardman, M. 89
Hargreaves, D. 6, 35, 36, 206
Hart, C. 5, 175
Harvey, D. 68
Hawthorne effect, the 123
Hazel, N. 178
Herbert, D. 21, 202
Hextall, I. 207
Hickey, M. 8, 67, 68
Hicks, D. 108, 109, 146
Higgins, S. 22
higher education institutions (HEIs) 4, 6, 11, 12,
    45, 46, 90, 205
Hillage, J. 6, 83
Hillcoat, J. 108
Hitchcock, G. 82
Holden, C. 109
Hopkins, D. 47, 49
Hopwood, N. 39, 168
Howell Major, C. 118, 121, 124
Howell, K. E. 125
Hughes, D. 82
Hulme, M. 40
Hurworth, R. 178

initial teacher education (ITE),
    current research context in 206–7
insider researchers 11, 129, 141
*International Research in Geographical
    and Environmental Education* (IRGEE) 19,
    21, 208
interpretivist theory 84, 86

Jackson, P. 22
Jansen, J. 120
Jessop, J. 142
Johnson, B. 9, 113, 114
Johnson, N. 88
Johnson, S. 89, 113, 114
Jones, M. 10, 11, 12, 19, 22, 146, 153, 201, 202
Jonson, R. B. 121

journals,
    classification of 19
        academic journals 19
        general journals 19
        professional journals 19
        specialist journals 19

Kallick, B. 193
Kapur, M. 62
Kellet, M. 140
Kemmis, S. 176
kennedy, C. 179
Kent, A. 91
Kincheloe, J. 87
Kirby, A. 17
Kirk, G. 57
Kitchen, R. 116
knowers 40, 41, 56, 60, 61, 126
knowing 40, 60
knowledge *see also* geographical
      knowledge
    basic premises 59
    conceptualizations of 54
    as a cultural product 60
    debates about 57–9
    influence of constructivism 59–60
    and knowers 40, 56, 60, 126
    realist perspective on 60–1
    as a social product 57, 59, 60
    types of 58
        content knowledge 58
        core knowledge 58
        procedural 58
knowledge growth 56

Lambert, D. 4, 10, 12, 18, 19, 21, 22, 26, 33, 37, 39,
      46, 48, 49, 50, 57, 68, 73, 87, 153, 155, 156,
      188, 201, 202
Lance, A. 199
Landsberger, H. 123
Laurence, F. 8
Lave, J. 9
Lawson, V. 8, 67, 68
Leat, D. 19, 22, 25
Leech, N. 9, 85
Lincoln, Y. S. 81, 124
Livingstone, D. N. 75
Locke, L. 156
Lofthouse, R. 19
Lotz-Sisitka, H. 55, 56
Lytle, S. L. 36, 40

McElroy, B. 208
McEwan, H. 33
MacFarlane, B. 130, 132, 135
McLaren, P. 87
McLellan, R. 182
Maclure, M. 6
McNiff, J. 118
McTaggart, R. 176
Mahony, P. 207
Manicas, P. 110
Marsden, W. 20, 201
Martin, F. 22, 33
mathematics education research (MER) 37
Maton, K. 60, 74
Matthews, J. 21, 202
Mauthner, M. 132, 135, 139
Maxwell, J. 119, 121
Meier, P. 178
Mercer, J. 129
Methodism 11, 145–7
    in geography education 145–6
Miller, T. 130, 131, 132, 134, 135, 136, 142
Mitchell, M. 88
Mockler, N. 135, 141
model,
    of teaching and learning situations **37**
Moore, A. 39, 40, 46, 47
Moore, R. 74
Morgan, J. 10, 11, 22, 53, 54, 57, 70, 73, 83, 87, 89,
      90, 91, 202
Morrison, K. 89
Morrison, M. 122, 124, 130, 137, 141
Morrow, V. 55, 56, 130, 131, 132, 140
Mouly, G. 105

Naish, M. 12, 83, 208
National Curriculum, the 54, 56, 58, 59, 95
    see GNC
Newby, P. 163, 164
Nundy, S. 25
Nuremberg Code of 1947, the 130
Nutbrown, C. 116, 126

Ó Dochartaigh, N. 166
Oancea, A. 7, 48, 83, 114, 124, 207, 209
objectivism 53
objectivity 61, 86, **115**, 121, 125, 163, 172
    see also reliability; validity
  of knowledge 57, 74
Ofsted 16, 23, 138
    inspections 46

O'Leary, Z. 9
Oliver, P. 129, 132, 134, 135, 136, 139
ontology 10, 84, 85, 103, 145
Onwuegbuzie, A. J. 9, 85, 121
Oost, K. 25
Osberg, D. 89
Osborne, J. 61

Perkins, D. 61, 62, 96
place, notions of 73
Pole, C. 130, 137, 141
Pollard, A. 209
Popper, K. 86
positivism, positivist 8, 38, 84, 86, 87, 88, 101, 103,
        104, 105, 108, 110, 125, 136
    post-positivist 38, 172, 176, 179, 181
Post Graduate Certificate of Education (PGCE) 3,
        5, 11
Post Graduate Diploma in Education (PGDipEd) 3,
        5, 186, 187, 190, 192, 193, 194
practitioner research 47–8
    and academic research 47–8
previous knowledge 56
principle of benificence, the 132
principle of non-malificence, the 132
Pring, R. 34, 120
procedural knowledge 58–9, 62, 96, 97
profession 32
    society's expectations 42
professional community 46
professional identity 46
professional knowledge 4, 17, 40, 41, 42, 46
    geography teachers' 32–3, 35, 36, 38
professional learning 4, 46
professional practice 31–2, 46
    research and 34
Programme for International Student Assessment
        (PISA) 68, 77n. 3
Purnell, K. 208

Qualified Teacher Status (QTS) 5, 11, 186
qualitative analysis **180**
qualitative data 39, 181, 201
quantitative data 39, 201

Rawding, C. 10, 77, 77nn. 4, 9, 95, 97
Rawling, E. 22, 25, 68, 69, 70, 71, 72
realism 56, 110
    social realism 58
reflection in action 40
reflection on action 40

reflectivity 126, 132
reflexivity 4, 114, **115**, 125, 126
regulated autonomy 70, 97
reliability 9, 20, 125, 153, 163–5, 176
        see also objectivity; validity
    aspects of 164
research 20 passim
    full-time/ part-time 152
    methodology 20
    reading 38
    research question/ aim 20
    systematicity of 20
research assessment exercises (RAEs) 6, 147n. 1, 205
research ethics 129–42
    and children 139–41
    context 130–1
    ethics of care 132
    final stages of research and 141–2
    informed consent 133–6
    privacy and confidentiality 137–9
    research integrity 132–3
research excellence frameworks (REFs) 6, 147n. 1,
        205
research paradigms (in education) 103–4
    interpretivist 103–4
    positivist 103–4
research project in practice 171–83
    communicating research findings 182–3
    data analysis 180–2
        qualitative analysis **180**
    data collection 176–80
        methods of **177**
    ensuring consistency 171–3
    literature review 173–5
    research questions see research questions under
            independent entries
    research strategy, choosing a 175–6
research proposal (writing) 113–26
        see also writing up
    considerations when writing **115**
        philosophical and theoretical
            considerations 118–19
    data collection and analysis 124–6
    features of a good propposal 113–16
    importance of context 117–18
    research design 120–2
    research methods 122–4
    research questions, arriving at 119–20
research quality,
    advanced conceptions of 209–10
        major dimensions 209–10

research questions 4, 8, 10, 11, 37, 38, 47, 101, 103,
        113, 114, **115**, 116, 117, 121, 123, 124, 125,
        126, 153, 165, 172, 174, 175, 176, 178, 181,
        182
    arriving at 119–20
    mapped to methods **179**
    proposed by GERC 23
    theory, methods and methodology, relationship
        between **172**, **173**
research-based dissertation,
    ethics and informed consent 161–2
    motivation and focus 154–5
    potential areas for investigation 155–7
    preliminaries 152–4
    realistic, the need to be 162–6
    researcher-supervisor relation 157–9
    working rhythm, developing a 159–61
researcher readiness 119, 121
researchers,
    teachers as 39–41
        implications 41–2
Richardson, K. 89
Rickinson, M. 22
Roberts, M. 10, 19, 22, 25, 36, 37, 69, 70, 71, 76, 87,
        97, 103, 201
Robson, C. 9, 38, 84, 85, 101, 102, 103, 104, 105,
        108, 110, 122, 163, 164
Rose, G. 68, 182
Royal Geographical Society 73
Ruddock, J. 47, 49
Russian doll principle, the 116
Ruthven, K. 39
Rynne, E. 33

Sachs, J. 9, 32, 34, 41
Savin-Baden, M. 118, 121, 124
Sayer, A. 68
Schön, D. A. 39, 41, 84
Schwab, J. J. 58, 62
Secord, P. 110
Sewell, K. 5
Shavelson, R. J. 83
Shenton, A. 125
Shulman, L. E. E. S. 32, 33
Silverman, D. 176
Singer, H. 138
Slater, F. 25, 38
Smith, E. 104
Smith, M. 19
social constructivism 53, 57, 60

social realism 58
social realist 21, 57, 74
Social Research Association (SRA) 130, 133, 137
Sockett, H. 33
Spellman, G. 22
Stables, A. 106
Stacey, R. 89
Standish, A. 72, 73, 74, 201
Steedman, P. 126
Stemhagen, K. 54, 55, 56, 62, 64, 96
Stenhouse, L. 39, 47, 49
Stenhouse's Humanities Curriculum Project 39
Strauss, A. 81
Stubbs, B. 105
students as co-researchers 125
students' understandings of geographical topics
    methods for accessing **178**
Sumara, D. 89
sustainable development 71–2, 181
Symonds, J. E. 124

Taylor, L. 11, 22, 84, 198, 201, 202
teacher professionalism 46
teachers,
    as knowledge workers 12
    professional autonomy for 46
    as professionals 46
    as researchers 12, 47–8
Teachers' Standards 46
teaching,
    as research-based profession 12, 206
Teaching Geography 19, 77n. 6, 208
theory 81–91
    in educational research 83
    in geography education 89–90
    roleof 97
    types of 83–5
        complexity theory 88–9
        critical theory 86–8
        empirical theory 86
        grand theory 86
        interpretivist theory 84, 86
thinking ethically 132, 142
thinking geographically 22, 53, 54, 58
Thomas, D. 6
Thomas, G. 82, 83, 84, 102, 103, 104, 105, 106, 107,
        110, 131, 132, 133, 153, 156, 160, 163, 164,
        190
Thomas, H. 19
Tolley, H. 200

Tooley, J. 6, 83
Towne, L. 83
Traianou, A. 130, 132, 135
transferability 9, **115**, 125
trustworthiness, concept of **115**, 124, 125, 141, 165, 176, 209

UN Convention on the Rights of the Child (1989) 139
UNICEF 140
Unwin, T. 75

validity 8, 9, 20, 33, 59, 61, 65n. 1, 85, 105, 125, 153, 164, 165, 176 *see also* objectivity; reliability
   aspects of 163
virtual learning environment (VLE) 191
Vithal, R. 120

Walliman, N. 153, 155, 157, 160, 161, 162
Walshe, N. 181
Watson, R. 135
Weeden, P. 10, 24, 39, 105, 106, 107, 146

Weis, L. 85
Wellington, J. 109
Wenger, E. 9
Wheelahan, L. 57, 59, 60, 65n. 1
White, R. 117, 178
Whitty, G. 6, 7, 32, 117, 147n. 2
Wiegand, P. 25
Williams, K. F. 142
Williams, M. 38, 84, 103, 153, 155
Wilson, M. 10, 11, 121, 122, 147
Winter, C. 22
Wood, P. 88, 89
Wooldridge, S. 201
writing up 185–95
   case study 186
   dissertation supervisor, use of the 190–1
   meeting deadline and standards 192–3
   pitfalls and practicalities of, the 186–8
   techniques and regimes for 188–90

Yates, S. 114
Yin, R. 176
Young, M. 56, 87, 97